Half-Time

BY THE SAME AUTHOR

The Little Wonder: The Remarkable History of Wisden
Hell for Leather: A Modern Cricket Journey
Bloody Foreigners: The Story of Immigration to Britain

A NOTE ON THE AUTHOR

Robert Winder was Literary Editor of the *Independent* and Deputy Editor of *Granta*. He is the author of several books including *Hell for Leather: A Modern Cricket Journey* and *Bloody Foreigners: The Story of Immigration to Britain*, and three novels. His most recent book is *The Little Wonder: The Remarkable History of Wisden*. He has completely missed the ball in all three of the sports featured in *Half-Time*.

John Wisden & Co Ltd
An imprint of Bloomsbury Publishing Plc

50 Bedford Square   1385 Broadway
London   New York
WC1B 3DP   NY 10018
UK   USA

www.bloomsbury.com

www.wisden.com
www.wisdenrecords.com
Follow Wisden on Twitter @WisdenAlmanack
and on Facebook at Wisden Sports

WISDEN and the wood-engraving device are trademarks of John Wisden &
Company Ltd, a subsidiary of Bloomsbury Publishing Plc

First published 2015
This paperback edition published 2016

British Library Cataloguing-in-Publication Data
A catalogue record for this book is available from the British Library.

ISBN: PB: 978-1-4729-0894-0
ePub: 978-1-4729-0893-3

2 4 6 8 10 9 7 5 3 1

Typeset in 12pt Stempel Garamond by Deanta Global Publishing Services,
Chennai, India
Printed and bound in Great Britain by CPI Group (UK) Ltd,
Croydon CR0 4YY

To find out more about our authors and books visit www.wisden.com.
Here you will find extracts, author interviews, details of forthcoming events
and the option to sign up for our newsletters.

Half-Time

The Glorious Summer of 1934

Robert Winder

B L O O M S B U R Y

LONDON · NEW DELHI · NEW YORK · SYDNEY

For Mary and Jim Winder

Contents

2013 and All That

There was a moment, when Lee Westwood stood on the seventh tee at Muirfield, near Edinburgh, on 21 July 2013, when it seemed as though a sporting miracle might be at hand. It was a roasting hot afternoon and, as the Englishman waited for Tiger Woods and Adam Scott to clear the green up ahead, he tried to gauge the strength of the wind. He was a third of the way through the final round of the Open; the thermometer was touching 30 degrees; and a birdie at the previous hole had given him a heart-stopping three-shot lead. His first major win could be just a few smooth swings away.

The salty grass, stiffened by spray from the North Sea, was wispy and scorched, the humps and hillocks were dry as hay, and the atmosphere shook with expectation. The sun-drenched gallery sported shorts and dark glasses in place of the usual waterproofs and umbrellas, and the main thing the spectators had to worry about, as they tilted their heads to watch white balls arching into blue sky, was the sunburn on their necks.

Most British sports fans, barring the odd Scot dismayed by the prospect of an English success story, had to pinch themselves, because a Westwood win was only one of three momentous possibilities jostling for headline space that day. Down in north London, England's cricketers (boosted by an innings of 178 by a young Yorkshireman, Joe Root) were crushing Australia at Lord's, a feat they had managed only once – *once* – in the entire 20th century. And further south Chris Froome was sipping iced bubbly as he pedalled his way up the Champs-Elysées to give Britain its second straight winner of the Tour de France. There was a carnival spirit shimmering in the freakishly hot air.

It was only a year since the bright, champagne-cork summer of 2012, when Bradley Wiggins's victory in the Tour de France (the first by a Briton) and the gold rush of the London Olympics had put a smile on Britain's sometimes grumpy face. Now, in the bewildering space of a single day, it was happening all over again. A few weeks earlier Justin Rose had become the first Englishman to win the US Open since Tony Jacklin in 1970; and the British and Irish Lions had roused themselves to beat Australia. And in early July an even bigger giant had been slain when Andy Murray ended Britain's 77-year wait for a male Wimbledon champion by beating the seemingly indestructible Novak Djokovic. The following morning he posed for photographs at the feet of Fred Perry, whose statue stands in the grounds of the All England Club, marking the last occasion, seven and a half decades earlier, when a home champion had lifted the trophy.

It didn't matter that Murray had won £1.6 million, whereas Perry won nothing apart from a silver cup. Nor did we care that he was Scottish, that three 'English' cricketers (Pietersen, Prior and Trott) were from the southern hemisphere, or that Froome was hailing his Tour de France victory as 'a great day for Africa'. Such was modern sport, and modern migratory life.[1] If Westwood held his nerve it would surely brush gilt on one of the more remarkable clean sweeps ever seen in sport.

It wasn't to be. In front of his 12-year-old son, who was in the gallery, Westwood fidgeted over his club selection before making a bizarre (and in retrospect rash) attempt to fly a nine-iron 200

---

[1] As always, there is an awkwardness involved in using 'Britain' and 'Britishness' to refer to the sporting successes of 'English' figures (even those, like Froome, who are Kenyan-born). It is well understood that the terms are not interchangeable. But there is no evading the fact that, in 2013, an Englishman was also, by definition, British.

yards. Perhaps he was fired by the memories of the very same afternoon four years earlier, when he bogeyed three of the last four holes in the 2009 Open at Turnberry to miss out on a playoff by one stroke. Either way, it was risky.

It doesn't sound plausible that a whole life can change while a golf ball hangs in the air, suspended above a sea of upturned faces. But something like that happened when Westwood, with that distinctively bowed front arm of his, thumped down through his tee shot, firing the ball high into the blue haze. Convention demanded that, a few brief seconds later, it would thud down into the green, drawing a shout of approval from the gallery; but this was not a conventional moment. At the summit of its flight it seemed to stall and lose momentum; then it plummeted like a spent firework into the bunker that guarded the front. Westwood's Open dream crashed into the sand with it. Phil Mickelson was halfway through one of the great rounds of his life, and two hours later the famous silver claret jug had once more been dashed from the Englishman's lips.

But this was only a blip – it could hardly dampen the burst of euphoric flag-waving inspired by this astonishing weekend. Up and down the land, channel-hopping couch potatoes watched the pageant unfold and became punch-drunk, even confused, by all this success. Was that Froome grimacing at his tricky lie in the sand? Was that Luke Donald clinging on to a catch in the gully? Was that Stuart Broad juddering up the Champs-Elysées in a buttercup jersey? When it emerged that the Royal and Ancient was blaming the relatively modest crowd at Muirfield on the improbably hot weather, it added a further dimension of unreality to the weekend's events – everyone knew that the Open was supposed to be played under grey skies, and in gale-force drizzle.

It seemed no less than the occasion demanded that Prince George, the royal baby-in-waiting who had been keeping the world's media camped outside a London hospital for a week or more, should choose this golden moment – the day after Super-Sunday – to come into the world. It added royal glamour to the national rejoicing, and the papers led the cheers. 'A *tour de force* for British sport,' cried the *Independent*. 'How we've become a nation of winners,' trumpeted the *Daily Mail*. Even the *Financial Times* gave a nod of approval: 'Britain misses the treble,' it observed. 'But not a bad afternoon.'

The *Daily Telegraph* went so far as to couch its response in solemn historical terms with the question: 'Has British sport ever touched such glorious heights?'

Without wishing to spoil the party, there was a simple answer to this: yes. Marvellous as 2013 seemed, there was indeed a precedent. If Lee Westwood *had* found a way to win at Muirfield he would have done no more than echo the amazing triple success of 1934. Back then, in the space of three heady weeks at the end of June and start of July, Hedley Verity at Lord's, Henry Cotton in the Open and Fred Perry at Wimbledon had pulled off a spectacular treble of their own. If that wasn't enough, Dorothy Round won the women's title at Wimbledon as well, making it a British one-two – a tennis honour that was rare then and hasn't been matched since. In this light, the summer of 2013 – Lord's, Wimbledon and close in the Open – was good fun ... but a near miss.

There was an extra dimension to the summer of '34, though. The years since the end of the First World War had been tense. As is well known, something profound perished in the bloody mud of Flanders, something to do with faith and self-esteem. The patriotic zeal that led millions to sign up, the trust in the officer class and political elite – these were cracked, perhaps beyond repair. No one could forget the way the papers had described the fateful first day of the Somme, when 30,000 young men (sons, brothers, dads, pals) were massacred in just one hour after being ordered to walk – on *no account* run; vital to keep in formation – into the hot spray of machine-gun fire. To keep morale high the newspapers spoke of terrific gains, high hopes and eager heroes ... and never again would they be believed. D. H. Lawrence wrote: 'Each one of us had something shot out of him.' And then came the General Strike, the Wall Street crash, and the once-mighty pound sterling came loose from its moorings. Mass unemployment stalked the grim industrial landscape, and it was hard to be optimistic about anything.

Even in 1934 Britain was only beginning to emerge, dazed and blinking, like a fawn on wobbly legs, from that long tunnel. According to the experts the slump had touched bottom, but not everyone could see this – there were still hunger marches sweeping into London. And out in the wider world the dreadful silhouettes of new demons were darkening the public mood as tangled ideas about war, peace, social progress and imperial decline quarrelled in the mist. Not surprisingly, in such an atmosphere the simplicities of sport were very appealing. But on the day of Henry Cotton's marvellous victory in Kent (the same day that Perry was beating the Czech giant Roderich Menzel in the second round at Wimbledon) Germany's Chancellor, Adolf Hitler, was eliminating his enemies in a so-called 'Night of the Long Knives'. And while Verity wondered what to do about Bradman, Stalin was planning a purge of his own, and Mao Tse Tung was preparing to undertake the Long March. The world felt heavy and uncertain.

These juxtapositions are more than ironic; they are connected. The fact that the world was once more marching to a martial drum, and so soon after the war to end war, added intensity to the thirst for harmless fun and the hunger for national self-respect. No one thought that sport could be an antidote to war as such – that would have been foolish – but there *was* an interest, amounting to a need, for the sort of high spirits that escapist entertainments such as these could generate. And in 1934 it was beginning to dawn on the more thoughtful onlookers that in some hard-to-imagine way it might, to use a sporting analogy, be only half-time in the greatest and nastiest game of all: the struggle with Germany. When the Great War finally ended nothing seemed clearer or more important than that such things must *never* be contemplated again; but now – incomprehensibly – it was beginning to look as though these years of peace were just a pause for breath, a lull. Sometime soon, the whistle would blow and the same dreadful game would resume. Anything that lifted the mood was absolutely fine by them.

The problem was, home success was in short supply. There hadn't been a local Open winner since Jim Barnes in 1925, and brilliant American golfers like Bobby Jones, Walter Hagen and Gene Sarazen were making the prospect seem ever more forlorn. The lawns of Wimbledon belonged to a new generation of Americans, Australians and the quartet of French champions known as the 'Four Musketeers'; there hadn't been a British winner since Arthur Gore in 1909. Most painful of all, given cricket's claim to be a metaphor for English supremacy, England hadn't beaten Australia at Lord's since 1896. In the winter of 1932–3 Douglas Jardine's team had bludgeoned Bradman and company in Adelaide and Sydney, using Harold Larwood's electrifying fast bowling as the spearhead of an intimidating new tactic: Bodyline. But decency would not permit them to try anything like *that* again, in front of civilised English audiences, so the odds on a domestic victory at the so-called home of cricket looked slim indeed.

All of that was about to change. Just after midsummer's day, a quartet of English stars stepped into the spotlight to make the nation's heart race. First, the Yorkshire left-armer Verity took care of Australia, taking 15 wickets (14 in one day) to clinch the win. Then a snappy young English golfer, Cotton, led from start to finish in the Open at Royal St George's, smashing records as he went. Perry and Round made it a perfect full house when they powered their way to glory on the lush grass of Wimbledon.

It was an extraordinary shot in the arm, and, though it came at a time when there was no such thing as live television coverage, BBC radio, newsreels and newspapers kept the population thoroughly enthralled. All these heroes remained more distant and mysterious than they possibly could today, but this remoteness gave them the allure of legendary figures, like knights of old. Few knew what they looked like beyond the hazy likenesses on cigarette cards. But everyone knew who they were.

The modern world has not proved much better at remembering them either. At the time of writing, the 'detailed' timeline on the Wimbledon website mysteriously fails even to mention Fred Perry's debut win, though it finds room for the victories of Jack Crawford in 1933 and Helen Wills Moody in 1935.

The black and white images that survive as evidence of what happened conjure an era barely recognisable today. But in fact they do carry some noticeable echoes of modern anxieties. Then, as now, the clouds of economic gloom were starting to lift; then, as now, sporting glory could rebuild morale, perhaps even boost the dream of recovery. We no longer use the same language. Today's political leaders talk about a 'long-term economic plan' or 'boom and bust' while in 1934 the Chancellor of the Exchequer, Neville Chamberlain, could turn to Dickens to help him make his point in the House of Commons: 'We have now finished the story of *Bleak House*,' he said, 'and are sitting down this afternoon to enjoy the first chapter of *Great Expectations*.' His point was simple – the sky was clearing – and the sporting glories that followed his remark were a hint that perhaps it was true, perhaps Britain *could* start enjoying life again.

As the *Daily Telegraph* put it, revelling in the happy 'triumph heaping on triumph … success in golf, in tennis, in the cricket field', it was a sign of 'recovered national confidence'. This notion was taken up elsewhere. The *New York Times* ran a piece, 'Bully for John Bull', which made the very same point: 'It's about time they declared a Bank Holiday over there, to celebrate the comeback of Great Britain in sports.'

So, yes, the sporting summer of 2013 had a precursor. It was 1934, a genuine *annus mirabilis* for English ball games that burst like a star shell over one of the darker points in our national story. Naturally, the people involved were blissfully unaware of the baleful events that would soon throw it all into such stark relief.

It would be a mistake to imagine that we can think about the summer of '34 in terms that seem natural to us eight decades later, but some things have not changed. The public was as greedy for success then as it is now – perhaps even more so, given the simpler patriotism forged by the wartime us-and-them mentality. Yet the whirling sporting drama of 1934 has been overlooked by most discussions of the period. Many respectable accounts of life between the wars do not even mention it. Eminent scholars such as Paul Johnson, Arthur Marwick and A. J. P Taylor ignore characters like Verity, Cotton, Round and Perry, even though they made a deeper impression on the public mind than the usual suspects on the political merry-go-round. Neither the Liberal MP Charles Masterman nor C. L. Mowat, authors of two prominent works on these decades, had anything to say about these obvious highlights of British life at this time.

In 1963 the Trinidad-born C. L. R. James, a Marxist expatriate in London whose many trenchant analyses of Caribbean history were dappled by a profound love of cricket, made a point of rejecting the assumptions behind such a stance in *Beyond a Boundary*, a classic essay that put cricket at the heart of the Caribbean struggle for political and cultural liberation. His refusal to feel abashed – he took his own enthusiasms seriously – led him to reject all history that relegated his beloved game to the margins.

> *A famous liberal historian can write the social history of England in the nineteenth century, and two socialist historians can write what they declared to be the history of the common people of England, and between them never once mention the man who was the best-known Englishman of his time. I can no longer accept the system of values which could not find in these books a place for W. G. Grace.*

Consciously or not, he was echoing what the cricketer-author Sir Home Gordon wrote in a memorial tribute to Grace that was published by MCC in 1919:

> *In the midst of the excitement over the first Home Rule Bill a distinguished diplomatist observed that there was only one man more*

talked about in England than Gladstone, and that was Grace. This unique reputation will have to be considered when the social and moral history of the past fifty years comes to be written ...

In James's view, the measure of WG's importance was that he charmed his way into people's dreams and ideas about themselves further than anyone else; though his own roots were in the urban professional class, he seemed to typify the rustic charm of Merrie England in a vivid and enjoyable form. He stamped his bearded likeness on it and pushed it, like a toy yacht, into the future. As James put it: 'he brought and made a secure place for pre-industrial England in the iron and steel of the Victorian age.'

These days it is not unusual to rate popular culture alongside opera, ballet, poetry or anything else – the old hierarchies have lost their grip – but this was a bold remark in 1963. Not many of the histories written after this time have been willing to take it on board, however. Modern accounts of the period continue to gloss over the role played by men and women with sticks and balls. John Stevenson's *British Society 1914–1945*, part of the *Pelican Social History of Britain* series (1984), mentions Perry as an aspect of 'glamour', refers to the interwar years as a 'golden age' for cricket (a term usually used to describe the period *before* the Great War), and skips everything else. Juliet Gardner's 850-page *The Thirties* also cites Perry chiefly in connection with trousers, and ignores the rest. Martin Pugh's *We Danced All Night*, a detailed chronicle of life between the wars, gives Cotton one line ('the first British player to take golf seriously as a career'), which is not quite correct – Harry Vardon had won six Opens by then – while overlooking the other champions. Piers Brendon's rich and detailed panorama of the thirties, *The Dark Valley*, has no time for ball games. And Richard Overy's *The Morbid Age* allows nothing to distract his cast of high-minded intellectuals from the spectre of more war. Yet even the highest of those minds revelled in the ebb, the flow, the human drama, narrative interest and sheer pleasure of games. As the great Cambridge mathematician

G. H. Hardy said: 'If I knew I was going to die today, I think I should still want to hear the cricket scores.' Most afternoons, he would float free of higher mathematics and wander down to Fenner's to watch the young scholars at their games.

No one would suggest that mere popularity is a worthwhile index of importance – the fact that car crashes, avalanches and burning buildings draw crowds doesn't mean that we should have more of them – but this neglect is pointed. Sport is a major industry – as big as law, accountancy and publishing, according to some estimates. One recent EU report found that its economic impact is more significant than agriculture, forestry and fishing *combined* – not so surprising when one factors in the gigantic betting pyramid which it supports, and the upside-down scale of commercial priorities inspired by insatiable media interest. Top football managers earn more in a week than the Prime Minister is paid in a year, while the mass movement of sports fans fills planes, trains, cars, buses, stations, bars, pubs, restaurants and shops every day.

There is also the effect on morale – what modern social surveyors call the 'feel-good factor'. This, like the impact on the national self-image, is not easy to quantify, but palpable. Just as Britain's scintillating victories in the Tour de France ignited a burst of enthusiasm for cycling, and just as England's nail-biting win in the 2005 Ashes against Australia sent youngsters racing out into parks wanting to be Freddie Flintoff, so the many triumphs of 1934 inspired a surge of simple happiness and pride.

It is easy to go overboard in these areas. But while it would be an exaggeration to say that sport has supplanted religious faith, its emergence as a mass-market spectacle *has* coincided with the thinning of church congregations, and the two do have things in common – a sense of ritual, the worshipful attitude of fans, chanting, the veneration of icons and public ceremonial (hymns, speeches, minute's silences and so forth). If Marx were alive now he might well mutter that *sport* was the opium of the people – and is performed in cathedrals (stadiums) designed to remind us of an epic, ancestral past.

It is no small thing, in other words. It asks and answers questions that lie close to our deepest thoughts about meritocracy: who is the best, the quickest, the strongest, the most skilful or the most together – even: who is the smartest? It gives us dancing parables of biodiversity, celebrating hulking rowers and tiny gymnasts, beanpole high-jumpers and hefty shot-putters alike. And it does this by blending the important with the light-hearted. Sometimes – on the biggest international stages – it can feel huge and all-encompassing, blotting out normal life in favour of something more charged. At other times it feels pleasurably negligible, of no great consequence whatever.

Either way, sport matters. Emily Davidson threw herself before the King's horse in the 1913 Derby for precisely the same reason that Trenton Oldfield, 99 years later, swam out into the muddy Thames to disrupt the University boat race. Both knew that the public was watching; both were seeking the maximum exposure for their cause. This, too, is why first-class cricket and other sports were cancelled when war came – not because they were shallow, but for the opposite reason: because they really did occupy a unique place in British life. Idle pursuits would not have been a distraction to anyone.

In passing we might note that there is another, more pedestrian reason why sport makes so little impact on senior historians. Put simply, they tend to be academically gifted people who preferred books to games at school, and rebel against the weary Victorian faith in physical pursuits (*mens sana in corpore sano*). Nothing wrong with that. But it does lead to a point of view quick to see sport as trivial, even vulgar.

It is especially tempting to feel this way about the heady victories of 1934, since there really was plenty of other news. Hindsight, which has excellent eyesight, has rightly preferred to focus on the fact that the world was mired in economic misery, and that new tyrannies were flexing their muscles across Europe and Asia. Britain, the once-famous workshop of the world, was grinding to a halt, while its vaunted Empire was reaching the confused and dispirited end of its life. George Orwell called the thirties a 'riot of appalling folly', and Ronald Blythe, in *The Age of Illusion*, brooding on the poverty and dictator-worship that dominated the summer of 1934, called it 'rotten in a way no year had been before or since'. Who could care about games?

The answer is: millions of people. Because if sport is anything, it is a vibrant form of storytelling. And the early decades of the twentieth century were a time of widespread illiteracy; not everyone was gripped by books or plays, and moving pictures were a novelty. For the man in the street the most accessible drama was sport: Blackburn v Bolton, Wales v Scotland, England v Australia. It was our lads against your lads, and may the best team win.

CHAPTER ONE

Early Days

It begins like a children's book. Once upon a time, in a faraway land long ago, there lived three little boys. The oldest, Hedley Verity, was born on 18 May 1905 in a western suburb of Leeds, no more than a stone's throw from Headingley, the home of Yorkshire cricket. The house stood in one of several roads of brand-new brick cottages, built in the early years of the century to house textile workers from the mills along the River Aire. So in his infancy he could hear through his open window, without even knowing what it was, the splash of applause coming over the summer rooftops. And when he moved a few miles out of Leeds at the age of four the family still took their annual holiday in Scarborough, so Hedley and his father (a coal merchant, also named Hedley) could walk to the ground on North Marine Road to watch Yorkshire take on the MCC, or see the Gentlemen try their luck against the Players. One day …

Two years after Verity was born, and 50 miles to the south, on the Cheshire salt field that was fuelling the chemical industry on Merseyside, Henry Cotton came into the world. He was born in Church Hulme, near Knutsford, where King Canute – so the story ran – had once forded a stream. His mother, Alice le Poidevin, was from the Channel Islands (like the famous golfers Harry Vardon and Ted Ray), while his father, George, was an agricultural engineer in Cheshire – boilers for greenhouses, milk churns, potato sorters and other devices. The family's cottage on Macclesfield Road was hard by the station, so young Henry and his brother Leslie were railway children. Towering above the field on the far side of the road stood an awe-inspiring sight – a massive Victorian viaduct over whose 23 arches ran the Crewe–Manchester line, higher than the trees and kissing the clouds in a storm of steam and whistle. There was something about these giant red-brick limbs that stirred his imagination – the way they strode across the valley, 100 feet up, conquering the landscape in vast green steps …

Up in Stockport, in 1909, an ambitious cotton spinner named Samuel Perry decided to name his son Fred. The house is roughly where today's M60 cuts under the Stockport Viaduct; back then it was a cottage beside the River Goyt. Sam Perry's job would soon take the family north to Bolton and west to Wallasey, a fishing village that is now an industrial port on the Wirral, a mile or two seaward of the thrumming waterfronts of Liverpool and Birkenhead.[1] Wallasey was golf country – home to Major Stableford, deviser of the recreational scoring system used by the entire golf world – and the links of Hoylake were only a few miles to the south. But the young Fred Perry, alone in his room, didn't notice. He played draughts as he watched the boats come and go.

Even in these sketches it is clear that the three central figures in this story have much in common. They were born within four years of each other in a unique environment, the clanking industrial zone of northern England that was still – many years after Dickens and Engels groaned over its many miseries – the thundering blast furnace of Britain's booming power. Verity, the oldest, grew up in the heart of textile-humming Yorkshire; Cotton and Perry came from the other side of the Pennines. But all of them had north of England blood in their veins, which made them kindred spirits.

As chance would have it, Perry actually shared a birthday (18 May) with Verity. But that wasn't all. Both boys lived in tiny

[1] The Wirral was in Cheshire until 1974, when it became part of Merseyside.

terraced houses built to withstand cold winters – only Cotton was free to wander the fresh pastures of rural England. But when Verity moved to the wooded hills around Rawdon, half an hour up the Aire valley, he, too, had space to run around. The children's area in the old house was divided between his toy soldiers and his sister Grace's board games, but upstairs, alone in his room, he would practise his stance, rehearsing endless strokes in the wardrobe mirror; or he would whip away with a skipping rope to improve his strength, over and over again. The sound of his feet thudding on the floor became part of the daily music of the house.

Verity had been going to Headingley with his father since he was eight years old, and was entranced from the first. A few years later he was playing in his own right, at Yeadon and Guisely Secondary School, and would catch the tram to watch grown-up cricket in Bradford and Leeds, worshipping at the altar of local heroes such as George Hirst and Wilfred Rhodes, and sometimes – perhaps above all – Surrey's Jack Hobbs. This habit led him into tricky waters; on one occasion he dodged a day of school and, according to his headmaster, 'only escaped a sound punishment by a small margin'. It helped that he was already, by then, a likeable boy: quiet, careful and industrious.[2]

Cotton and Perry also had fathers who enjoyed their boys' sporting hopes. And this paternal involvement did not cease when the boys grew into long trousers. 'Always remember,' George Cotton would say, urging Henry on to bigger and better things, 'that the best is only just good enough.' When Fred Perry was a teenager, his teetotal father Sam promised him £100 if he could reach his 21st birthday without touching alcohol. And Hedley went to sleep each night beneath a plaque on the wall above his pillow, which carried the defiant reminder: 'They told him it

---

[2] 'Not once did I hear him boast,' said the lenient headmaster, William Rigby. He thought that young Hedley was 'reserved, a good type'. In sparing the rod, however, he may have devised a punishment more agonising than a mere beating: he banned Verity from cricket for the rest of the summer term.

couldn't be done.' All of them, in other words, were expected to work as hard as they could, and to do well.

Although Verity, Cotton and Perry were born in the early years of the 20th century, there is a case for saying they drew their first breaths in more traditional, nineteenth-century air. There were stirrings of the great shifts in science and technology that lay ahead, but so far as most people were aware the new century did not truly dawn until May 1910, a few days before Fred Perry's first birthday, when King Edward VII died and a curtain fell upon the gilded Edwardian past. Until then, the old ways held good.

The months that followed the royal funeral suggested the arrival of many new ideas. In November an arresting show of paintings, 'Manet and the Impressionists', opened in London; the following year Chekhov's *The Cherry Orchard* had its British premiere, along with first appearances for Diaghilev's *Ballets Russes* at Covent Garden, and a cubist drawing by Picasso. The ingredients of modernism were flickering into life.

And it wasn't only artistic circles that felt the impact. There were strikes on the docks and railways, while the suffragettes were smashing windows to draw attention to their own deep grievance. The social landscape was shifting, and new political groups were stirring civic life in ways that challenged the traditional order of things. In short, a new mindset was being forged, one that signalled a sea change in English life: it embraced religious nonconformity, equality, co-operative effort, self-reliance and civic pride.

Verity, Cotton and Perry were all children of this spiritual revolution. All had fathers who were lay preachers – Hedley Verity Senior in the Congregational Church, George Cotton and Sam Perry in the Wesleyan tradition. They were part of the same morally resolute and upwardly mobile force in English life: Verity's father began as a tram driver in Leeds before becoming a coal merchant and urban district councillor, full of the common-sense wisdom known as 'Yorkshire caution', while Sam Perry had political hopes – in Wallasey he was Secretary of the Co-operative

Party, a progressive wing of the Labour movement, with its office in the Liver Building across the estuary.

As a result, all three had a well-mannered upbringing. The inscription on the stone water fountain near Verity's birthplace in Leeds said: 'Drink and be Grateful', and to grow up at this time was to be surrounded by admonishments of this sort. Cotton's father insisted on the importance of thank-you letters, while Perry's had a thing about shaking hands and looking people in the eye. When Verity Senior met England's captain Douglas Jardine years later, the most important thing he wanted to express was his pride in the fact that in his son he had 'bred a better man than myself'.

It does not seem a coincidence that all three of these sporting stars came from such a precise strand of English society. They breathed the same cold air, inhaled the same *Zeitgeist*, drank the same mother country's milk. They were not working class in the old proletarian sense; but neither were they part of the elite – the well-heeled, white-collar world of law, government and finance. They were the new bourgeoisie, the thrusting make-something-of-yourself class that, like Oliver Twist, wanted more: more toys, more fun, more time, more education, more everything. In due course both Cotton and Perry would cast themselves as gifted outsiders trying to break into the inner sanctums of their sports, but neither was a humble proletarian, hammering, as part of a mass uprising, at the closed doors of the establishment. They were something else – individualistic members of the aspiring urban middle class, what modern politicians like to call 'decent hard-working families' – energetic, clean-cut and ambitious.

At the height of the Industrial Revolution it was sometimes said that what Manchester thinks today, London thinks tomorrow. London was merely the administrative capital of Britain's empire; the great cities of the north were its humming engine room. This was still partly true at the beginning of the 20th century. Yorkshire and Cheshire were not provincial locales – they were part of Britain's propulsion unit. But though Verity, Cotton and

Perry did not drift in from the margins, they *were* part of a social upheaval that prized financial independence and self-help while also nurturing co-operative ideas and movements. This allowed them a dream of personal advancement never before imagined in Britain. A generation earlier Hedley, Henry and Fred might have been the kind of desperate, soot-stained labourers described by Dickens and Engels; indeed, they were still surrounded by the stick figures of Lowry's landscapes. But as they grew into their respectable Christian names they were walking into a new world.

The fourth character in this story, Dorothy Round, is the odd one out. Though born in the same period as the others (1908) and in a similar place – Dudley, a Worcestershire satellite of Birmingham[3] – the fact that she was a woman changed things markedly.

Her father was a successful building contractor in the Midlands, but if Round's early years were comfortable (her home had a tennis court) she shared with Perry, Cotton and Verity the fact that her family was staunchly Methodist – taking the Sabbath seriously, putting aside not just games but novels and other childish things. Dorothy's own literary preference was for religious books, and in later years, when she travelled around the Midlands to sports events, she would often speak at prayer meetings. Just as Eric Liddell, at the Paris Olympics in 1924, refused to run on the Sunday, she too publicly swore off ever playing tennis on the Lord's day.

Like her three famous contemporaries she had a sports-loving father, who built her a special on-court practice board so she could work on her game. Her three brothers took precedence, of course, but she was at home with a racquet in her hand from infancy

---

[3] The Birmingham area actually had an older tennis history even than Wimbledon: a hybrid of rackets and pelota, the game was born on the croquet lawns of Edgbaston, and in 1874 an English solicitor (Harry Gem) teamed up with a Spanish businessman (Juan Perera) and two doctors to create Britain's first tennis club at Leamington Spa.

onwards, and her brothers made sure she grew used to a hard-hitting game. When, aged 11, she won a local doubles tournament, no one was very surprised. Had she been a boy, she might have been pushed to take the game even more seriously, but she was content to play in an amateur spirit. Tennis, she later told the *Sydney Morning Herald*, was 'just a jolly game which I enjoyed'. She was clearly gifted, and liked other sports – hockey, badminton, gymnastics – but her ambition was to be a 'gymnasium teacher'.

When one of her brothers put her down for the Worcestershire juniors competition, she went along in a give-it-a-go spirit ... and won. And people sat up when, on holiday in North Wales, she went in for a local event at the last minute, turned up wearing her school blazer and won that, too. She was only 15, and one of the players she beat was a Wimbledon regular named Joan Strawson. At the British hard-court championships she fared less well – on her debut she won just seven points in the first set, and heard a contemptuous voice in the crowd saying: 'Who is she, anyway?' But the Lawn Tennis Association was well aware that a fine young player was rising in the Midlands.

While her achievement in winning Wimbledon in 1934 was every bit as terrific as Fred Perry's, however, there was no getting round the fact that women's tennis was not at this time comparable in scale or impact to the men's game. Women under the age of 30 had not even won the right to *vote* until 1928, and it wasn't just that women's tennis was wrongly seen as a junior form – it really was a frail, fledgling version of itself.

Still, there *were* hints of a new dawn – the stylish Frenchwoman Suzanne Lenglen won Wimbledon every year but one from 1919 to 1925 (and the French Championship five times into the bargain) as she single-handedly raised and buffed up the image of women's tennis – partly through her tremendous play, and partly thanks to her dashing skirts and dramatic bandannas. In 1926 Lenglen even paved the way towards the idea of women *professionals* by playing exhibition matches in America for money, though this was to raise funds for war-damaged France as much as for herself.

In one way tennis was more equal than many sports, thanks to its social importance. But this wasn't saying a lot. The women's game was still a demure affair, a fashion parade – a matter of risqué new skirts, shocking bare forearms, innovative necklines and so forth. Even over-arm serving had until lately been thought unfeminine,[4] and when in later years Round started winning titles, the papers made quite a point of telling readers that she liked knitting, made her own jumpers, loved children and had been popping down to the shops on her own since she was, oh, so high. No one ever talked about Fred Perry in such homely, domesticated terms.

But while it is easy to shake our heads at the disparity, we can't avoid the fact that Round's impact as a sporting celebrity could not, given the social fabric of the time, rival that of the male stars whose doings dominated the headlines. Though a brilliant and pioneering player – genuinely so, since she was forging a path trodden by few women, at a time when suffragette marches were a fresh memory – she could not send hats spinning into the air like a Verity, a Cotton or a Perry. It wasn't her fault; it was just the way things were. But there is a significant point of historical etiquette here: though it would be wrong to regard her efforts as lesser than the men's, neither would it be accurate to imagine they had equal weight, since she was in a less competitive sport, with fewer participants and a lower level of public interest. To project our sense of sexual equality on to the past would be to misrepresent it; the newspapers did take pleasure and pride in Round's victory, but it didn't occur to them that women's tennis was anything but the smiling baby sister of the men's game. We can sigh over the imbalance as much as we like, but we should not pretend that things were otherwise.

---

[4] Ellen Stawell-Brown caused quite a flutter when she took to serving over-arm at Wimbledon in 1906, and it took a while for the new method to catch on. But it did mean she was able to pass on some useful tennis tips to her grandson, Tim Henman.

It is a reminder, if nothing else, that the past really is a foreign country, and that they really did do things differently there. In the early years of the last century, most Britons had never even visited the next county, the next town or the next village; many lived in horizons bounded by the nearest hill. The railway was busy changing all that, but the motor car was a new-fangled toy, aeroplanes were a futuristic fantasy and hardly anyone had a telephone. People's hopes and habits were not the same as ours.

Indeed, as John Maynard Keynes famously observed in *The Economic Consequences of the Peace*, pre-war Britain was a profoundly complacent place: 'The inhabitant of London could order by telephone, sipping his morning tea from India, the various products of the whole earth, in such quantity as he might see fit, and reasonably expect their early delivery upon his doorstep. He could invest in business ventures far around the world, and spend the fruits of other men's labour on his own comfort and amusement. He could move through foreign parts without a passport, purchase whatever he pleased with his super-strong pound, own his own house and conduct his affairs without interference.' Best of all, the lucky fellow at the centre of all this imperial plenty could think this state of affairs 'normal, certain and permanent'.

Such fellows could hardly have been more wrong.

CHAPTER TWO

Children of the Great War

Verity, Cotton and Perry had something more important in common than a coincidence of social background. All three boys grew up in the sombre shadow of the First World War, and though they were too young to fight – Verity, the oldest, was 13 when the war ended, and the closest to being recruitment fodder – they were old enough to have their imaginations and their emotional reflexes influenced, if not shaped, by the conflict.

This is not the place to retell the horror story that was the Great War, and it would be clumsy to attribute the success of the three sportsmen to the sombre mood of the time – there were thousands of games-mad boys who never scaled such heights. But we do need at least to register the fact that the roots of their 1934 triumphs drew nourishment from this soil. The world in which they were raised was the home front of a nation at war, and since that nation's boys were the prime target of the recruitment drive by newspapers, pulpits and politicians, theirs was not a normal upbringing.

In one sense they were fortunate: unlike the children of younger parents, they never had to face the giddy terror of waving father off to face the music, or gasp at telegrams saying that he would never return.[1] But what they personally saw or experienced in

---

[1] Though Henry Cotton's uncle Sidney *was* called to arms (his name is on the Roll of Honour in St Luke's church). He survived, but young Henry would have been well aware of the fear that struck families whose men were in the trenches.

the four-year course of the war is irrelevant. The social landscape of the entire country, the nervous system of daily life in Britain, was being irrevocably shaped by the enormous struggle with Germany, and everyone was affected, however hard they tried to ignore it.

As it happened, the signs were impossible to miss. The Parliamentary Recruiting Committee printed 54 million recruiting posters, more than one for every citizen ('Fight for King and Empire ... Take up the Sword of Justice ... Rally Round the Flag!'), and war fever often took even more direct expression. The Order of the White Feather was founded in August 1914 with the intention of shaming so-called cowards, and it wasn't fussy whom it targeted – it often picked out teenaged boys.

The youth of Britain was thus besieged on two fronts. On the one hand they were urged to be young lions, aflame with bash-the-Hun team spirit and a desire to do their duty; on the other, they were supposed to feel guilty. This is what boy-culture was like – warlike fantasies mixed with white-faced trepidation. And to an extent that was not at first clear, this really was a boys' war. Many decades of indoctrination (Wilfred Owen's 'old Lie') had managed to fire a whole generation of youngsters with public school, muscular-Christian ideas about sacrifice ('Now God be thanked for matching us with His Hour' – Rupert Brooke), while luring the malnourished children of the industrial class with the promise of a square meal. The mixture was effective. By the last year of war, half the 1.75 million men on the Western Front were 18 or under. And by this time the average life expectancy of a subaltern on the front was barely six weeks.

Some of the new recruits were underage by some distance. It has been estimated that 250,000 boy-soldiers were taken into uniform by a military caste happy to turn a blind eye to dates of birth. One, Sidney Lewis, was waved through as someone who could pass for 17 by a patriotically-minded doctor, when in fact he was only 12.

In this context, a 13-year-old like Hedley Verity would certainly have had some idea what he might have to get into. On Boxing Day 1914 the *Observer* printed a cheerful set of schoolboy howlers intended to reveal how little some children knew about the historic events swirling over their heads. Q: 'What is the Iron Cross?' A: 'A medal the Kaiser gives his soldiers for brutality.' Q: 'Why did St Petersburg change its name to Petrograd?' A: 'So the Germans won't know where to find it.'

Cotton and Perry, too, as children of serious-minded, literate households, would have been at least dimly aware of the cataclysm erupting around them. Even if they did not scan the newspapers or follow the endless false dawns through which our brave armies were always advancing to victory, they could hardly have evaded the drip-drip of war talk. It was there in the 'Beastly Hun' atrocity stories used to stiffen morale, in which German nuns and nurses dashed out children's brains, or offered parched Tommies water only to slosh it on to the ground. It was there in the cinemas – an estimated 20 million people (half the country, in just six weeks) saw the new film *The Somme*, and glimpsed for themselves the horror of the trenches. And it was there in the legion of war rumours – such as the one about the 'Angel' of Mons, for instance, who hovered over our brave troops, or the 100,000 Russians who, it was said, had landed in Scotland and were marching south to join the fray.[2]

The national propaganda effort (presided over by the novelist John Buchan) went to great lengths to spread such messages, using papers, magazines, paintings, adventure stories, cigarette cards, lectures and mobile-cinema trucks to splash cautionary tales. The Hun was burning cathedrals ... severing children's hands ...

---

[2] In *Memoirs of a Fox-Hunting Man*, his account of his own gilded life before 1914, Siegfried Sassoon remembered that 'everyone' was gossiping about the imaginary Russians – even as they warned that 'the Germans might land at Dover any day'.

crucifying prisoners ... slicing away nurses' breasts.[3] And he was poised to invade. A devilish attack could happen any minute – not for nothing were clear nights becoming known as 'Zeppelin weather': huge balloon-bombers the size of two football pitches were drifting this way.

It worked: everyone learned to hate the Germans. Perfume emporia had to post signs pointing out that their ravishing Eau-de-Cologne wasn't *really* from Cologne; the London and North Western Railway changed the name of one locomotive from *Dachshund* to *Bulldog*; and German Shepherds were reclassified as disputed canine territory – Alsatians. William le Queux's alarmist 1915 thriller, *The German Spy System from Within*, sold 40,000 copies in a week, while Buchan's *The Thirty-Nine Steps* ran for months on the London stage. Almost everyone had a friend who had a brother who knew a fellow whose cousin's sister claimed to have actually met a secret agent.[4]

Once the war bogged itself down in the mud of Belgium there was no need for such cultural pressure: everyday life on the home front was thoroughly impregnated by war. Churches seemed to be entirely given over to funerals, while the pinched food ration – the modest butter allowance and filthy 'war bread', a grey loaf padded out with beans and potato – became a grim fact of everyday life. The tight meat allowance meant that youngsters had to get used to

---

[3] The young Robert Graves, in *Goodbye to All That*, worked on the assumption that such stories were 'wartime exaggeration'; but that left lots of room for genuine alarm. He did not believe it when the newspapers claimed that Belgian priests were being hung upside down and used as the clappers inside bells; but he was 'outraged' by the more credible accounts. He had a particular reason to feel sensitive on this subject: his own name, on the Charterhouse school list, was Robert von Ranke Graves.

[4] There was so much 'invasion literature' that P. G. Wodehouse was driven to satirise it, in 1909, in *The Swoop*. 'It was inevitable,' he wrote, keeping a straight face, 'in the height of the Silly Season, that such a topic as the simultaneous invasion of Great Britain by nine foreign powers should be seized upon by the press.'

liver, tripe, offal and other delicacies. And as a result of DORA – the Defence of the Realm Act – a once-free country was taking its first steps towards being a nanny state. Landmark buildings were requisitioned, land reassigned and men conscripted. Kites and bonfires were banned, and pub hours regulated. There was a pulse of stirring poetry in the air ('Not a drum was heard, not a funeral note'), the clocks were adjusted (winter daylight began an hour earlier) and the street lamps were dimmed. Lakes and ponds were drained so that moonlight would not glimmer to the sky; and travel was restricted. Holidays were cancelled and employment reformed around a whole new industry: munitions. The world felt harsher, drabber, poorer.

Though the propaganda effort was intense,[5] it was not true that 'no one knew' how awful things were over there. Yes, the papers were censored: honesty was discouraged for reasons of morale, and editors bent over backwards to print good news. There were endless tales of gallant British advances and manoeuvres, and an equal number about Germany's 'medieval war manners'. Victory was always being presented as imminent – the idea that it would all be over by Christmas remained the official line, year after year after year. But this was a new kind of war, one that engaged the whole population, and even in the opening months the truth slipped through. The *Cheshire Observer* liked printing first-hand stories by any local lad (13,000 had signed up by the end of 1914) who had made it safely home. One, Eric Wetherby, returned from the hell of Mons and said, 'It is the worst thing I ever saw. You simply cannot describe it.'

Quite a few such tales slipped through the net, especially in the early months, when the net was not tight. According to one

---

[5] It was reported, in a disquieting item in *The Times* in 1917, that Germany had built factories for melting down human bodies. Such stories were believed, though they were not true – which meant that when similar rumours floated across the Channel in the Second World War they were dismissed, although this time they were all too real.

eyewitness in the Cheshire papers, the Germans were stacking up the bodies of dead comrades as ramparts for their snipers. Another, describing a trudge through a shattered wood, said: 'One of the men thought he had seen a piece of bacon, but on close inspection it turned out to be a man's leg.' Yet another related the terrifying vigil imposed on British snipers, who had to lie alone and trembling in the muddy darkness of no man's land, using wet turnip leaves for camouflage, as they waited all night for one clear shot at the Hun. 'It was not war,' declared a soldier on witnessing a stretcher party blown apart by shellfire. 'It was murder.'

Life was not necessarily rigid for children; on the contrary, thanks to the decline in supervision caused by male conscription and the number of women in the workplace, juvenile delinquency boomed. 'They run wild, unobserved,' ran a letter to *The Times* in 1915. The streets were full of martial signs that boys like Verity, Cotton and even the youngest, Perry, could not have missed. There were recruiting offices everywhere: the one in Chester used a tramcar festooned with flags to cart newcomers from the castle to the station, while the one in Leeds bore the words 'For King and Country' in giant letters on the side, with a resonant destination on the front: Berlin. There were tented villages for new recruits, who paraded in town squares and parks, and solemn funerals everywhere – not to mention interminable roll calls of the dead in churches and newspapers. Soldiers visited schools to spread the gospel of self-sacrifice; street corners filled up with floral tributes; people with sunken eyes wore black armbands; and a hefty chunk of the nation's children lost their dads – by the end of the war Britain had 350,000 fatherless boys. The whole country, it seemed, had gone khaki.

Some of the images on Britain's streets were disquieting. The war years spread over 40,000 amputees and 270,000 wounded men across English society, filling the hastily requisitioned hospitals. The workers labouring in the TNT factories (most of them women) were becoming known as 'canaries' thanks to the pallid yellow skin they developed on the production line; there were thousands of Belgian refugees in shelters; and gangs of German prisoners of war cowered at railway stations en route to the internment camps. Men paced the streets with sandwich boards – 'Be Ready to Defend Your Home and Women from the German Huns'. And moments of intense military importance were often marked at home – in December 1917, for instance, when every church steeple in the land pealed out to celebrate the 'victory' at Cambrai.

These and other echoes hummed in the British bloodstream. In the early months of the conflict the seaside venue for the Verity family's annual summer holiday, Scarborough, was shelled by German ships trying out their strength – the trains into Leeds were soon full of people trying to escape the bombardment. Two years later, the whole area was shaken by the news that the Leeds Pals, the Yorkshire regiment recruited to do its bit for King and Country, had lost 15 officers and 233 men in only a few blinks of an eye on the fateful first morning at the Somme. 'We were two years in the making,' wrote Private A. V. Pearson, 'and ten minutes in the destroying.'

When carriages full of wounded troops from Flanders began to arrive in Yorkshire, crowds numbering 6,000 or more thronged outside the railway stations to see what these unfortunates looked like. And though Verity himself was now safely tucked away in the hills at Rawdon, the war burst into fiery life in December 1916, when the nearby Barnbow Works, which employed 16,000 workers, most of them women, blew up. Barnbow produced 24 million shells and half a million tons of high explosive for the war effort, and the blast shook a huge area, killing 35 workers and wounding hundreds in a home front echo of Belgium. A year later, just before Verity's 12th birthday, a test pilot, William Ding, crashed his plane in front of a crowd of 1,000 people at a Leeds airfield.

It didn't matter where people lived. Cotton grew up in rural Cheshire, nowhere near the front line, but it was the same story there. The Chester Regiment sent 1,000 men to Mons in the first weeks of the war, and three weeks later only 200 were alive. Here, too, hospital trains full of dazed young men with shattered limbs started rolling into Chester station. Local people put on orchestra concerts for the wounded (and for the needy Belgian refugees) and big crowds gathered in the Roman town square to listen to speeches and sing 'Land of Hope and Glory' (written in 1902). Henry Cotton might even have heard whispers about the Gretna Green disaster of 1915, when a military convoy collided with two passenger trains, one of them the express to Glasgow, killing over 200 and injuring 200 more.[6] For all he knew, that doomed train might have rushed over the towering viaduct across the field from his front door.

Liverpool felt even hotter blasts. As a youngster, Fred Perry knew all too well that there was danger in the sky – Liverpool suffered air raids even in 1914–18 – and on Saturdays he himself, along with his classmates at school, had to practise safety drills using a Red Cross flag in a field. The great River Mersey was a hooting cavalcade of ships, hauling consignments of young lives to the cauldron on the Continent; it was a common sight to see these vessels breasting the swell as they rode out of the estuary into the Irish Sea. In 1918 Perry went on a school trip to welcome home two troop carriers – *Iris* and *Daffodil* – back from the Zeebrugge Raid, a daring escapade that had been a costly attempt (more than 200 died) to block the entrance to Bruges by sinking three hulks in the harbour channel. The Mersey ferryboats had been in the thick of the action. It was nice to have a day off, though there was a catch – 'We were all handed Union Jacks,' Perry recalled, 'and had to congregate on Merseyside and wave them furiously.'

---

[6] On their return to Edinburgh after the accident, some survivors, dishevelled men of the Royals Scots, were mistaken for enemy prisoners and pelted by children.

Henry Cotton was the only one of these three boys pushed from home and hearth. His own family had to watch as Henry's uncle joined up, but he was one of the lucky ones: he returned (and his name is on the memorial at St Luke's in Holmes Chapel). But even if, safe in the folds of the Cheshire countryside, young Henry could let the war pass over his head, things changed when his father moved south to take a job at the London Salt Company, supplying local authorities and fish merchants. The family settled in south London, first in Peckham, then Dulwich. The war was even closer here, and to avoid the German airships overhead, with their lethal cargoes of incendiary bombs, Henry was sent to Reigate Grammar School in Surrey. This was close enough, on calm days, to catch the blast from Ypres and Passchendaele. The thunderous pounding at the Somme, in July 1916, shook windows and bedsteads as far off as Croydon.

But it was the oldest, Verity, who was the most mindful of what war meant. When it ended he was 13, alarmingly close to becoming howitzer fodder, and he was already thinking of making the summer game his life. Some fathers might have had a tantrum over a stand like this, tried to knock sense into the lad, but Hedley Senior backed his son's dream as long as he pursued it with diligence. In some respects he was a hard taskmaster: when he loaned Hedley money to buy encyclopedias he wanted repayment in weekly instalments. He soon relented – the debt could be worked off by cleaning books and boots. But the one thing he would not tolerate was a casual attitude. When Hedley came home from matches he would ask: 'Any criticism? Any faults?' The whole point, so far as he was concerned, was to be always learning, always improving.

So it was that one day, as Verity sat on a gate with Frank Whitaker, a friend from the village who used to let him practise with the students from the Baptist Theological College in Rawdon, he confronted the fearful facts of life.

'Do you believe I can play for Yorkshire?' he asked. 'No one but my father does.'

By way of reply Whitaker rolled up a trouser leg to reveal an ugly line of wounds. He, too, had nursed cricketing hopes until shrapnel had raked his leg a few weeks before Armistice Day. Both of them knew he had been lucky: his cricket fantasy may have died, but he had at least come home; he could still swing on gates.

Perhaps the most inescapable consequence of the war, however, for all such boys and girls – was the immediate cancellation of top-level sport. 'This is not the time to play games,' Field Marshal Lord Roberts declared in 1914. First-class cricket was stopped in its tracks by a notorious letter in *The Sportsman* of August 1914, by W. G. Grace: 'It is not fitting at a time like this that able-bodied men should be playing cricket.'

In all more than 200 cricketers marched off to war, and many did not return. The most famous losses were Warwickshire's Percy Jeeves (the name immortalised in P. G. Wodehouse's valet), the great googly merchant Reggie Schwarz of South Africa, and Kent's Colin Blythe (a left-arm spinner, like Verity), who died at Passchendaele in 1917. But every school, village, club and town lost a player or two. Verity would have felt keenly the loss of the Scarborough Festival, which was cancelled because it was, said MCC, 'hurtful to the feelings of a section of the public'. Youngsters like him were forever tripping over news of this or that player who had volunteered, or died.

All sports lost notable names. Rugby had to mourn David Bedell-Sivright of Scotland – one of some 30 internationals to be killed, while Ronnie Poulton-Palmer was one of 26 England players (captain in 1914) who never returned. His last words, after he stopped a sniper's bullet in 1915, were: 'I shall never play at Twickenham again.'

Tony Wilding, a New Zealand tennis player who won Wimbledon four times running before the war (and was also, in the way of things back then, a first-class cricketer) was killed by a direct hit on his dugout at Neuve Chapelle. And Captain John Graham, part of an outstanding golf generation at Hoylake, died at Ypres ('No greater blow has fallen on the ancient game,' wrote the *Glasgow Herald*, 'since Lieutenant F. G. Tait laid down his life on the South African veldt'). Graham had been Leading Amateur in the Open no fewer than five times before the war, without quite having the game to beat Vardon, Taylor and Braid – the so-called 'Great Triumvirate' that dominated golf in the early years of the century. Lord Annesley, the amateur champion of Ireland and a son of Co. Down, was yet another victim, killed on an air raid over the Channel.

Every leading cricket-playing county suffered, and Yorkshire was no exception. A few heroes made it through unscathed: Jack Wilson, who played nine times before the war, won a medal bombing German submarines at Zeebrugge in 1915, and destroyed a Zeppelin near Brussels a few weeks later. But it was impossible to ignore the enormous number of war dead. One of the county's finest ever players, Second Lieutenant Major Booth from Pudsey – an all-rounder who took 181 wickets in 1913, some of which young Hedley would have seen – was a casualty, and he was far from alone. There were lots of white roses among the poppies. Booth served alongside several of his Yorkshire team-mates: Arthur Dolphin, Roy Kilner and Abe Waddington. When he fell, his remains were later identified by the MCC cigarette case in his uniform.

Football was slow to hang up its boots, a fact that may have helped relegate it below rugby in the esteem of the upper classes. But in due course the footballers who joined the fray suffered heavier losses than anyone. Some 2,000 joined up, and hundreds died. Spurs lost 11 players, Newcastle seven, West Ham five. Seven members of the Heart of Midlothian team of 1913–14, the most successful in Scotland's history, perished. Donald Bell, of Crystal Palace and Newcastle United, won the Victoria Cross in 1916, but died five days after the action that led to his recommendation.

At Alleyn's, the private school to which he had won a scholarship, Cotton would have sat through regular readings of the war list, with all the names of all the schoolboys who had given their lives for their country. As someone from a less favoured background Verity might not have been *quite* so caught up in the pathos of the famous schoolboys who fell – Howell of Repton, Poole of Rugby, Whitehead of Clifton ('the perfect flower of the public schools', as *Wisden* described him) and so on. But cricket was by no means a trivial pursuit in Yorkshire, so when the club President, Lord Hawke, declared it a 'strict condition' of employment that the county's leading players should do war work, it was clear that something enormous was afoot. It was nice for fans that the Bradford League kept going (indeed thrived, attracting men like Hobbs, Barnes and Woolley) though to Hawke this, too, was a 'scandalous' breach of decorum, and the *Yorkshire Post* conceded that it was 'out of harmony with the spirit of the times'. Either way, the 1917 game in which a big crowd saw Hobbs strike 132 against Barnes in Bradford was one of the great days in Yorkshire folklore. The sound of the ball flying into the neighbouring roofs and windows echoed across the county.

There is much about the past that remains forever hidden. We do not know if Verity was watching football at Elland Road the day the call went out for recruits, and 500 men marched on to the pitch to loud applause. There is no evidence that he was one of the Boy Scouts sent to guard Eccup Reservoir, or detailed to harvest the flax needed to make linen for aeroplane wings. It is possible that he rattled a tin can in the town centre (Leeds raised £33,000 this way), since lots of children did so at this time. And he just might have been in the 40,000 crowd at the Town Hall on Armistice Day, to listen to the police band and watch fireworks – the *Yorkshire Post* reported that the whole city was 'alive with singing, merrymaking and shouting'. But even if he took no part in such things, and stayed in the nets at Rawdon, grooving that deliberate high action which in time would bring him so many wickets, the war would have been stealing into his soul like a ribbon of smoke, or the sound of distant thunder.

Of course we can't draw anything like a line of cause-and-effect between the ghastly nightmare of Flanders and Verity's arm ball, between the choking splutter of doomed gas victims in the Ypres Salient and the Perry backhand, between the smashed victims of Neuve Chapelle and Cotton's silky ball-striking. Nor can we take it as read that boys like Verity, Cotton and Perry were keen readers of news reports or poems. George Orwell, himself a schoolboy during these years, later claimed that the uproar on the Western Front made less impression on him than the sinking of the *Titanic*, and that his abiding memory of the war was ... margarine. But he was aware, ever after, of a sense that something momentous had been happening, so we can take all of the newspaper war talk to be representative of the tense, fraught climate of opinion through which they moved. The youth of Britain grew in the shade of world-shaking events that touched everyone, even those who looked the other way.

It is well understood now that the Great War produced a pronounced shift in the British state of mind. At the time, however, the picture was murky – hardly anyone could say just what this savage fight, with its obscure origins in Austria and 'Servia', was about. But by the time the boom of gunfire faded there were few illusions left. In 1918 Siegfried Sassoon spoke for many when he wrote, in *The War Poems*:

> *You smug-faced crowds with kindling eye*
> *Who cheer when soldier lads march by,*
> *Sneak home and pray you never know*
> *The hell where youth and laughter go.*[7]

[7] Some modern historians recoil from the verbal power of lines such as these, and speak disparagingly about the 'poets' view' of the war, as if its sensitivity to suffering made it less profound than the 'Generals' view' that the men were expendable.

The lesson seemed clear, and on the first anniversary of the bitter end, in November 1919, the *Daily Herald* delivered a prayer that many felt to be necessary: 'Swear to yourselves, this day at 11 o'clock, that never again, God helping you, shall the peace and happiness of the world fall into the murderous hands of cynical old men.'

It took years for the full implications of all this to become clear – at first there was only a vague sense that this war had been no plumed, glorious affair – but it was clear that the Britain blinking its way into the 1920s, broken-spirited and angry, was not the land that had marched off to war. The years of what that dogged chronicler of dismay C. E. Montague called 'mud and stench and underground gloom' had taken their toll. A generation of Britons had been exposed to a life 'squalid without precedent'.[8]

Nothing seemed the same. Tracts with unsettling titles like 'Tradition Lies in the Dust' or 'Is There a God?' appeared on station bookstalls. An Englishman's home was no longer his castle; on a war footing, the state had assumed a power over individuals it would not lightly renounce. The social make-up of the population was new, too. The women who poured into the workplace were not willing to return to home and hearth like quiescent pets – and since nearly 10 per cent of their menfolk under the age of 45 had vanished, women were in any case still in great demand as workers. As a result, the war helped to clinch what years of suffragette activism had fought for: the vote.

There was some reluctance to admit it, but the old order was finished.

It would be easy to overstate things. The children of the Great War were lucky: too young to fight, they were neither shell-shocked nor traumatised. But neither were they unaffected. The

---

[8] In *Disenchantment* (1922), Montague, a *Manchester Guardian* leader writer, was one of the first to mince no words in his depiction of the war's grim futility. His title contained the tacit suggestion that Britain was, before all this, an enchanted realm.

war was by far the biggest influence on their young lives, moulding their sensibilities in deep, mysterious ways. It is thus not fanciful to see its echoes in the energetic zeal displayed by the generation of sporting men and women who came to the fore afterwards. The years following the Armistice were not easy; life was too hard (and too short) to be wasted on anything half-hearted. Even sport was serious.

CHAPTER THREE

The Roaring Twenties

A year after the war ended Hedley Verity left school and started at his father's coal firm in Guiseley. He was only 14 years old but already convinced that his future lay elsewhere – on the cricket pitch. After a few months in the depot, shovelling coal and playing with a cricket ball at lunchtime, he threw up his hands. 'It's no use,' he said. 'I've made up my mind to some day play for Yorkshire.' Fortunately, the *Yorkshire Evening Post* was already calling him 'one of the most promising cricketers in the Leeds district'. Perhaps he could escape life at the coal face after all.

It was proving hard to get noticed by the county coaches, though. He had not yet found his true *métier*: he was a medium-pacer who tried to swing the ball a bit. And when he played his first game for Rawdon First Eleven in 1921, he didn't have the happiest of days – he was out for nought and didn't bowl. But he already had too much control for most Second Eleven batsmen. On one occasion one of the gruff elder statesmen of the team ground his boot into the wicket on a perfect length and told him, 'Tha' wants ter pitch 'em there.' Verity obliged, hitting the damaged spot time and again and taking seven wickets; and the dressing-room could enjoy a good laugh at what had, after all, been a blatant piece of pitch-tampering. But when he went for trials in Leeds, Bobby Peel, the Yorkshire all-rounder, looked at him and groaned, 'Can't you bowl faster than *that*?' For the first time, Verity thought about changing to slow bowling: though tall, he was not quick. But he persisted as a seamer until, in the same

Headingley nets four years later, George Hirst, the England left-armer, also suggested that he take up spin.

Hirst was disappointed that Verity appeared to lack pace, since he seemed built for speed, but he admired the boy's approach to the game and saw signs of a rare natural gift. 'He takes to cricket,' he told Verity's father, 'as a duck takes to water.' This was music to a proud father's ears, naturally, but what pleased Hedley Senior above all was evidence that his son was happy to listen to an experienced elder: 'He was always willing and eager to learn,' he said later. 'If any man deceived him, he studied carefully how it was done so that he might try it on someone else.' Not that young Hedley was the kind of bowler who much liked to experiment: he preferred to nag away, wearing batsmen down with unflinching accuracy, like water dripping on stone.

Verity Senior still had an unswerving faith in his son. He urged his daughter Grace to come and watch an early match on the grounds that 'It might be the start of a famous career.' He was well aware of his son's utter dedication. Young Hedley, he wrote, was 'so fully occupied in the cricket field that he had no time for anything else. Any friends he found must, if they wished to retain his friendship, go with him to the cricket field.'

Far to the south, in London, the Cottons were settling into their new life. George was a keen weekend golfer – 16-handicap – and one of the first things he did for his sons was buy them memberships at Aquarius Golf Club in Dulwich, a brand new nine-hole course laid out on the grassy roof of the Beechcroft reservoir (Europe's biggest water tank, no less). The boys took to the game at once, and within a year or two were among the best players not just in the club's junior section, but in the adult lists, too. And while Leslie was clearly very good, his younger brother Henry was something else. At the age of 11 he rather sweetly autographed a photograph of himself holding his golf clubs, as if he were already a champion. By the time he was 13 years old he had a handicap of four, and in 1923 won three competitions, including the overall club championship, the Hutchings Trophy. At weekends, the brothers would play 27 holes in the morning, a further 27 in the afternoon, and then go round with their father in the evening. George Cotton had built a dozen garages in Dulwich to profit from the post-war boom he foresaw in motor cars. One of these he converted into a dedicated golf practice net, and the seeds of Henry's future were planted then and there.

At this age Henry was good at cricket as well as golf, useful enough to captain the Under-14 side at Alleyn's. He liked nothing better than to take a day return to The Oval and sit on the boundary – like Verity his boyhood hero was Jack Hobbs. He would keep the score, calculate the great man's average, and fantasise about being out there himself one day. But that summer he found himself in the eye of a cricketing storm. Along with three friends he objected to lugging the team's kitbag on the train back from an away match at Marlow, and for this outrageous breach of *esprit de corps* was sentenced to be caned by prefects. He was rescued only when his father kicked up the daddy of all fusses, in which he denounced the school's punitive culture as cruel and disproportionate.

It turned into a heated row, complete with testimony from doctors and solicitors, and earnest letters flying to and fro. Henry ended up withdrawing from cricket altogether. And while some boys would have responded by knuckling down and keeping their noses clean, Cotton did the opposite. With an unusual degree of *amour propre* he declared that he was done not just with cricket but with school. He intended to be a professional golfer. His brother Leslie had the same ambition, and they were both in earnest.

On the other side of London, close to the palm houses at Kew, another sports-loving son of Cheshire was starting to make a name for himself … at table tennis. In 1917 Sam Perry became the first National Secretary of the Co-operative Party, and when it decided to move its headquarters south to London, near Charing

Cross, he moved with it, settling in Brentham Garden Suburb, a pleasant new estate of some 620 houses in Ealing, west London. The war was not quite over: indeed, a few days after the family left the North-West, more German bombs fell on Liverpool. But this was a fresh start.

Brentham was a social experiment based on co-operative, Arts and Crafts principles. The idea derived from William Morris's belief that ordinary men and women deserved beauty in their surroundings, and called for a cluster of well-built houses wrapped around an enticing range of shared facilities – parks, recreation grounds, social clubs, trees, flowers, whist drives, concerts, sports fields, a kindergarten and a church. It was a dream of communal, recreational living brought to life in suburban Middlesex.

As far as the teenaged Fred Perry was concerned, Brentham was 'paradise', and it was here that his sporting talent first revealed itself. Table tennis was a relatively new pastime, first played in England in the 1880s (created, the story went, by tipsy Empire types who built nets out of books after dinner in the officers' mess), but the Brentham Institute had a table, and Perry – on the small side, and somewhat fearful on the cricket pitch (in his own words a 'worse than bad wicketkeeper') – was soon addicted. He won the inaugural World Championships in a hall near Fleet Street in 1926,[1] and the two World Championships after that as well. But by then he was gripped by a whole new ball game: tennis. On a trip to Eastbourne in the summer of 1923, he had slipped away from his family and spent hours gazing at the well-heeled having fun on the grass at Devonshire Road. He was captivated. It wasn't just the game – it was the clothes, the handsome players, the Daimler cars, the whole farrago. It was a revelation. As he said later, tennis was a game which, in those days, 'the lower middle

---

[1] It sounds grand, but in fact this was a fledgling event. Planned as a purely European tournament, it turned into a World championship when half a dozen Indians pitched up unexpectedly and the good-hearted powers-that-be adjusted the format to let them in.

class had never seen or played'. He was only 14, but a gorgeous new vision of life was swimming before his eyes.

The first sporting stirrings of these three young enthusiasts took place against a shaky background. Absorbed in their games, the boys were probably oblivious to all such matters, but the years following the war were peaceful only in name, and the national scenery was shifting fast. Jubilation over the Armistice gave way to a more jittery mood as strident politics clashed with a hedonistic party scene. And the reservoir of optimism ran dry fast. As R. H. Tawney, who explored the links between Protestantism and winner-takes-all finance in *Religion and the Rise of Capitalism* (1926), put it: 'In April 1920 all was right with the world. In April 1921 all was wrong.'

At first it seemed as though sport could help people find their way back to normal life. Cricket returned in the summer of 1919: in front of huge crowds, Yorkshire won the Championship, thanks to 164 wickets from Wilfred Rhodes, and Surrey's Jack Hobbs scored over 2,500 runs. It was almost as if nothing had changed, and *The Times* was delighted to report that 'all is well with our great game'. But even cricket was no longer what it had been in those golden summers before the war – the roll call of the fallen was too long, and too fresh – and nor was anything else. Tennis, golf, rugby, football ... they all resumed, but there was no hiding the fact that people had more important things to worry about – not least the flu epidemic brought home by the troops (the epicentre was later discovered to be the holding centre at Etaples, near Le Touquet) which was on its way to killing a quarter of a million survivors of the war.

Abroad, there were upheavals almost everywhere. After surviving the German assault (at the cost of nearly four million lives) Russia was locked in civil war as it turned itself into the Soviet Union. Prohibition in America (imposed in 1919) put gangs of racketeers and mobsters on to the streets in a tussle over the right to have a stiff drink. Ireland's struggle for freedom was renewing itself with a vengeance that did not end with independence in 1922. And Italy gave the world its first dictator when Benito Mussolini (also in 1922) outlawed political opposition and declared himself Il Duce.

In Germany the bohemian carnival of Weimar was collapsing under the weight of indebtedness imposed by Versailles (the terms of which Churchill called 'malignant and silly'). The result was the famous hyper-inflation: when Berlin printed a flood of new money (the strategy now known as 'quantitative easing') the proud Deutschmark melted. In 1921 it took just 60 of them to buy a dollar; two years later it took more than four trillion – a meaningless number. One visiting US Congressman, A. P. Andrew, wondering how much he should leave as a tip in a restaurant, gasped when he was told that 400 million was about right. A beer? Four *billion* marks. Citizens shopping for eggs pushed wheelbarrows stuffed with cash, only to discover that the barrow was more valuable than the money it held; people who had once enjoyed bulging bank accounts woke to discover that their life savings might not even run to a loaf of bread.

The Great War had only been over for four years, and Europe was still counting the cost. 'Seven hundred thousand of the beauty and pride of Britain,' wrote the historian Charles Masterman, 'who might have changed the world a little for the better, lie silent and cold.' Had the war settled border disputes? No. Had it brought financial stability? No. Had it enriched our spiritual and cultural life? Hardly. Had it spread fairness or soothed fears? Emphatically not. Had it, he asked, put an end to war? Oh dearie me.

But even in this demoralising context, the wrenching misery created by Germany's economic trauma was something new. In 1924 D. H. Lawrence, on his travels, wrote a 'Letter from Germany' which suggested that something unimaginable was growing in the forests of the north: 'At night you feel strange things stirring in the darkness ... the old flow, the old adherence is ruptured.' That is when a bizarre saviour stepped into the picture.

Adolf Hitler, released from the prison where he had written *Mein Kampf*, celebrated his freedom in 1924 by listening to Wagner and buying a fast Mercedes.

On the home front, Britain tried to restore democracy through the so-called 'Khaki Election', called just three days after the Armistice in November 1918. And when Lloyd George made a famous pledge to create a 'land fit for heroes' there was a brief sense that a new world might be built. But peace was far from peaceful: the land was soon pock-marked with strikes, riots and protests as a million soldiers, nerves fried by shrapnel, demanded something better than a return to how things were. In a way that only became clear later, Britain suffered what future generations would call a backlash. For years they had been told they were fighting for 'their' country; now it began to dawn on them that they owned not a stick of it, not a single blade of grass.

Women were marching for a brighter future, too, and industrial workers refused to let their captains turn the clock back. The population that had gone obediently to war did not return quietly – quite the contrary. The disbanded armies found themselves in an ever-lengthening dole queue – by 1920 almost 10 per cent of the workforce was idle. And war imagery was still ever-present: tender memorials were still being unveiled; people were still singing 'Abide With Me' and 'O God, Our Help in Ages Past'; and when the Tomb of the Unknown Soldier was revealed in Westminster Abbey on Armistice Day, 1920, more than a million people gathered in the streets to salute.

There were still deeper forces moving in the social undergrowth. What Einstein had done for the laws of physics (subverting, against all common sense, the old Newtonian certainties) Freud was doing for private life. The English version of *The Interpretation of Dreams*, with its amazing suggestion that even our selves were beyond conscious control, had been published before the war, in 1913, but it made few waves with the public until afterwards, by which time the awful scale of the conflict echoed the idea that we were ruled by vast commotions we could not fathom. Marxist thinking, more obviously revolutionary, made a similar claim: the engines of history lay concealed beneath the surface of everyday events. The effect of these thinkers and their disciples was great. Nietzsche had pronounced the death of God a generation earlier, in 1886, and as Europe's faith in a benign deity dwindled, people couldn't help but seek other patterns to live by – be it in physics, economics or the reflexes of the mind.

Perceptions such as these found expression in the literature of the time. Where writers such as Dickens, the Brontës, Trollope, George Eliot, Henry James and Hardy had dramatised the trials and tribulations of individual men and women – on the basis that the trajectory of single souls was where the meaning of life resided, modern readers took a more quizzical view. Proust won the Prix Goncourt in 1919 for the second volume of the memory-work that would eventually grow into *A la Recherche du Temps Perdu*. Closer to home, Aldous Huxley (in *Crome Yellow*, 1921) was beginning to hint at the bleak dystopia that would emerge a decade later as *Brave New World*. And through writers such as Joyce (*Ulysses*, 1922), Mann (*The Magic Mountain*, 1924) and Woolf (*Mrs Dalloway*, 1925) literature was finding new voices. E. M. Forster even had the nerve (in 1924) to examine the British Empire, in *A Passage to India*. A generation of authors seemed to be seeing the world as grey, anxious and treacherous – rather like the 'unreal city' of T. S. Eliot's *The Waste Land* (1922), where fear could be seen in 'a handful of dust'. Lytton Strachey had delighted his Bloomsbury friends in 1918 by sketching the clay feet of his *Eminent Victorians*; but now everyone was at it. These may not have been the most widely read works of their day,[2] but they did suggest an edgy *Zeitgeist*. Some were attracted by the utopian

---

[2] The bestselling novel of 1922, in most accounts, was *If Winter Comes* by A. S. M. Hutchinson, the story of a Scottish nobleman's unhappy marriage; it was rivalled in 1924 by Margaret Kennedy's *The Constant Nymph*, a daring treatment of a girl's sex fantasies in the Alps which might be called an early example of chick lit.

thinking coming out of Russia; others feared that this could all too easily take a despotic turn. Nothing was certain.

This unhappy strand of the national scene culminated in the General Strike of 1926, a howl of despair in which nearly two million workers downed tools. But there was always a brighter thread running alongside this anxious public mood. The men and women who had survived the war wanted to celebrate, and were not willing to be lectured on morals by the whiskered old fellows who had led them into the trenches. Exciting new gadgets – cars, telephones, radios, picture houses, planes, watches – were pouring out of the factories and begging to be adopted and enjoyed. Why wait?

So while in Britain the twenties did not roar quite as loud as in speakeasy America or the decadent fleshpots of Berlin, there was a moderate frenzy of pleasure-seeking: jaunty music, bright lights, novel fabrics (*nylon!*) and new drinks – coolers, fizzes and highballs. The first 'nightclub' was launched in 1921, and was followed by the first Gin and It. A spasm of John Bull patriotism led by Horatio Bottomley tried to turn the clock back to the so-called good old days, but for the most part it was a fine time to be a vegetarian, a nudist, a spiritualist, a cabaret dancer, a free-love fanatic, a swimmer, a poet, a wizard or an artist's muse. The sudden, chronic shortage of men gave women, intoxicatingly, the upper hand – anyone could be a coquette or a heartbreaker. Girls only had to smile to be taken to a continental café for enticing treats – frothy coffee and chocolate éclairs; you could get a whole brick of vanilla ice cream for twopence. They even developed a vivacious feminine idiom of their own: handsome young men were NST – Not Safe in Taxis. A new word emerged to describe this heady cocktail – *glamour*. Or, as a sneering poem of 1926 ('The Woman') by Jacques Reval put it:

In greedy haste, on pleasure bent
We have no time to think or feel
What need is there for sentiment
Now we've invented sex-appeal.

None of this did anything to change the fact that on the less well-favoured side of the street there were sallow beggars at bus stops, hostels for indigent children and glum queues at soup kitchens. Life was rough. People might be tripping about in silk gowns in the bright lights of Mayfair, but in the slummy backstreets of Britain's cities they would do almost anything for a slice of bread and margarine, or a mouthful of brawn. Some servants stayed in their posts without pay just to have a roof over their heads.

But an early form of compassion fatigue was gripping the young – they could hardly be expected to moan, like, for *ever*. So the first thing the unlocking of Tutankhamen's tomb in 1922 inspired was a craze for all things Egyptian, and the party set laughed the nights away at risqué parties and Cleopatra-themed balls. They took snazzy holidays, too, in resort hotels in the South of France, or chased the winter sun to Davos and St Moritz – and why not, when a pound could buy as many as 200 precious Swiss francs? Even politics was alluring: androgynous women in chic hats tripped off to be bilingual secretaries at the League of Nations, and there were peace conferences in the Alps.

If the age had a symbol, it was the transatlantic steamship. The *Titanic* disaster was so long ago – and modern liners had lifeboats, don't you know! On the *Aquitania*, the swankiest of all the Cunarders (though it was her sister ship, *Mauretania*, that won the Blue Riband for transatlantic speed) the menu in the first-class grill warned that 'the motion of the ship precludes carrying the older red wines'. She was a byword for opulence. Bright platoons of stars – actors, royalty and sports personalities – wrapped themselves in mink and diamonds as they admired the ocean view. That vivacious girl with the lipstick and the cigarette holder might be Clara Bow, and, hang on: that handsome devil in the tuxedo, with the champagne cocktail – wasn't that Jay Gatsby?

After the grinding years of mud and ditchwater, who could be blamed for wanting to gun the engine a bit? The brainy scientists of the new, unstable Einstein-universe were using complex arrangements of mirrors to measure, of all things, the speed of *light*. And there were practical consequences to this. When the war ended there were 100,000 cars in Britain; by the 1930s, thanks to William Morris in Oxford and Herbert Austin in Birmingham, there were more than a million, gliding about on roads glittering with a neat new gizmo: Catseyes. In January 1926 a Scottish vicar's son named John Logie Baird sat in his attic room above Frith Street, in London's Soho,[3] watching the faces of his friends as they stared at his bizarre new contraption: television.

Zippy new aeroplanes were competing for the Schneider Trophy, and in 1924, the year Harold Abrahams and Eric Liddell were winning gold medals in the 'Chariots of Fire' Olympics in Paris, the Flying Scotsman starred at the British Empire Exhibition in Wembley. Ernest Eldridge was pushing a Fiat that resembled Chitty-Chitty-Bang-Bang up to a juddering 124mph, while Malcolm Campbell was setting frantic speed records on the beaches of South Wales in his famous *Blue Bird*. It was also the year of the first winter Olympics (in Chamonix), with its exhilarating new possibilities for high-speed jinks in playgrounds of snow and ice; and Charles Lindbergh became the first man to fly across the Atlantic. In 1928, not to be outdone, Amelia Earhart proved that a woman could do the same, landing in South Wales to become the most feted female pilot in the world. Few wished to ruin things by pointing out that she did not lay so much as a finger on the controls herself.[4] Britain saw its first Grand Prix in 1926, and in 1927 Major Seagrave's *Sunbeam Mystery* touched 200mph at Daytona Beach, Florida.[5]

All of this exciting information was brought to the public's attention in an innovative way via the burgeoning popular

---

[3] Above what is now Bar Italia, a much-loved landmark in London's Soho.

[4] An omission she made up for in 1932, when she *did* fly solo across the Atlantic.

[5] In 1929 he pushed his own record up another notch by registering 231mph in a purpose-built car that came to symbolise speed for decades: *Golden Arrow*.

press. Ushered in by Alfred Harmsworth's *Daily Mail* in 1896 and Arthur Pearson's *Daily Express* in 1900, the mass-market in news flared into exuberant new life in the post-war years, thanks not least to the rivalry between the papers and their famous owners (Lord Northcliffe and Lord Beaverbrook). Other publications – such as the *Star*, the *Daily Sketch*, the *News of the World*, the *Evening News*, the *Evening Standard* and the *Daily Mirror* (launched by Lord Northcliffe in 1902 as predominantly a women's journal) – were quick to join this rapidly expanding market, all eager to put a light-hearted gloss on things. After the long years of sacrifice and pain, who could begrudge Britain a burst of levity? 'Sixty Horses Wedged in Chimney' ran the headlines, 'Slimming Made Girl Steal', 'I'll be Mayor And Still Sell Fish And Chips'. New methods of printing and distribution made it possible to smack these upbeat products down on millions of doorsteps every day. The *Express* was especially committed to a cheerful view of life, and its keen sense of news as entertainment (it was the first paper to feature a crossword) was perhaps best summed up in a famous 1920 headline (28 May): 'The World Is Getting Better'.

There were few more appetising ways to express this frolicsome spirit than through sport, and no one (with the possible exception of the Mountbattens) symbolised it so colourfully as the Prince of Wales. He was yet to display the full extent of his boredom with royal matters by divorcing them in favour of Wallis Simpson. His jet-setter's diary sent him from resort to resort, growing, as one columnist put it, ever 'more tanned and more tired'. But he was a noted playboy – a dapper Prince Charming – inspecting battleships in Navy whites before dancing the night away at a high-society fancy-dress do. He was handsome, energetic, frivolous and frantically in demand. As one ditty, popular with the ladies of the era, put it:

> *I danced with a man who danced with a girl*
> *Who danced with the Prince of Wales …*

It was in keeping with his role as the iconic leader of this fun-seeking new world that the Prince adored outdoor pursuits. The *Illustrated London News* pictured him golfing in South Africa and applauded the fact that he possessed to the full 'that thoroughly British characteristic – a love of sport'. It was true. He was forever being snapped in dashing poses: skiing in Norway, fishing for tarpon in New Zealand, handing out silver cups at race meetings (sometimes tackling the jumps himself), hunting tigers in India, breasting rapids in Japan, riding to hounds in Gloucestershire or shooting duck in Canada. A keen golfer (in 1926 he was captain of Royal Mid-Surrey, on the edge of Kew Gardens), he took lessons from James Braid, once writing to him after an almost-great day at Walton Heath: 'with the chance of breaking 80 I couldn't stand the nerve strain, and fluffed the chip.' At Oxford, which he attended despite offering scant signs of ever having read a book, he tried his hand at football, polo, roulette and tennis.[6]

He was everything a proper young modern Prince was supposed to be. The tattered old idealism of King and Country was being refreshed by images of these spirited pleasures. As depicted in the media, they suggested a healthy, virile and youthful new world. It wasn't the whole truth, but it did suggest a country that was being renewed.

Where did sport sit in this spidery web of contrasting impulses? Like everything, it found itself torn between the two. If Hedley Verity and Dorothy Round represented the troubled, doubtful, gloomy post-war state of mind – they were grave, serious and responsible in everything they did – then Henry Cotton and Fred Perry leaned towards the flashier end of things. They were products of, and leading figures in, the go-getting, fun-loving culture that was starting to edge across Britain like a weather front.

[6] Though in this his brother outdid him – in 1926 the future George VI played in the Wimbledon doubles with Louis Greig, losing in straight sets in the first round.

There were other tensions playing through them. On the surface, sport was one of the ways the country could put on a happy face again, but even here it was divided along class lines. The first FA Cup final at Wembley in 1923, in which West Ham played Bolton in front of the King, collapsed under the crush of public enthusiasm when something like 300,000 fans tried to press into the new stadium (they were dispersed by a mounted policeman on a grand white horse). The more aristocratic pastimes, meanwhile, were quick to capture the very different fizz and snap of the new world, the one chock-full of celebrities spraying champagne, the one on the wireless to which millions were now listening[7], the one that was reached by Pulman carriage and chauffeured motor car – youthful, athletic and suave.

Underlying all these things was a thirst for simple pleasures. The Great War had been a battle of machines, a production line of death, so it was not surprising that it created an equal and opposite longing for rural pursuits. The revival of sport was like the appearance of new grass in spring – it chimed perfectly with pastoral dreams. So when Stanley Baldwin was elected Prime Minister in 1924 it was no coincidence: he was said to represent, in some quintessential way, the homely English countryside. *The Times* said he had 'the fragrance of the fields, the flavour of apple and hazel'.

---

[7] The BBC was launched in 1922 (14 February) and caught on fast. By 1924 it could claim a million regular listeners, rising to 2.5 million in 1927. On special occasions it could bring the country together like nothing else in history. In 1924 over six million listened to King George V's speech from Wembley, the first time they had ever heard their monarch's voice. It was, in these early days, very highbrow. The invisible reader of the nine o'clock news delivered the broadcast in full black-tie evening dress.

CHAPTER FOUR

Practice Makes Perfect

The first thing Hedley Verity had to learn about cricket was patience, because it took ten years of diligent effort at various league clubs before he could fulfil his ambition to play for Yorkshire. This lengthy apprenticeship would not have sat well with many players, even then, but Verity lived up to his Bunyanesque surname and was a byword for persistence. He did have some well-placed admirers in Yorkshire cricket, however, and when George Hirst recommended him as a cricket professional to Accrington, in the Lancashire League, in 1927, it was the first big step towards making the game his career. Though young, he always had the serious air of an older, more experienced man, and he was devoted to practice, understanding from an early age that to succeed as a bowler he had to be more than occasionally dangerous: he had to be unerring.

After just one season at Accrington, where he played all right without setting any houses on fire, he moved to Middleton, near Manchester, where he immediately felt happier – not least because the club agreed that he could be released if Yorkshire ever came calling. But league cricket was serving him well: it was a school of hard knocks, full of people whose lives depended on the runs they made and the wickets they took: no one was indulged simply because he was fresh and keen. Before long, he was working on his fitness with renewed determination and spending hour after hour in the nets, aiming at a single spot on the turf as he mastered the arts of spin and drift.

It took a while, but after one more quiet season he emerged, like a butterfly from a chrysalis, in 1929. That year he took 100 wickets and scored a century – all the while helping to mow the outfield and fix the pavilion roof. Summoned to play for Yorkshire's Second Eleven as a stand-in, he caught everyone's eye by taking five for seven. His domestic life took a stride forward, too. Just before the season, in March, Verity had married Kathleen Metcalfe, a bookbinder he had known since infancy. His sister Edith was bridesmaid.

He was a 25-year-old professional, a baritone in the Benton Congregational Church and a husband, but his dream of playing for Yorkshire remained just that. A modern player would be tempted to give up, but there was no reason to be too dismayed by this apparent failure. Everyone knew that the path ahead was blocked by the great Yorkshire left-armer Wilfred Rhodes, who seemed in no hurry to bring down the curtain on a glowing career that would end up yielding 4,187 wickets and nearly 40,000 runs. Rhodes had been a star since the end of the nineteenth century – taking 6 for 63 on debut in 1898 – and had opened the batting for England (with Hobbs) in a partnership of 323 against Australia in 1912. After the war he picked up where he left off, taking 163 wickets in 1919. And in 1929 he was not close to finishing: he was merely en route to becoming, at 52, the oldest man to play Test cricket for England.

He was a hard man to dislodge, in other words, and Verity had no option but to wait his turn, keeping himself fit by taking his dog, Prince, for long walks and running with his faithful skipping rope. It meant that when his chance did come (in 1930) he was ready. Filling in for Rhodes (who watched him very carefully, through binoculars) he bowled well against Sussex at Huddersfield (three wickets) in May, and followed this up with eight against Leicestershire and nine more against Glamorgan.

If he was nervous, he didn't show it. Even at this age he was all steadiness, and his placid, otherworldly quality brought him 64 wickets in this, his first full summer as a county cricketer.

When the national bowling averages were published in September he stood at the top, and the grapevine hummed with talk about this polite, quiet destroyer they had unearthed up at Headingley. The wise old owls were quick to call him 'the new Rhodes', or 'another Wilfred', and Rhodes himself anointed Verity as his successor with a nod: 'He'll do.' Verity's reply was in the same practical vein. 'Both of us are left-handed and like taking wickets,' he said. 'Let's leave it at that.'

Rhodes did not wander off into the cricketing sunset. In the years to come he would spend many hours discussing the finer points of left-arm spin with his replacement, and Verity was all ears. According to Hirst, he absorbed the wisdom of Rhodes 'as a sponge takes water'. In the spring of 1931 *The Times* gave his emergence an official stamp of approval by naming 'young Verity' as a player of 'great promise' and expressing its confidence that 'the heritage of Peale, Peate and Rhodes will not be wasted'.

There seems to have been something precious – even dislikeable – about the young Henry Cotton. Even as a schoolboy he would insist, when his friends paid a penny to take the train or a tram, on taking a taxi. He knew his mind, and didn't care who knew it. But Henry was lucky, because, just like Verity's father, George Cotton was tolerant and supportive, as well as demanding. He took the liberty of writing to J. H. Taylor, the famous professional at Royal Mid-Surrey. His sons were thinking of becoming professionals, he said – might Mr Taylor be so good as to have a look at them, with a view to seeing if their ambitions were in any way realistic?

Taylor was at this time one of the most celebrated golfers in Britain. He had won five Open titles between 1894 and 1913, and come second six times. When it came to golf he knew rather more than the score. But while in modern times such a brazen request from a father would be comical (*Dear Tiger, I wonder if by any chance you might be willing to cast your eye over my son ...*) at that time a golf pro occupied the same social rung as a gardener or a cook: there wasn't much he wouldn't do for a shilling.

Taylor agreed, and took the boys round Royal Mid-Surrey, a course he had helped mould. A photographer captured the moment, the two youngsters flanking the senior pro, a golfer so sturdily built he was unable to cross his legs. Taylor was still a formidable player – he had been attached to the club since 1899 but had not yet given up winning tournaments (aged 53, he would come fifth in the 1924 Open at Hoylake). And his post-round report was interesting. He could see that the older brother, Leslie, had the stronger game at present, but it was the younger lad who caught his eye. Henry had an impressive level of concentration, he said, adding that he might go far. Years later, in *Golf: My Life's Work* (1943), he echoed his own words by calling Cotton 'the most outstanding British professional since the days of Harry Vardon … he has raised the game to new heights', without mentioning the part he had played at this early stage.

Before long Henry and Leslie Cotton were assistant professionals at Fulwell, a Taylor-made course near Twickenham. The weekly wage was 12s 6d – just 65 pence in today's money[1] – and the duties were mundane: wiping clubs and shoes, sweeping the floor and sanding hickory shafts. This last was a chore, but Cotton told himself, as he scraped away, that it was good for his wrists. He was already beginning to reject the mantra that hands needed to be kept quiet in golf: strong wrists were a crucial part of his own method, and he was adamant that the right hand should be used to the full. He practised through his lunch hour, and then in the net in the garage at home. 'I doubt whether anyone,' wrote

[1] This translates into a salary of £32 10s per annum – no great shakes. If we follow the Bank of England's inflation-adjustment measure (multiply by 50) it means that Cotton was earning £1,625 a year – a sum unlikely to make an assistant pro whistle now. But it was a start. When he went to Langley Park he earned £2 10s a week (£130 a year – £6,500 in today's terms): no king's ransom, but not bad for a 19-year-old. And money went further in those days: the price of an 'average' house was £500 (£25,000 today), and a chap could get lunch in a London tearoom – beef with all the trimmings, with bread and butter pudding and custard – for 1s 6d. A cup of tea was twopence.

Bernard Darwin, grandson of the evolutionary thinker, noted Cambridge Blue and senior golf writer for *The Times*, 'devoted as many back-breaking, hand-smarting, brain-tiring hours to the acquiring of golfing shots as Cotton'.

There was an additional difficulty connected with his new role. As an up-and-coming amateur and golf club member, he had once been part of the game's privileged elite. The tipsy old buffers in the members' lounge had been only too happy to buy the lad a ginger beer and take pleasure in his many successes. As a professional, however, he suddenly found he was *persona non grata* in the comfortable bars and saloons of these same clubhouses – they were amateur-only, men-only precincts. It was ironic: the more he improved as a golfer, the lower he sank in the social hierarchy of the game. As a teenager he had been clubbable; as an expert he was not even allowed into the rooms with nice carpets. It was a pointed education in the way the world worked. He could play golf with the Prince of Wales, but never join him for coffee afterwards.

He was something new – a professional with the hinterland of a member – and it gave him a withdrawn air that resembled loneliness. He was no traditionalist, out to preserve the good old ways. He bridled at traditional tweed jackets and caps, preferring racier silks or cashmeres; and he chafed at the charade by which amateur spectators would tuck into steak and kidney pudding in the clubhouse grill, while the professionals over whose games they had been oohing and aahing had to make do with a sandwich in the car park, washed down with tea brewed on the gas ring where the glue was warmed.

Apart from anything else, it made for an awkward relationship with his peers. Not much of a mixer anyway, Cotton and his brother were misfits. Most of their fellow professionals were rude mechanicals – even the greatest of them, like Vardon (the son of a Channel Island garden labourer) and Taylor (an orphan who started as a caddie). Henry and Leslie were cut from a very different cloth – they were well-spoken, in a hurry and going places. After just nine months at Fulwell, Cotton moved on, once again thanks to Taylor. On the latter's recommendation he was appointed assistant professional at Rye, and not long after that, at the tender age of 19, he became the head professional at Langley Park in Kent. He was the youngest man ever to fill such a post.

Langley Park was not far from Beckenham, so Cotton could live at home. He caught the No. 37 bus to Herne Hill, took the train to Beckenham Junction and rode the last four miles on a heavy bicycle (good for his legs, he hoped). He spent his free hours on the putting green, tapping balls hour after hour. An admirer of the great Abe Mitchell, who swished the ball away 'with a terrific flash of the hands', he sought to strengthen his grip by any means possible, scything clubs through heavy, wet grass with one hand. At Rye he had sometimes been known to practise by the light of the moon. Now, back home in Dulwich, he pounded balls into his father's garage net till all hours, stopping only when his raw, bleeding fingers could not take any more punishment.

Since his ambitions lay on the course, this was not unusual. But the class-ridden contradictions of golf affected Cotton mightily, pouring petrol on his already burning ambition. He may have been well-born for a golfer, but no working-class artisan was more industrious – sometimes he practised for so long that he found it hard to stand up, and he developed a pronounced question-mark stoop in his shoulders. It wasn't easy, refining a style of his own, and it involved jettisoning plenty of time-honoured rules. But through long and determined practice he acquired a superlative motion of well-calibrated fluency and snap. Distilling the swing down to its essence, bracing his body to unleash his hands, he polished it down to one languid move. According to Darwin, he played with 'a lovely smoothness and ease', combining 'immense power with absurdly small effort'. He started waltzing round golf courses with what Henry Longhurst in the *Sunday Times* called 'tireless mechanical accuracy'. A notice in the *Melbourne Age*, many years later, agreed: Cotton's golf was like Winston

Churchill's English: 'You could not match it, but you could not fail to be the better for trying.'

Longhurst, who followed Cotton's entire career both as a reporter and a friend, felt there was little the man couldn't do with a golf club. 'We often used to challenge him to take his drive from a bad lie on the fairway, simply for the aesthetic pleasure of seeing the ball fly away as though fired from a rifle.' In an echo of Robin Hood and the silver arrow, he once hit a shooting stick 20 yards away with a one-iron. Not bad.

It has often been said that Cotton was the pioneer who dismantled the snobbish idea that professionals were no better than servants, and it is true that he played his part. But he was pressing at a door that was already ajar. Club members still tended to treat golf professionals like jobbing labourers – barely better than caddies or chauffeurs – just as, in cricket, the amateurs looked on the professionals as mere tradesmen, no matter how brilliant they were. But there were nuances to these distinctions. The golf professional stood in relation to his amateur employer rather as Jeeves did to Wooster – *he* was the suave expert on whom the day depended; the Eton and Oxford-educated aristocrats were simply well-heeled twerps. So the gulf *was* narrowing. The three aces who made up the Great Triumvirate were all made members of the clubs they represented in honour of their great victories.

In the winter of 1928–9 the 21-year-old Cotton went to America to gain experience. He put his resources together, raised £300, and sailed west on the *Aquitania*. He made an immediate splash, coming third in his first tournament in California, the Sacramento Open, and in the course of his travels made enough money to recoup his expenses. But it came as a shock to see how far he lagged behind his American opponents when it came to hitting the ball. Two of them in particular, Sam Snead and Tommy Armour, urged him to seek extra yardage by abandoning his left-to-right fade in favour of a more powerful draw shape, and he knew they were right. He set about flattening his swing at once. Without saying a single word, Armour taught him an even more precious lesson about the value of persistence. Serving with the Tank Corps at Ypres, Armour had lost the use of his right eye in a mustard gas attack, and had metal plates in his head and left arm. The resolve he now brought to his golf career was humbling to those who had escaped such horrors. In 1920 he won the French Amateur, and in 1927 added the US and Canadian Opens, too. He was bad-tempered, but who could blame him? There was a saying in sport that a winner was just a loser who hadn't given up, and there was no more shining example of this than Tommy Armour.

In California Cotton found something else he liked the look of: dollar bills. He was much taken by the flamboyant Walter Hagen, and at the Hollywood Plaza he couldn't help noticing that when the Haig's manager paid the bill he did so by snapping open a briefcase stuffed with cash from exhibition matches. It was not the only magical thing about the big-spending, breeze-shooting Hagen. In London he would use the roof of the Savoy as a driving range, sloshing balls into the Thames with a merry grin.

'That's what I want,' Cotton remembered thinking. 'Silk shirts with monograms and two-toned shoes, beautifully-made suits and golf cuff-links.'

News of Cotton's impressive showing in America soon filtered back across the water, and the next thing he knew he was selected to join Britain's elite team of professional golfers for the Ryder Cup at Moortown, Yorkshire, in the spring of 1929. He was part of a winning squad, too, even securing one of the singles points that helped secure a 7-5 victory. Suddenly he was a talked-about force in the game. The *Evening News* asked him to write a column, and Gamages, the famous sports shop in London's Holborn, invited him to join a celebrity sales team that included grandees like Vardon and Taylor to give in-store ball-striking tips. The golfers developed a cruel routine in which they confused visitors by dishing out contradictory advice. Taylor would tell some poor student to follow through more, while Vardon would urge him to shorten that finish. The poor man would wander out of the shop, recalled Cotton, with a 'glassy-eyed stare' – whether because he was bemused or angry, no one could say.[2]

But his fellow professionals were beginning to form a dimmer view of young Henry. Golf was a sport that prided itself on its considerate etiquette, a game in which players 'addressed' the ball, 'approached' greens and 'read' putts like respectful members of an al fresco Sunday school. And while it didn't help that the papers kept calling him 'the public school golfer', Cotton didn't help himself much either. When he partnered his brother in the Midlands Open in 1929, *The Times* thought he talked too much. 'The art of foursomes play,' it advised, trying to be tactful, 'is to have implicit faith in your partner, and to offer advice only when it is asked.' The paper hinted that had he been less domineering 'the margin of victory would have been more convincing'. Other papers ran snide cartoons, and the *Observer* said there was 'no question' that 'Cotton has not been altogether popular with his fellow professionals, and with certain sections of the public'. He was aloof, it suggested: 'his only concern has been with his score.' We can see in such criticisms the same reflex that led people to disparage other lonely stars (Geoff Boycott or Nick Faldo). Much as England hungers for sporting success, it dislikes monomaniacs, preferring an offhand or buccaneering quality in its talismen.

The invitation to winter in Argentina, with its pleasant southern-hemisphere sun, thus came as a great relief. And when Cotton arrived at Mar del Plata he was intrigued to discover that a rather striking young woman, Isabel-Maria Estanguet de Moss, had put herself down for no fewer than 50 lessons with him. He was quick

---

[2] In 1928 Cotton was asked to give similar golf demonstrations and lessons at a new store in Dublin. He was sceptical – 'What did I know of golf at the age of 21?' – but gave it a go, only to be pole-axed when one man ('thoughtless beyond belief') caught him full on the leg with a wayward drive. Exhibitions of this sort were soon, thanks to just such incidents, banned by the PGA, though not for health reasons alone: golf's professionals tended to see big-city sports stores as rivals to their own club shops.

to point out her failings (which didn't include the fact that she was the daughter of one of Argentina's richest men – the family ranch was said to be larger than Wales); she, with her notoriously short temper, was quick to put the visiting hired hand in his place. She was married to a leading diplomat, but this inconvenience didn't stop them becoming *very* close friends, a development Cotton celebrated by winning the Mar del Plata championship.

The following year was a disappointment. Cotton's upward momentum stalled, and he blotted his copybook by opting out of the 1931 Ryder Cup team after a row about travel arrangements. The selectors were insisting that the players sail back to Britain together, as a group, while Cotton wanted to stay on in the United States and make a bit of cash. The argument became a *cause célèbre* when another leading player, Percy Alliss (father of the commentator, Peter), was also rendered ineligible thanks to his position as the resident professional at Berlin's Wannsee Golf Club – the setting, a decade later, of the hideous meeting at which Reinhard Heydrich would announce the 'final solution' to the Jewish question. It meant that two of Britain's best players weren't playing. When Cotton went on to decline a request to play for England against Scotland, while agreeing to accompany the Ryder Cup team as a newspaper reporter, it sparked a surge of ill feeling. The friendly editor of *Golf Illustrated* went so far as to write to him ('pal to a pal') to point out that 'there is a feeling among the public that you are high-hatting them ... You have taken your individualism far enough for the time being.'

Advice like this didn't make Cotton mend his ways. On the contrary, it made him feel even more isolated and out of kilter with the times. So when he was offered the chance to become the resident professional at Waterloo Golf Club, in Belgium, on the edge of Wellington's famous battlefield, he leapt at it. The Secretary of Waterloo approached Cotton to see if he might recommend someone, and was surprised when Cotton suggested ... himself. Thanks to his Channel Island mother, he spoke fair French, and felt at home on the Continent. He saw it as financially useful – he could charge higher fees in Belgium. And it was a gilded opportunity in another way: Isabel Moss was also in Belgium – her husband was the ambassador in Brussels. All things considered it was, he said later, 'a very good decision, one of the best I have ever made'.

It was Mar del Plata all over again: 'Toots', as everyone called Isabel, became Cotton's favourite student, taking a lesson every morning and playing with her teacher in the afternoon. Soon she was an eight-handicapper herself ('I got her to play quite decently,' said Cotton, 'by telling her she was no good') and they were a couple. She bought him a fabulous blood-red 1929 Mercedes-Benz cabriolet, which he drove proudly from tournament to tournament. He convinced himself that driving was good for his hands, if not his back, and loved the splash and dazzle it made when he rolled it into new venues. He especially liked pulling up in front of signs saying NO PARKING.

As Walter Hagen had shown, there was a fair bit of fun to be had with a car like this. Back in 1920 Hagen had bemused the members of Deal at the Open Championship by responding to the ruling that he was not allowed in the clubhouse (the marquee was surely more than adequate, the members felt) with a chauffeur-driven Rolls which he filled with food from the Ritz, and used as his personal picnic spot and changing room.[3] Cotton was much taken with this stunt and started turning up in a white Rolls of his own, setting up elegant luncheons (hampers from Fortnum & Mason) beneath the 'astonished gaze' of the startled members. But the burghers of Waterloo did not stand on ceremony so stiffly as their British counterparts; they did not follow the Anglo-Saxon habit of banning golf professionals from the clubhouse, and were even

---

[3] Hagen went on to come a none-too-impressive 55th, which a few grouchy old-timers in the clubhouse judged to be exactly what he deserved. But they hadn't heard the last of him: he ended up winning the Open four times (two of them, in 1922 and 1928, just up the coast at Royal St George's) in a dashing wardrobe of expensive clothes – always remembering, as he famously put it, to smell the flowers along the way.

happy for Cotton to turn the club shop – traditionally a mechanic's cave of boiling kettles, string, gluepots, files and grinding tools – into a dapper gentleman's outfitter. Before long it was a smart emporium of pricey silk sweaters, two-tone brogues (he was paid £25 to lend his name to the so-called 'Cotton Oxfords') and zebra-skin chairs.

CHAPTER FIVE

Anyone for Fred?

Fred Perry's father must have sighed when his son announced he wanted to play lawn tennis. He was not an out-and-out socialist so much as an evangelical progressive who wanted the Co-operative Party to bring 'a more Christian-like spirit' to the Labour movement. But he did have left-leaning ambitions, and they certainly did not include kowtowing to the kind of blue bloods who liked biffing balls about on lawns. He was busy with his own career, however; he had contested and lost two General Elections in Stockport in 1920 and 1922, and was about to win Kettering (in December 1923) as a joint candidate for the Co-Operative and Labour Party.[1] So he wasn't up for a fight.

When he good-humouredly spent five shillings on an 'antiquated' second-hand tennis racket for his son, it quickly became a prized possession. But the young Perry was still primarily a ping-pong player, and at the family home in Pitshanger Lane he created a bespoke practice facility by pushing the kitchen table up against the wall and using it to play endless rebounds to himself – ping-*pong*, ping-*pong*, ping-*pong*, ping-*pong* … As he swatted the white ball to and fro, incessantly, patient hour after bloody-minded hour, he began to absorb the reflexive talent that would later help him

---

[1] It is worth reflecting, when we are tempted to see history as the inexorable unfolding of events, that if Sam Perry had won Stockport in 1920 he would have moved north, and the story of Brentham, Perry and Wimbledon might have been very different.

succeed in the larger form of the game: he learned to take the ball early, virtually on the half-volley, with a strong wrist, quickening the tempo with zippy topspin until the rally sounded like a train racing – clickety-*clack*, clickety-*clack*, clickety-*clack* – on bright new rails.

There is an echo of Verity here. Just as young Hedley was open-minded enough to listen to the Yorkshire coaches urging him to switch to spin, so Perry was fortunate in having a mentor, Pops Summers of Brentham, to set him on a new path. Summers urged young Perry to master this knack of taking a tennis ball on the rise, and kept him at it when he was struggling to pull the move off ('I broke a lot of windows').

It is telling that all four of our budding champions shared a tireless devotion to practice. Something in the post-war emphasis on pure, whole-hearted endeavour, combined perhaps with the scarcity of rival attractions (no television) produced a quartet of exceptionally driven young athletes. Just as Cotton would wrestle with clubs to strengthen his hands, so Verity would shovel away at his heap of coal with a vengeance, to build up his muscle power and endurance. Just as Round would thwack away at the special wall built by her father, and just as Verity would bowl lumps of coal at the garage door, so Perry would bat balls to and fro in a lonely pursuit of excellence. Modern sports science talks about 'repetitions' as if the idea of grooving the muscle memory were some arresting new discovery, but to these apprentices the idea that practice made perfect was so obvious it barely needed stating.

It took Perry months of determined effort to turn his quick-fire table tennis flick into a weapon that could work in lawn tennis, too. 'Literally hundreds of people would come in relays and hit quiet shots with me,' said Perry. He failed and failed and failed. And then, one shining day, in a flash, in the same way that a beginner cyclist discovers how to balance on wheels, he found it! It was a Sunday morning at the Herga Club in Harrow, a moment so golden he never forgot it. Everything fell into place; suddenly he was fizzing tennis balls away like tracer shells, and his forehand was a magic wand – 'that battered old racket could spit flames'. In time this new stroke would become his chief characteristic, his signature shot. In meeting the ball so early, and on the move, he harried his opponents to distraction. And by stealing a march on his rivals in this way he adjusted the whole rhythm of tennis, changed the dimensions and music of the game. As the actor-fan Peter Ustinov said: 'He took the ball so early it seemed almost as unfair as bodyline bowling ...'

Table tennis offered him another unorthodox move: it embedded the habit of using a backhand chop on the forehand, achieved by flicking his hand anti-clockwise under the wrist. This turned out to be an effective volleying method for balls close to the body. But it was taking the ball on the rise that was the breakthrough. At a stroke, Perry rewrote the coaching manual, and reshaped the choreography of tennis for ever.

It was enough to make him switch games for good. 'I was a world champion at nineteen,' he wrote in his memoir with a haughty shrug, as he turned his back on table tennis, 'so I decided to retire.' Once again he had the support of his father: the MP for Kettering could see that his son risked becoming a jack-of-all-trades by trying to play too many games at once. He encouraged him to give up table tennis once and for all. 'What else is there to win?' he told the budding star. 'Why not concentrate on tennis?'

Fred needed little encouragement. After a minor run-in regarding the way he used the Brentham bowling green as a practice lawn, he played at the Herga Club, which had a more ambitious juniors section, and then the even more upscale Chiswick Park club, in whose stunning 18th-century Palladian landscape (the inspiration for New York's Central Park) he prospered.[2] This outdoor game

---

[2] The fact that he was welcome at both of these well-bred clubs, without any demur, suggests that the famous snootiness of English tennis at this time was not quite so cold and exclusive as we sometimes think. It always had a soft spot for the better player.

wasn't so very different, was it? He gripped the racket just as he had gripped a table tennis bat, and quickly tuned himself to the tempo of the larger format. He couldn't practise against the kitchen wall now, so used the garage door instead, honing his strokes with lonely patience. In 1926, only three years after hitting a ball for the first time, he entered the Middlesex juniors with a Brentham friend, still using the same old racket, and won the doubles.

That May the country ground to a standstill when the General Strike was announced. It lasted less than two weeks, but it was still a momentous event, especially for a left-leaning politician such as Sam Perry. His son declined to be distracted by it, however. 'Tennis was of much more importance to me than a strike,' he wrote. That autumn he was playing in the British juniors at Wimbledon, and that trusty old five-shilling racket fell apart in his hands. But he had a generous new friend at the Herga Club, a Slazenger representative who was happy to supply him with the latest tennis equipment.

It didn't take long for Perry to come up against the supercilious mindset of English sport, however. When he turned up to play in a schoolboys' tournament at London's Queen's Club, having read in the evening paper that it was open to all schoolboys, the stewards sneered at his modest credentials – Ealing County? Was that *really* a school? They seemed to be much more respectful to the young gentlemen from Eton, Marlborough and Rugby. But this merely sharpened Perry's will to win. As it happened, he did look the part – he was already dashing and handsome – but his accent gave him away as someone who hadn't been to the right school. In later years his father would make much of this incident, and in 1935, at a Manchester dinner in his son's honour, he made trenchant political capital out of it. If only tennis were open and democratic, he said, why, hundreds of ordinary boys and girls could do just as well as his boy. Emphasising that Fred had learned the game at public clubs rather than public schools, he held his son up as a political talisman: proof of what could be achieved without a privileged background 'through facilities that were open to the average youth'.

Perry himself didn't much care. Just as Cotton had one or two airs and graces not *quite* in keeping, some felt, with his new station in life as a lowly professional, so Perry was no great admirer of the Corinthian code. 'I'd always been regarded as an upstart,' he conceded years later, in his autobiography. 'I freely admit I wasn't a good loser ... I was someone who didn't have the right credentials for the noble game.'

The weakness of British tennis was becoming a national issue. In 1927 the President of the LTA, Lord D'Abernon, asked whether 'any sensible Englishmen' could tolerate for much longer a situation in which home-grown players did so badly at Wimbledon, and suggested that 'regaining supremacy in international competition had great urgency and real importance'. It was still assumed that the shining lights of the future would, as a matter of course, come from Oxbridge, but there *was* an increase in the funding of tennis clubs, and Middlesex was a prime beneficiary. Perry spent the next two years playing on the club circuit in west London, improving all the time without, as he put it, 'setting the Thames on fire'. It didn't help that in 1928 (aged 18) he was still only 5ft 3in – not tall enough to become a big power server. His father prescribed swimming, believing it would stretch him out, and, as luck would have it, in two years he gained nine inches. In 1929 he entered Wimbledon for the first time, winning two rounds, but he was about to face his first crisis. He wasn't able to earn money from tennis, so in these years he worked first (through his father's good offices) at the Co-operative Wholesale Society, and then at Spaldings in Cheapside, near St Paul's. Things came to a head in January 1930, when he was denied the leave of absence he needed to play in the annual hard-court championship in Bournemouth. It turned out that his employer was planning to go and watch the tournament himself – he could hardly permit this cocky young trainee to go as well, just to *play* in the damn thing.

Once again, Sam Perry MP rode to the rescue. Some fathers may have felt that a cold dose of reality was just what the boy needed, but Perry felt the opposite. He told his son to resign from Spaldings at once, and offered to pay his wages for one whole year, so he could at least see how far he could go. Effectively he was sponsoring his own child, a touching but risky move bordering, in some eyes, on turning professional. But since his gilded amateur rivals, such as Bunny Austin, themselves enjoyed a helpful cushion of family money, who could argue?[3] Fred Perry was a free man. He had a year to prove himself – and the way he was playing it might not take that long.

It took only a week. He reached the final in Bournemouth, where he lost (in five sets, after failing to clinch a match point) to the British number one – Bunny Austin.

His semi-professional status was controversial enough to inspire a few mutterings in Parliament, but Sam Perry dealt with them firmly. 'Should it not be the aim of all of us,' he said, 'to give our children a better chance than we have had?' This was the voice of a new, aspiring social class, the voice of Brentham – a new note in English society. And it was only the beginning. That June, Perry played at Wimbledon and, in the third round, beat the number four seed, an Italian baron (and First World War ace) named Umberto de Morpurgo. It earned him a match on the game's hallowed Centre Court, and Perry loved it ('nothing in the world can prepare you … it suited me right down to the ground'). He lost the match, but impressed the watching public *and* the selectors, who picked him for a Great Britain team set to tour America that autumn.

He won plenty of admirers in Westminster, too. 'Many of my Conservative friends,' wrote his father, 'were evidently impressed that the son of a Co-operative member of Parliament should bear

---

[3] 'I feel not a scrap of envy,' wrote Perry of Austin in 1936, by which time the pair had won the Davis Cup together. 'But few of us can manage Repton and Cambridge.'

himself so smoothly in the royal presence.' It all meant that when Fred went to visit his father at the Houses of Parliament he was welcomed by no fewer than three Prime Ministers: David Lloyd George (premier at Versailles, now leader of the Liberals), Stanley Baldwin (Conservative Leader of the Opposition) and the present incumbent, the Labour Prime Minister Ramsay MacDonald. On this they could all agree: England stood badly in need of a new tennis champion, and if Sam Perry's boy was made of the right stuff, then the best of British luck to him.

The other turning point, in 1930, was that Perry celebrated his 21st birthday, collected the £100 his father had promised him for remaining abstemious, and followed Henry Cotton's example by embarking on a tour of America. Unlike Cotton, he was not alone. He boarded the *Mauretania* at Southampton in the white blazer of the Great Britain tennis team. Though young, he was already part of the game's elite group. The only cloud on his future was his reputation for tantrums. As Dan Maskell put it, he was 'a stubborn and somewhat truculent character'. Perry himself was happy to admit as much. 'I was a strange kind of cat,' he said. 'A loner. I was bloody-minded … wanted to do things my way.' This bad-tempered attitude of his was so obvious that he was taken aside by the team captain, Leslie Godfree, in the middle of the Atlantic Ocean, and told that he was expected to 'adhere' to a higher standard of conduct.

'If you want to have it your own way,' Godfree told him, 'you'll be on the next boat back to England, and you will never play for your country again.'

Perry nodded. The trip, he said later, was a thrill – he loved the 'speed and hustle and dash' of America; in his autobiography he remembered in particular the glitz and the glitter, and confessed: 'wealth, and display that money can buy, dazzled me.' But this forceful piece of advice on manners was more important, from a tennis point of view, than anything else. The tour 'changed my game and my attitude', he said. He didn't win much, but practised hard (his backhand in particular) and knew that his game was improving fast. When he reached the last 16 of the US Nationals at Forest Hills, he was not surprised: indeed, he believed he had the ability to go much further. And he was mesmerised by the social side of American life. Tennis seemed to be a glossy magnet for wealthy men: half the people Perry met seemed to own copper mines or railroads. They had yachts and butlers, and threw wonderful parties. It wasn't a bit like Ealing.

In another echo of Cotton's itinerary, he headed to South America after that, winning in Brazil and then, in Argentina, capturing his first National championship. A dutiful son, he wrote to his father that he had 'put 15' (i.e. a point) on his game, proud to be able to send home an example of what Sam Perry liked to call 'traditional Cheshire grit'. But the voyage back was a bitter one: at the farewell dinner he tried lobster for the first time and was confined to his cabin, groaning and sickly, all the way home.

One reason why Perry had been keen to spend this particular winter abroad – it may also explain the softening of his demeanour – was that in early 1930 he lost his mother to a nervous ailment. The news hit him hard: to the end of his days he refused to play on the anniversary of her death, and it turned him off politics, too – he maintained that it was the strain of electioneering that had undone her. What made it worse was that, a year later (while he himself was in America), his father shocked him by marrying his secretary after a high-speed romance that raised a few eyebrows in Brentham. It made the old house in Pitshanger Lane a bit less homely, so far as Perry was concerned.

But the trip to America filled him with energy, and in April, at Queen's Club, he won through to the trials for Britain's Davis Cup team. Two months later, when Wimbledon came around again, he was the number five seed. Don't say anything, people were whispering, but we might just have an actual-proper-genuine-real contender here.

He certainly had the brassy streak of a champion-in-waiting. On his first visit to the All England Club in 1930 he had paused below the famous Kipling inscription over the Players' Entrance, the noble credo of amateur sport – 'If you can meet with triumph and disaster / And treat those two imposters just the same' – but had simply shrugged.

'You know,' he muttered. 'I only ever think about triumph.'

The All England Club had been holding an annual championship on the smooth lawns of Wimbledon (initially on Worple Road) since 1877 – it was already historic – but it had come a very long way since a few hundred spectators paid a shilling to watch the first final. It wasn't until 1922 that it moved into its beguiling new premises in Church Road and became an international event; before long some 15,000 people, many of them members of the smart set, were making a daily trek down Church Road. They didn't have many Britons to cheer for. Tennis in the 1920s was dominated by the four French 'musketeers' (Henri Cochet, René Lacoste, Jacques Brugnon and Jean Borotra) who beat all comers with swishes of Gallic flair – between them they won all six titles from 1924 to 1929. The new No. 1 Court opened in 1924, swelling the capacity, but even this was not enough to keep up with demand. In 1927 tickets were held back for anyone willing to queue – and a tradition was born: fans filled the road at dawn. This Wimbledon queue became an annual spectacle, with thousands swarming the pavement. Some 22,000 tried to squeeze in on Saturday that first year, 2,000 of whom were turned away. By the 1930s a crowd numbering some 200,000 pressed in – as much to be seen as to watch the games. Gentlemen wore ties; ladies wore long drifty dresses; everyone wore hats. It was the next best thing to a society wedding.

In later years it seemed that Perry had been in the vanguard of this sudden fondness for tennis, and this was true. But he was a symptom of the game's growing popularity as much as a cause. In 1925 there were 1,620 clubs affiliated to the LTA; five years later there were over 2,500. Tennis was fashionable as well as fun. John Betjeman was not the only one to drool over the sun-burnished limbs of his lissom tennis partners ('Miss Joan Hunter Dunn,

Miss Joan Hunter Dunn / How mad I am, sad I am, glad that you won'). Being a serious player was really something, with all these slinky girls clustering around: Daddy's girls, chorus girls, poor little rich girls, show girls, 'It' girls and nice girls. Many relished the way tennis created opportunities for outdoor games with the opposite sex. Who *wouldn't* want to be Fred Perry, with all that going on?

One young girl who was few of these things was Dorothy Round. In her teens she lived at home, playing tennis with her brothers on the family court and emerging as something out of the ordinary on the Midlands circuit around Birmingham. She won her county colours at the age of 17, made her Wimbledon debut the following year and in 1929 reached the second round and struck people as a 'steady' sort of player. That year she also won the Midlands Counties Singles championship, which led to her being selected to play for England against Scotland. In 1930, aged 19, she performed strongly enough in the Wightman Cup trials (the match between Britain and the USA that had been running since 1923) to be hailed by the *Observer* as having 'better strokes, better strategy and higher courage' than anyone else on show.

Like Perry, she took her game across the Atlantic (in 1931 and 1933), losing to Helen Jacobs in the semi-final on the second of these trips to announce herself as one of the coming forces in the sport. But there was still an old-fashioned feel to the way her burgeoning game was discussed in public. When she was filmed skipping with a rope (just like Verity) to improve the speed and lightness of her footwork, the commentator could not resist adding that this was how to keep 'that perfect slim and supple figure'.

Meanwhile, the crowds attending sports events were growing all the time. In 1923, as we have seen, a famous white horse was needed to control the crowd at the Bolton v West Ham FA Cup final. And that summer the nation held its breath as Jack Hobbs, the 40-year-old master, inched his way closer to a 100th first-class ton. The British Empire Exhibition of 1924 (at Wembley) included a sculpture of Hobbs made out of New Zealand butter. Big audiences lined the Thames for the boat race, too, and enormous numbers crammed the inner rings of many racetracks.

There was something in the air, and it seemed to be driving lots of people to amazing new heights. It wasn't a coincidence that these years saw repeated attempts to conquer Everest, if only to show that the imperial spirit still had sap in its veins – the roof of the world being the so-called 'third Pole'. The 1924 expedition ended badly when George Mallory (who had taught and befriended Robert Graves at Charterhouse) vanished near the summit with his young partner, Sandy Irvine. But the pair became terrific national heroes in their dramatic death – martyrs to an epic idea and dream, like the fallen of the Great War. The King himself attended the memorial service in St Paul's Cathedral.

And it didn't stop others from undertaking similar adventures. In 1926 a 19-year-old American girl named Gertrude Ederle became the first woman to swim the English Channel. The newspapers at once christened her 'Queen of the Waves', which created a ripple of patriotic alarm – weren't *we* supposed to rule these wave thingies? – but who cared? She was cheerful, fit, sporty and buoyant. It didn't matter *that* much that she was the daughter of German immigrants in America. Happy days were here again.

CHAPTER SIX

Depression

In 1928 there was something like the bursting of a dam in the British public's sense of its own past. Not that there had ever been barbed wire marking what could or couldn't be said about the war – the first volume of Ford Madox Ford's *Parade's End*, whose aim was 'the obviating of all future wars', was published in 1924, and there was some gut-wrenching poetry about the pity of it all. But few wanted to express much beyond sheer grief. It was still too raw; no one wanted to rake over all *that* again.

Cracks began to appear in this consensus soon after the 1926 General Strike – a brief but shocking eruption of despair. Stanley Spencer's 1927 murals of shell-blasted men, in a chapel at Burghclere in Hampshire, tore another hole in the vow of silence; and in 1928 the Apollo Theatre found itself with a palpable hit when R. C. Sherriff's *Journey's End* also presented a downbeat view of war. Almost every theatre in London turned down this play (where was the satin-clad leading lady?) but thanks to a dashing young actor named Olivier it transferred to the Savoy Theatre and ran for 594 performances. By 1930 it was playing on a dozen stages across Britain, and many more overseas. It seemed there *was* room for work that tried to unvarnish the truth, after all.

Before long there was a rash of such creations. In that same year, Siegfried Sassoon's *Memoirs of a Fox-Hunting Man* contrasted the lazy pre-war summers of a well-born Sussex squire with the shock of front-line work; in *Undertones of War* the soldier-poet

Edmund Blunden spoke of the 'socket-eyed despair' that haunted him at Ypres; Richard Aldington's *Death of a Hero*, hailed by his friend Lawrence Durrell as 'the best war novel of the epoch', took a swipe at the complacent Edwardian officer class; and Henry Williamson recalled the smashed bodies at the Somme and asked, in *The Wet Flanders Plain*: 'Who could have imagined that the Big Push was going to be this?'

The following year, 1929, saw the ghoulish comedy of Robert Graves's *Goodbye to All That*, which presented the war as a barrage of bad jokes and worse food. This was the year of *All Quiet on the Western Front* by Erich Maria Remarque, which sold four million copies in 28 languages before becoming a film. And in 1930 Frederic Manning, in *Her Privates We* (a title borrowed from *Hamlet*), depicted the camaraderie of men under fire in a new way.

It was not yet routine to portray officers as cowardly hypocrites – the so-called 'lions led by donkeys' argument – since it was clear that the well-born had fallen at the same grotesque rate as the ranks. But the chorus of candid voices did lead to a stark reappraisal. For a decade it had seemed ignoble to question the way the war had been fought – an insult to the sacrifice. But Wilfred Owen's poems – compact horror stories in a sorrowful, shell-shocked rhetoric – were now becoming the accepted way to think. At the time of his death in 1918, only five had been published, and the 1920 collection, edited by Siegfried Sassoon and Edith Sitwell won him only *bien-pensant* admirers. But the 1931 edition, with the memoir by Edmund Blunden, won many new readers and cemented his place as the eloquent spokesman for a resonantly sad world view.[1]

---

[1] Not everyone was persuaded. As late as 1936 W. B. Yeats, editor of *The Oxford Book of English Verse*, decided to exclude all poetry inspired by the nightmare of Flanders on the extreme aesthetic grounds that 'passive suffering is not a theme for poetry'.

By the time Vera Brittain's *Testament of Youth* came out in 1933, no one could be astonished by anything. But the book's potent mixture of anger and grief made it an instant hit: the first print run of 3,000 sold out on publication day. Virginia Woolf was said to have stayed up all night reading it. Even so, the feelings provoked by such works were not uniform; some preferred to thumb their noses at the reflective mood. The mass audience was not so interested in poetry, and with Sherlock Holmes gone it preferred Biggles, Agatha Christie, P. G. Wodehouse or Dornford Yates.

The other response was simply to pour another drink. Although large areas of Britain were still bent double under the weight of the depression, in the big city the party scene launched in the twenties bubbled along merrily. Smart London was all go. The Savoy Hotel published its own cocktail book in 1930, and there was a gleaming world of fast cars, automatic ticket machines and electric light. Men wore smoking jackets, held cigarette holders at striking angles and affected the nonchalant charm of Noël Coward. And sport came to the fore, too. Clean-limbed, suntanned, upwardly mobile sporting stars were the poster children of a new age. It was no surprise when Ethel Wigham, the picture-book daughter of a Scottish-American millionaire and the 1930 'Deb of the Year', turned down the Earl of Warwick, no less, in order to marry a swell American golfer named Charles Sweeny. So many people wanted to catch a glimpse of the wedding dress that the streets of Knightsbridge were blocked for three hours.

As if by magic, movie stars were starting to *speak*. People had been delighted by the silver-screen antics of Charlie Chaplin, Buster Keaton, Laurel and Hardy and the Marx Brothers, and were happy to gaze up at Rudolph Valentino. But these icons had nothing to say for themselves until, in 1928, Walt Disney and Mickey Mouse came along, and Tarzan started yodelling across a Hollywood jungle, and soon there was no shutting them up. It was still possible to sway along to 'Yes, We Have No Bananas' in music halls or to relish serious theatre, but motion pictures were the thing: Charles Laughton looked exactly like Henry VIII, Claudine Colbert *was* Cleopatra, and wasn't little Shirley Temple the cutest thing you ever saw? James Cagney, Joan Crawford, Fred and Ginger ... darling, they were all simply *wonderful*!

It was a sign of the fearful times, perhaps, that made audiences at this time hungry for horror, too. The golden age of science fiction (usually held to be the fifties) was some way off, though *Brave New World* (1932) was delivering an early glimpse of future terrors. And there were monsters elsewhere: 1931 saw *Dracula*, *Frankenstein* and *Dr Jekyll and Mr Hyde*; in 1932 there was *White Zombie*, *Vampyr* and *The Mummy* (with Boris Karloff); and 1933 was the year of *King Kong* and *The Invisible Man*.

Sport was part of this eruption of fun. While Verity was finding his feet in Yorkshire, cricket truly was a nationwide common pursuit. The London County Council owned some 350 pitches in 1929, used by more than 1,000 clubs. Combined with private clubs, it meant that cricket really was part of the marrow of English life. And the combination of games and poverty was giving birth to a new hobby: football pools. By the mid-1930s over five million people were filling out their match predictions and posting coupons off to Littlewoods and Vernon's. Since only 80 per cent of the sums paid in were paid out as winnings, it was a terrific way to lift money out of the pockets of the public – the prospect of a pools win easily outgunned the drab laws of probability.

Something even more remarkable was rising to prominence elsewhere. His name was Donald Bradman. Depression-era Australia was, like Britain, a ravaged land longing for a hero to bring some cheer to difficult, hardscrabble lives. The collapse of the world price for meat and wool had fractured the agricultural economy, and in 1932 unemployment touched as high as 30 per cent. The one commodity in plentiful supply was time, and with so much of it on everyone's hands, sporting occasions drew ever larger crowds: what had once been mere fun was fast becoming a major industry.

The first glory of this new age was the wonder horse, Phar Lap, who claimed 14 wins in a row in 1930–31 – indeed, was so terrific that someone tried to shoot him a few days before the Melbourne Cup. And now Don Bradman (he was only 22, but had already notched two Test centuries) was giving Australia something new. No product of smart schools, he was a self-taught, small-town boy who thus seemed *especially* natural and Australian: a bright-eyed wallaby with a bat, an off-the-peg legend. He had sent up a flare in January, scoring 452 not out for New South Wales against Queensland, and the world had taken notice – partly because it was a record, partly because it took only 415 minutes. Now, as the new decade dawned, he was on his way to show the mother country a thing or two about this bat-and-ball game they thought of as theirs.

He began the 1930 tour of England with 236 against Worcester-shire (at a time when games between touring sides and counties meant something) and then, in the first Test, hit 131. This was only a prelude, a clearing of the throat. At Lord's he made 254:[2] at Headingley he plundered a century before lunch on the way to 334 – a Test record; and at The Oval he notched 232. In all he took some 3,000 runs off English bowling that year, and the grand old men of MCC vowed to stop him next time, by hook or by crook.

'There would seem no limit to his possibilities,' wrote *Wisden*, and his reputation in Australia knew even fewer bounds. As a man and a team-mate he was not universally acclaimed: some found him cold. But as a public performer he was without equal. No politician, scientist, writer or artist, no explorer, musician, actor or aviator attracted the attention he generated. Crowds gathered at railways stations for a glimpse; if he ever took tea in a café an

---

[2] On the day of this innings, an Indian political firebrand named Jawaharlal Nehru was arrested following a protest in Delhi. It was the height of the civil disobedience in India inspired by Gandhi and his followers. Not one of England's better days.

audience would gaze through the window. First-time visitors to Sydney would be asked if they had seen the harbour, the bridge … and The Don.

Jack Fingleton, a team-mate, called him not only 'genius absolute' but 'the most discussed man in Australia … the continent's number one idol', and this was no exaggeration. Swarms of spectators – many who cared little for cricket till now – filled grounds to bursting point just to see him in the flesh, and often drifted away when he was out. At his wedding in 1932 the church was besieged by raucous well-wishers who forced their way inside and climbed on to chairs in search of a better view of their hero; the police tried to put up barriers, but they were knocked aside in the stampede.

There have been hundreds of testimonials to his impact on the Australian imagination, but few are more often quoted than the observation by the novelist Thomas Keneally, who wrote of his schooldays: 'If we spoke of literature we spoke of Englishmen. Cricket was a great way out of Australian cultural ignominy, for while no Australian had written *Paradise Lost*, Bradman had scored a hundred before lunch at Lord's.'[3]

How could a pint-sized little prodigy achieve such resonant effects? According to one contemporary, Philip Lindsay, by 'stiffening the sinews and exalting the heart'. These are areas of life beyond the reach of most political leaders. No amount of juggling with the interest rate or the tax code can create such a stir. Lindsay's phrase was quoted approvingly by C. L. R. James, in *Beyond a Boundary*, in support of his own faith in cricket as a rich cultural event. For James, the task of stiffening sinews and exalting hearts was for the likes of Learie Constantine, who

---

[3] This pithy tribute is often used to dramatise Australia's so-called 'cultural cringe'. Alas, Bradman never did score a century before lunch at Lord's, though it sounds like the kind of thing he ought to have done. The hundred he struck before lunch in 1930 was at *Leeds*. But Keneally is a fine novelist, and no doubt was speaking figuratively.

scored over 1,000 runs in England in 1928, and, as a black-skinned colonial, 'revolted against the revolting contrast between his first-class status as a cricketer and his third-class status as a man'. And no Australian needed to look beyond Bradman for such things: he was God in whites.

There was only one cloud on his horizon. At the end of the 1930 tour, in the final Test at The Oval, he and another young hero, Archie Jackson, were going along very nicely, thank you, when rain began to spatter on south London. By the time play resumed the wicket had become spiteful – in those days it was uncovered and open to the elements; cricketers had to take the rough with the smooth – and a layer of moisture was visible on the rain-darkened turf. Batting was going to be hazardous. In truth there was little point even taking the field: it was 6.25, and by the time the batsmen had dawdled to the wicket (to the jeers of the crowd) there would only be time for one over.

What an over it was, though. As Jack Fingleton described it in *Cricket Crisis*, his eyewitness account of the Bodyline saga, Larwood started banging the ball in short and was glad to see it bouncing 'viciously' from the wicket. And England saw something they had never thought to see: as the ball spat past his ears, the great Bradman was visibly unnerved. So what if he was the best player of all time? So what if he went on to get a double century in this match? There was a chink in the fellow's armour, after all. This, wrote Fingleton, was the moment the Bodyline story really began. When England sailed to Australia two years later, they did so 'with a glint in their eye'.

The boom in all these entertainments, cricketing and otherwise, widened the already substantial gap between the British public and its leaders. It wasn't the first sign of such a gulf – and was no greater than the abyss that lay between a Victorian factory hand and an earl. But modern media – newspaper, magazines and radio – made it more obvious. Heavy industry was failing, but new, lighter businesses (chocolates, stockings, hats, bags and dancing shoes) were doing well. So while many people (those with jobs or incomes) partied the night away in air thick with streamers, cigar smoke and alcohol, swapping stories about the new driving test or the greyhound track, society's elders seemed different. When they appeared on newsreels and in photographs they belonged still to an age of high winged collars, frock coats and top hats. A. J. P. Taylor thought the 'most considerable achievement' of Neville Chamberlain as Chancellor of the Exchequer in 1932 was to shift the interest rate on war loans from five to three and half per cent. News like this was not the sort of thing to cut much ice with café society.

Nor could it compete with scandal. This was the time when newspapers began to put reporters in divorce courts to lap up whatever saucy gossip they could find. And the most eagerly followed trial, in the summer of 1932, concerned a Church of England vicar called Harold Davidson, the Rector of Stiffkey in Norfolk, who took it upon himself to 'rescue' girls who had fallen into vice before, it was said (without much proof, but who cared?) performing his missionary duties a little *too* keenly.

But by this time the party was coming to an abrupt end. In May 1931, Credit Anstalt (founded by the Rothschilds, and at one time the biggest bank in Austro-Hungary) went bankrupt, even though it had widely been considered, in a phrase perhaps not quite in circulation at that time, 'too big to fail'. The faraway Austrian source of this eruption reminded some of the dark day in 1914 when an equally little-known Viennese institution, Archduke Franz Ferdinand, had been assassinated in Belgrade. If such a thing could happen in a bright imperial capital stuffed with grand buildings, sublime orchestras, waltzes and cafés, throbbing with fur coats and brain doctors, then nothing was safe. Other banks started to topple as well, and before long they were falling like dominoes. By September more than 300 had capsized in America alone, and things got worse in October, when 500 went under.

In truth, this was no bolt from the blue, but the dying ember of the bonfire of debt that still smoked in the rubble of the Great War. But the 1931 bank collapse triggered a chronic slump. The engines driving the 'civilised' world broke: trade halved, industrial output shrank, unemployment soared, crop prices withered, businesses failed and currencies buckled. The only thing that seemed to prosper in the poisoned atmosphere was the market in violent solutions: angry nationalist parties flared to life everywhere.

The resemblance with the depression of our own times is striking. Both began with a financial collapse (1929 and 2007) caused by wild money-trading, and a stock market bubble; both were triggered by the crash of a bank – for Credit Anstalt read Lehmann Brothers. Both turned into a slump when fearful depositors created a sovereign debt crisis – leading in 1931 to a run on the banks, and in 2008 to the Icelandic-Irish-Greek insolvencies that gave the euro the jitters. In the 1930s Europe's countries raised tariff barriers in a risky attempt to protect their own home industries against cheaper foreign imports, and embarked on a tit-for-tat devaluation of their currencies. The only element missing in this new version of a familiar story was, perish the thought, an arms race.

At the relatively grand old age of 26, Hedley Verity was still a novice county cricketer. But his first season as a Yorkshire regular (1931) began in spectacular vein: he took 35 wickets in the first five matches, and showed no signs of slowing down. By the end of the season he had taken 188 wickets, enough to earn an England debut against New Zealand in which he claimed 4 for 75 and scored 24. These efforts, along with his 10 for 36 against Warwickshire – on his 26th birthday – made him a *Wisden* Cricketer of the Year (along with Bill Bowes). The bible of cricket was fulsome but cautious. 'He still has a great deal to learn,' it wrote, urging 'continuous practice'. But it was clear to everyone by now that when conditions were favourable he was near-unplayable. In the *Manchester Guardian* Neville Cardus wrote that he had 'a beautiful action – supple, upright and economic'. Those long years of resolute practice acted like sandpaper on his original talent, honing his easy bowling action into a movement of deceptive simplicity and cunning.

The following year, 1932, yielded a further 162 wickets including *another* full house – his famous 10 for 10 against Nottinghamshire: still the best bowling analysis ever achieved in first-class cricket, bar none. Yorkshire won the County Championship in each of his first three seasons, 1931, 1932 and 1933 – and it wasn't a coincidence. Best of all, it was achieved in such a courteous fashion. With his sticking-out ears, long face and receding hairline, Verity looked like a vicar, and there was something so diffident in his manner – when he appealed, even the umpire could hardly hear it – that almost everyone was disarmed. He was a strong, silent type, but mild and kindly, too.

Henry Cotton liked Waterloo, even though his position there meant missing some British events. It was an evocative place full of English echoes: the fairways had been laid out by Harry Colt, the noted architect of Hoylake, Sunningdale, St George's Hill and Wentworth, on the very slopes where Napoleon's *Grande Armée* of 1815 had met its match; and this was not the only reminder of such deeds. The first shots of the First World War had rattled into the air at Liège, and, though no one knew it yet, in a few years' time French forces would run into the invading Germans at Charleroi, barely a three-iron away. And the British would endure their baptism of fire at Mons, a day's trudge to the south.

It was a blood-soaked landscape, in other words, resonant with British bravery, but it was also a fine golf course and a pleasant place – the *tarte au sucre et fromages* was, according to people who knew, *sans pareil*. It suited Cotton's personality, because he was still something of an oddity in Britain, where he couldn't avoid being ill at ease on both sides of golf's social divide. The toffs looked down on him because he was a professional (and his relationship with 'Toots' was semi-scandalous; though a devoted and obvious couple, they couldn't marry until she obtained a divorce in 1939). The pros, meanwhile, saw him as a toff, so he couldn't rely on their camaraderie either.

The Fred Perry who returned from *his* travels in North and South America (almost in Cotton's footsteps) was no longer the wide-eyed youngster who had left Ealing, but an athletic tournament winner with an ambitious gleam in his eye. In the Davis Cup trials in April, at Queen's Club (whose lawns he had gate-crashed for the schools championship) he was the star attraction. And though he lost a five-set final to Bunny Austin it was Perry who caught the eye. He was, ran one report, 'a Goliath rejoicing in his strength'. When he reached the last 16 of the French Open a few weeks later, even casual observers were beginning to sit up and take notice.

If he was intimidated, he didn't show it. He cruised through five matches with hardly a false step and became only the second Englishman to make a semi-final in a decade. But his opponent, the American Sidney Wood, was living out the sort of dream Perry had in mind for himself: he was arriving each day in a Rolls-Royce arm in arm with Noël Coward and also the screen goddess Gertrude Lawrence, who turned everyone's head by waving a lace handkerchief at her tennis-playing beau. Perry could hardly help feeling belittled by such a show, and Woods breezed past him before winning the final, too. Still, the point had been made: England had a serious competitor at last.

In Britain the northern industrial heartlands were so much more buffeted by economic hardship than the Home Counties that another chasm was yawning – the famous north–south divide. Malnutrition boomed: rickets, scurvy and tuberculosis had a field day. The hunger marches on London reached a crescendo after 1931 thanks to the 'Means Test' – a sensible-sounding measure (help should be limited to those most in need) that became a hated excuse for state interference. Unemployment money *was* available, but only for those who passed a humiliating government inspection. As Orwell put it in *The Road to Wigan Pier* (1937) the Means Test gave 'encouragement to the tattle-tale and the informer, the writer of anonymous letters and the local blackmailer'.

In 1931 the scale of the flight away from sterling left the government with no option but to abandon the gold standard and give up trying to strap the pound into the tough valuation against gold that Churchill had imposed in 1925 (a doomed attempt to bring the creaking economy to the heel of monetary discipline). At a stroke, the pound fell against the dollar by a quarter – disquieting for those with fat sterling bank balances or savings (interest rates fell from 6 to 2 per cent) but good news for borrowers and exporters. But there was a long way to go before the skies lifted. In 1933 unemployment topped six million, creating the despairing world captured by Walter Greenwood's novel *Love on the Dole*. The *Manchester Guardian* called this work 'the real thing' and hailed Greenwood as a great local author: the Salford in his fiction was the same ashen zone that had inspired Friedrich Engels's *The Condition of the Working Class in England*; it would later become even better known through L. S. Lowry's paintings. Edith Sitwell, for one, declared herself 'terribly moved' by the dramatisation of such biting poverty.

Picking up on this theme, in the autumn of 1933 an immigrant London publisher, Victor Gollancz, sent the Yorkshire playwright J. B. Priestley (himself a wounded veteran of the Somme) on a tour of England. The project was probably inspired by George Orwell's *Down and Out in Paris and London*, which Gollancz also published that year – after it was turned down by Faber's T. S. Eliot. Priestley criss-crossed the country from Bristol to Hull and from Brighton to Middlesbrough, taking the national temperature not in a big-picture, macro-economic way but at street level. He found many different Englands – plush south, stricken north, the lawnmowers of suburbia, the blighted docks, the cheap new world of car showrooms and bingo halls. The resulting travelogue, *English Journey*, described in a 'rambling but truthful' fashion a land that was not quite green and not especially

pleasant either. In so doing it found a readership in the mood for
impish self-examination, knocked *Thank You, Jeeves* off the top
of the bestseller list and led Orwell to think about doing a follow-
up – in Wigan maybe.

All such musings were made to seem parochial by the spectre
of something drastic stirring in the wounded heart of Europe.
In the early days of his rise to power, Adolf Hitler seemed an
implausible, pantomime figure whose wilder comments need not
be taken too literally. But he had made alarming headway, and
Britain's newspapers were starting to chronicle his doings with
keen interest. At the beginning of 1933 he became Chancellor of
a coalition in which his Nazi Party held a third of the seats, and
a month later, after a convenient fire demolished the Reichstag,
he declared a national crisis and claimed dictatorial powers. He
had banned the Communist Party and trade unions, withdrawn
from the League of Nations, rejected the terms of the Versailles
settlement (which were, many Britons agreed, harsh to the point of
vindictive); and launched a red-hot weapons programme, trebling
the size of the German army. His followers were burning books
by Jewish authors, and hardly anyone in power was objecting.

In truth it looked awfully like a warpath, and some people
seemed to know as much. In January 1933 Winston Churchill told
dinner guests at the German Embassy that Hitler showed signs
of wanting to renew hostilities at the earliest opportunity, and
though not in Parliament himself he pressed for a firm response,
beating the drum whenever he could. 'Those bands of Teutonic
youths, marching through the streets and roads of Germany, with
the light of desire in the eyes to suffer for the Fatherland, are not
looking for equal status,' he wrote in the *Daily Mail*. 'They are
looking for weapons.'

It was not a message Britain wished to hear. Although life still
felt militarised to a high degree (many Great War veterans hung
on to their rank, so the nation's schools, offices and golf clubs
were full of Colonel Smiths and Major Browns) the martial echoes

were nostalgic rather than pugnacious. If anything, the mood was vehemently anti-war. So it wasn't a surprise when the students of Oxford University, in February 1933, voted *not* to fight for King and Country no matter how grave the provocation (a pledge they abandoned when the time came). They may have thought that they were doing nothing more than speaking up in favour of peace as a matter of plain decency, but the debate suggested a failure of patriotism, and made for strong headlines.[4]

One figure making only a minor dent on the public mind was Joseph Stalin. He had been the world leader of the great communist experiment for years now, and during the financial slump it was tempting to see him as the standard-bearer for a more optimistic and equal way of arranging human affairs. True, there were nasty rumours about his fondness for the grim world of secret police, foreign spy networks, labour camps and firing squads; and the man was laying claim to some highly unusual titles – 'Brilliant genius of Humanity … Gardener of Human Happiness … Father of Nations'. There was loose talk, too, that some parts of the Soviet Union – the Ukraine, in particular – were in the grip of a truly astonishing famine. But it was hard to tell quite how bad this was: there were conflicting accounts, and who could say which of them to believe?

On the one hand there were brave young journalists like Malcolm Muggeridge, who travelled to Moscow for the *Manchester Guardian* and saw enough to demolish every vestige of his sympathy for the communist project – it was 'the most terrible thing I have ever seen … the essence of destruction'. His own paper was startled, and did not print his reports, so he wrote

---

[4] Winston Churchill was among those who groaned at the news: in a speech to the Anti-Socialist and Anti-Communist Union he called it 'abject, squalid, shameless'. He shuddered aloud to think how this vote would be seen overseas: 'My mind turns across the narrow waters of the North Sea and Channel, where great nations stand determined to defend their national glories or national existence with their lives.'

a book instead. But Gareth Jones, a Welsh journalist (and former adviser to David Lloyd George) was making similar claims. In a series of articles for *The Times*, the *Western Mail*, the *Manchester Guardian* and the *Evening Standard* he painted a harrowing picture of a Moscow-orchestrated plan to wreck, in the name of class struggle, the Ukraine's vast farms. Jones did not mince his words – 'The famine is an organised one ... The Bolsheviks are destroying Russia' – and in a famous press release swore that the cry all across 'all parts of Russia' was: 'We are starving!'

Not everyone wanted to hear this sort of thing: it contradicted the still-fashionable hope that communism might usher in a better world. Writers like George Bernard Shaw were ardent supporters of this utopian dream, thought Stalin was, too, and rallied behind him. Sydney and Beatrice Webb, founders of the Fabian Society, the *New Statesman* and the London School of Economics, also rose up in defence of the Man of Steel; Beatrice denounced Stalin's critics as 'absolutely wrong' and, in a phrase that in time became notorious, referred to the casualties of Stalin's agrarian plan as 'cutting out the dead wood'.

It was the same story across the Atlantic. The *New York Times* bureau chief, Walter Duranty, mocked the Muggeridge–Jones view as 'malignant propaganda'. And *his* reports from Moscow had won a Pulitzer Prize in 1932 – surely *he* could be trusted. When he wrote, semi-admiringly, that the *kulak* class of private farmers (numbering over five million) of *course* needed to be 'liquidated or melted in the hot fire of exile', he may not have intended readers to take it literally. But that was what was happening: mass murder on an epic scale. Even the Tsar-induced crop failure of 1892, a callous failure of governance that helped ignite revolution, killed only 300,000–400,000.[5]

---

[5] In 2010 a Ukrainian court made a historic (and rather provocative) statement by finding Stalin guilty of genocide for this long gone, but far from forgotten, crime.

It was hard to feel sure about anything much, with these currents sloshing to and fro. The world was shrinking – people were saying it would soon be possible to eat lunch in London and dinner in New York – and its seams were popping. Even the Empire wasn't what it was. As James Morris later put it in his history of the Pax Britannica, it was starting to lack charisma: 'By the 1930s it was more benevolent than it had ever been, more idealist in an unassertive way, more sympathetic to its subjects, less arrogant, more humane; but it was becoming a somewhat dowdy presence in the world.'

The Imperial Conference at Westminster in 1930 gave the major British colonies a new status as autonomous 'dominions' rather than subject peoples in an Empire, but while this was presented as an innovative new order, everyone knew it meant the end of the old ways. The ocean-spanning Victorian empire, built on the power and clamour of the piston engine, was running out of steam. Mohandas Gandhi visited London in 1931 and made an enormous impression with his homespun style, renouncing the Ritz in favour of plain lodgings in Poplar. But few (even those who had read Forster's *A Passage to India*, which ridiculed British India) knew what to make of this holy vegetarian; he held an unsettling new moral mirror up to Britain's imperial nature, making it seem shrill, cruel, not quite Christian. Since then Gandhi had been fasting and praying for Indian peace and self-government. Things were changing all right.

CHAPTER SEVEN

Rising Stars

After his remarkable first season in county cricket, it was no surprise when Hedley Verity was asked to board the Orient liner *Orontes* at Tilbury and take his place on the infamous 1932–3 tour of Australia. It would go down in history as the Bodyline tour. Under the proud leadership of Douglas Jardine, England unleashed a barrage of vicious bowling at the Australians (Bradman wasn't the captain, merely the figurehead) with field settings derided in most quarters as unsporting. That brutal over at The Oval in 1930 had not been forgotten; Jardine was reported to have studied footage of The Don's edginess and cried: 'I've got it! He's yellow!' Over dinner at London's Piccadilly Hotel, with Nottinghamshire's captain Arthur Carr and the two fast bowlers, Bill Voce and Harold Larwood, he refined the strategy. He knew he commanded a bowling attack menacing enough to bang the ball in fast, from round the wicket, with a tight cordon of fielders on the leg side. But he needed to ready the team mentally as well. According to some accounts, on the long voyage to the southern hemisphere he urged his players to refer to Bradman, easily the best batsman in the world, as 'the little bastard'.

The idea of targeting a batsman's chin instead of his stumps was a sour break with cricket's much-vaunted principles of fair play. It provoked intense barracking at the games, and led to a furious diplomatic row. Jardine became the single most hated epitome of cold-hearted English hypocrisy when, in Adelaide,

Australia's captain Bill Woodfull was struck a fierce blow in the ribs by Larwood. When play resumed Jardine simply strengthened the leg side and sent Larwood round the wicket to bowl more bouncers at the injured batsman. And a few balls later Australia's wicketkeeper, Bert Oldfield, had to be helped off the field with a fractured skull. The 50,000-strong crowd blazed with self-righteous anger, and one or two Englishmen looked askance at this as well. The usually placid *Wisden* called it 'a disgrace to cricket', and in a letter to his parents the young Gubby Allen (who had been born in New South Wales, but was now Eton, Cambridge and MCC) was moved to see the drama in military terms, confiding that Jardine 'was loathed more than any German who ever fought in any war'.

The controversy was especially bitter given the crumbling status of Britain's imperial sway in Australia. At first, reluctant to admit that a team representing the MCC could possibly behave dishonourably, England's spokesmen tried to persuade themselves (and the public) that Australia were over-reacting. But the row rumbled on into the summer of 1933, and when the touring West Indies gave England a taste of their own medicine at Old Trafford, it put things in a different light. Jardine took his punishment like a man, scoring a painful 127 against Learie Constantine and Emanuel Martindale in full cry, but Hammond was hit in the face, and the crowd frowned. It didn't like it any more than the Australians had – in fact it had the cheek to huff and puff.[1]

This echo of Bodyline made it clear to almost everyone (including *Wisden*) that perhaps the mother country *had* been punching below the belt after all.

Thanks to the express-train bowling of Larwood, and the icy calculations of Jardine, Verity's patient spin-bowling on the

---

[1] Constantine had recently matched Verity by taking 10 for 10 for his club, Nelson, a barnstorming display that led the *Pathé Gazette* to call him 'the coloured catapult'.

Bodyline tour attracted little attention. Verity's job was to keep one end quiet while the fast men recharged their batteries, and it was the bouncer war that captured all the headlines. But away from the limelight Verity did rather more than block things up. He bowled a series of long, well-controlled spells, picking up wickets all the time, and on one occasion came up with a cricketing tactic that was every bit as well aimed, though it was almost the strategic opposite of Bodyline.

It was a balmy Sunday afternoon; the rest day in Sydney, and the Test was evenly poised – England were 413 for 8 in response to Australia's 435. Drowsing by a river, Verity worried away at something he had noticed the previous evening – the dark marks etched into the wicket by the thudding boots of Australia's Harry Alexander.

'Think them over, Hedley,' Jardine had said. 'They may be useful.'

That's exactly what Verity was doing. *Wisden* would later say that he bowled with 'pensive' variety, and it was certainly his thoughtful side that came to the fore now. He could see that only one of the footmarks was of any use – but though it was on the correct length it was outside the right-hander's leg stump. The Australians, he thought, would never play at balls pitched there unless he bowled over the wicket – not his usual angle of attack. And even then he had a tiny strip no more than an inch wide to aim at – anything outside that the batsman could play with his pads.

But what would happen if he emptied the off-side field? Might Australia be induced to swish inside-out at balls they should more wisely leave alone? 'Mid-off, mid-on,' he said to himself, 'three or four short legs … Jove, how accurate I would need to be!'

It was tricky, but 'just possible', he thought. He said as much to Jardine.

Jardine was nervous about all the open space on the off side, but Verity felt that any shots aimed that way were fraught with risk … as long as he could hit that rough spot.

'It seemed our only chance,' he said.

The plan was hatched. It required Verity to aim at a little strip of dusty ground a foot long and an inch across. But first he would have to wait until the quick bowlers had seen what *they* could do with the wicket. To no one's surprise, Larwood made an early breakthrough; but then Bradman and Woodfull brought up the hundred for the loss of only one wicket. That's when Jardine threw the ball to Verity. It was time to give this crafty tactic a try. He set the field, and here came Hedley.

It is fair to say that things went well. The first two balls hit the tiny target and fizzed away from Woodfull. Bradman, frowning, accepted the challenge (as usual), went on the attack (as usual) and drilled three fours through the empty cover region. At that stage it looked as though England might have to give up and rethink, but then – blow me – Bradman tried the same thing again and was clean-bowled for 71.

Verity stood on the edge of the wicket, accepting the congratulations of the England team in his usual calm way. The fall of Bradman could always be counted on to send a shock wave through both the Australian dressing-room and the home crowd; the plan now was for Larwood to skittle the rest. But when he limped off with an injured foot, the spotlight again fell on Verity. Back to work he went, wheedling away in search of that scarcely visible weakness in the wicket, and once more he kept finding it. A little while later he had 5 wickets for 33, and Australia had been dismissed for 182. England knocked off the runs for two wickets, and that was that – another Test in the bag.

It was telling that Verity, invited to contribute a memory – 'The Best I Have Ever Bowled' – to a 1935 anthology, nominated this high-wire effort over his more obvious star turns (the two ten-wicket hauls, for example). And it won him the undying regard of his captain. 'Hedley has come through his first tour triumphantly,' Jardine wrote in a letter to Verity's father. He had been 'a real friend and a grand help to me'.

Not everyone rolled out the red carpet. In his early days Verity had been a proper batsman (in the fullness of time he would score over 5,000 first-class runs) and on this tour England recognised this ability and sometimes sent him out to open the innings. But back in Leeds his captain, Brian Sellers, was quick to remind him that there'd be none of this nonsense back in God's own county. 'You may be number one for England,' he said, 'but don't forget you're still number ten for Yorkshire.'

His team-mates were warmer. According to his friend Bill Bowes, Verity was so unerring that he bowled his arm ball (which did not spin, but kept curving in at the right-hander's stumps) only 16 times in a typical season – and took 16 wickets with it. To some, this spoke of something more than mere skill: it implied rare personal qualities. Norman Yardley went so far as to say that bowling, for Verity, was 'his prime means of self-expression'. In paying tribute to a 'thoughtful, studious and invariably kind' cricketer, he was echoing many such testimonials. In a nice irony, Verity was an out-and-out professional armed with the very attributes – modesty, steadfastness and the undemonstrative exercise of rare gifts – often presumed (at Lord's, especially) to be the province of the amateur code.

Belgium suited Henry Cotton's ambitions as a golfer down to the ground. For a man who had eyes only for major titles – he cared little for the bread and butter events – it was perfect. He could still make what Henry Longhurst called 'periodical raids' on Britain in that stylish car of his, designed to make a splash wherever he went.

A modern player would not operate in such a way – he would join the magnificent, five-star, private-jet travelling circus known as the tour – but the structure of professional golf was different back then. There was nothing like a 'tour': indeed, the prime obligation of a club professional was to serve his members at the weekend, so such tournaments as there were took place in the middle of the week. The prize money at these contests wasn't bad – the winner of the British Matchplay scooped £1,040, enough to buy half a house on Walton Heath – but it was nothing like today's jackpots. So the top players – Park, Taylor, Vardon – would often play one-off challenge matches for £100 a side. Cotton followed suit. In 1929 some 3,000–4,000 spectators walked the course to see him (with his partner Archie Compston) lose to the great Abe Mitchell and George Duncan for a £500 pot. And a year later he took on Mitchell in a singles match over 36 holes and wiped the floor with him, finding himself nine holes up with nine still to play.

The great names of the past were not finished yet. When Cotton went to Torquay for a par-3 tournament, his score of 55 was not close to matching the four-under-par total (50) of the six-time Open winner, Vardon, then in his 60th year. And some games were just for show: in 1931 Cotton played (and lost to) Bert Hodson at the gala opening of Llanwern Golf Club, a new woodland course near Newport in South Wales.

Cotton was a good match-player. Although he went down in the foursomes in the 1929 Ryder Cup, he was man of the hour when he beat Al Watrous in the Singles, on the 15th green, to secure a narrow victory for Britain (7-5). And in 1932 he carried off the British championship, sponsored by the *News of the World*, after being a finalist in 1931. It was after this dazzling effort that Bernard Darwin wrote: 'I have never seen such golf played – no, not by Bobby Jones, nor Sarazen, nor the Triumvirate.'

A year later Cotton beat Densmore Shute (USA) in a high-stakes (£500) match at Walton Heath – a victory that made him Golfer of the Year in the American press. He played Walter Hagen, too, at Ashridge, and when he lost (the American won six of the last seven holes) he invited Hagen to Waterloo for a rematch. Hagen accepted, but soon wished he hadn't: after oversleeping in Croydon he took a private plane to Brussels, raced to the course hours late, and in front of a large crowd that was 'fuming' at the delay, having paid 25 francs a ticket, watched Cotton nail a new course record 66 in the first round, and 67 in the second, to win with debonair ease.

But strokeplay – a four-round championship, with every stroke counting – was Cotton's *métier*. In this he was ahead of his time, but those long nights pounding away at the range or in his net, grooving his wristy swing into a relentless machine, made him a testing opponent over four rounds. Having said that, it took him several years to find his feet at the highest level. In the 1929 Open he was paired with Hagen, but shook hands on the 18th green to congratulate him on a course record (67) and a six-stroke win. In 1930 he couldn't get near Bobby Jones at Hoylake, and at St Andrews in 1931 led after 36 holes before falling back to equal tenth behind Tommy Armour. In 1932 he never found his best form and came tenth equal again; and in 1933 he led after *three* rounds but ended up seventh. It meant that he had three top tens in a row, no small thing, but it was less than he hoped for, and less than he promised.

In the early years of the new decade he suffered from painful stomach ulcers, which the papers called 'boil trouble', and also from what Cotton himself called a 'carbuncle' on his left hand. It was so tender he took to wearing a glove on it, creating an accessory that is now routine but was at that time quite unheard of. At the end of 1931 he treated himself to a few months in Biarritz, south-west France, to convalesce, and followed a faddish diet recommended by a French chef – raw minced steak, carrots and red wine. In January 1932 he announced that he was 'better in health than I have been in years', and it was true. His form was sharp and he was the leading home challenger for the Open. This still seemed a dream, however – the big prize really did seem an American possession. 'Let me win the British,' Hagen had said, 'and you can have the rest.' The gods must have been listening, because he went on to win it four times (in 1922, 1924, 1928 and 1929). Bobby Jones won thrice (1926, 1927 and 1930); Gene Sarazen took it at Prince's Club, Sandwich, in 1932, and Shute won in 1933.

This last was at St Andrews, the spiritual home of British golf. It hurt a bit that six of the top ten that year were American – it felt like a low water mark, and no one knew what it would take to disrupt this domination. But Cotton was the man most likely. He hadn't been able to play in the 1933 Ryder Cup thanks to his residency in Belgium, but he kept on showing flashes of rare ability. In challenge matches he would touch heights that made him seem 'almost flawless' (*The Times*), and other newspapers had taken to calling him 'the hope of Britain' or 'Britain's great chance'. All he needed was one of those weeks when everything clicks. He was already a high-profile figure in the game. His instruction book, *Golf!*, was called 'extraordinarily stimulating' by *Tatler* and 'intensely interesting' by *Golf Illustrated*. By now he was a fitness freak, putting himself through strenuous drills to correct the deformation (right shoulder lower than left) caused by more than a decade of serious golf. He was getting close to cracking this fiendish game.

Fred Perry's growing success brought a number of trappings in its wake. Though he was still an amateur (the opportunities in professional tennis were at this time limited only to the most famous players) one of the pleasant quirks of amateur status was that players *were* allowed to write for cash. Articles and columns by Perry began to appear in the *Evening Standard*, which insisted on calling him 'the brilliant young London player'. As his reputation grew (Australia's Jack Crawford was referring to him as 'England's most promising colt') Perry thus found himself able to afford a car for the first time in his life – a dapper little Austin Seven, with a rakish sliding roof.

That autumn Perry went back to America, advancing to the semi-finals of the US Open. He made even more decisive inroads into his future, however, when he went on to California and fell in love with it – the landscape, the sunshine, the jazzy cars, the sun-kissed girls, the rustle of folding money, the whole film-star glamour of it all – Perry was especially thrilled to find that the movie crowd was 'tennis struck'. When asked to appear in one Pacific Coast tournament, he agreed on condition that he be granted a date with Jean Harlow. No problem. She was waiting for him when they reached the restaurant. On his return to Britain he used his new-found fame to help his father on the hustings in Kettering, and since his main job seemed to be to cuddle factory girls he was happy to do his bit. It did not work, though; his dad lost the seat.

By now Perry was rather more than a coming man; he was a champion-in-waiting. In the 1932 French Open he claimed his first title, winning the doubles with Austin, but the rest of the year was poor. He lost a quarter-final in Paris, against the big-hitting Czech Roderich Menzel, and went out of Wimbledon at the same stage, thanks to Jack Crawford. It began to strike Perry that he was, by following some well-intentioned advice from his elders, playing *too* carefully – failing to exploit his athletic superiority. He had no strategic advantage: he could not beat his rivals in a cerebral game. But if he could turn tennis into a pure physical tussle, was there anyone who could stop him?

Just as Cotton had worked on his health, so Perry adopted a strict new regime. That winter he trained with Arsenal Football Club, running 'hundreds of thousands' of laps of the Highbury pitch. It did the trick: by the summer of 1933 he had sharply raised the pace of his game and was looking like a new player. Though he lost in the quarters of the French (again), and came a bad-tempered cropper at Wimbledon, he went back to France that autumn with high hopes of helping Britain win the Davis Cup for the first time since 1912.

At this time the annual knockout competition between the 31 tennis-playing nations was a genuine World Cup of tennis, and just as prestigious as the individual trophies – if not more so, since it presented tennis as that highest of British things: a team sport. Perry had figured heroically in the 1931 contest, an exciting one that included a semi-final win over America at Roland Garros. First he turned the tables on Sidney Wood, the author of his downfall at Wimbledon, in four sets, and when Austin beat Frank Shields (grandfather of the actress, Brooke[2]) it put Britain through to face France in the final, which of course would be played in Paris – the Davis Cup was a 'challenge' in which the previous year's champion hosted the winner of the knock-out stage in a final playoff.

Few had expected Britain to get this far: the management had to cable London to send clothes, and the players were treated to a luxury golf break in Fontainebleau.[3]

France was represented by Borotra and Cochet – two all-time greats – and was firmly expected to win, as it had done for the last four years. But Perry sprang a surprise by beating Borotra, and when Austin did the same the Cup hung in the balance. After a few more twists and turns the tie stood at 2-2, and it all came down to Perry's decisive match against Cochet. Cochet was a well-known trickster: when opponents missed first serves he had been known to hit the ball into the stands and wait for it to be returned, creating a tense delay before the second serve. Combined with the quality of his tennis, this proved too much for the young Englishman, but although Perry lost the match in four sets he had done more than enough to be hailed as a near victor back in London.

In 1932 Britain fell at the semi-final stage, losing to Germany in Berlin, but, having gone so close in that 1931 event, Britain was again one of the favourites in 1933. This edition of the Davis Cup got off to a disquieting start, though, when Germany (under new, Nazi leadership) announced that 'non-Aryans' could no longer be involved in tennis – on or off the court. It meant that two of

---

[2] When Brooke Shields married André Agassi in 1999, it was more than a showbiz get-together: she grew up with tennis in her blood. The marriage, however, lasted only two years.

[3] Perry played enough golf to make him 'a keen follower but a bad exponent'. At the end of 1934 he would tell *Time* magazine that he was 'getting tired of tennis' and was thinking of taking golf more seriously. But he never did: it was harder than it looked.

Germany's finest players, Nelly Neppach and Daniel Prenn, were excluded from the game, since both were Jewish.[4] In a surprising departure, Perry and Austin went so far as to write a joint letter to *The Times* expressing their 'considerable dismay' at this news, but it didn't distract them from the business of beating Spain, Finland, Czechoslovakia and Italy in the qualifying rounds. They then put out Australia at Wimbledon – Perry did not even have to take to the court against Crawford – and once more faced America in a semi-final in Paris.

The first match went down in legend because Perry didn't just beat Ellsworth Vines: he literally drove him to his knees. At match point down in the last set, Vines collapsed in an unconscious heap and could not continue. It paved the way to a symbolic defeat which put Britain into another final against France – for the second time in three years. This time, British hopes were sky-high. The *Daily Express* declared that we were no longer the 'poor, despised back number of lawn tennis', and even the French seemed to feel there was something in this: when Perry walked into a Paris brasserie for dinner one night, the house band started playing 'God Save the King' as a mark of respect.

Perry and Austin were stronger now, and Borotra and Cochet were older, and when Perry ground down the latter in front of 15,000 roaring home fans it was a sign that things had changed. But Cochet avenged himself on Austin, the next two matches were shared 1-1, and once again it was up to Perry to try and prevail in the decider.

It started badly. His opponent, André Merlin, ran away with the first set. Austin, watching from the stands, was chain-smoking nervously, while his anxious wife puffed away on two cigarettes at once. But Perry fought like a cornered cat, pushed Merlin on to the back foot, and won the next three sets to secure a remarkable victory for Britain.

---

[4] Prenn's response was to flee to Britain, but a despairing Neppach committed suicide.

The teams celebrated by taking the trophy on a high-spirited tour of Paris nightspots and drinking champagne together. Cochet presented Perry with his autobiography, inscribed 'To Fred Perry – In memory of the victory, so well merited …' and King George V sent a fulsome message, too. Somehow the players made it on to the boat train, the *Golden Arrow*, to Victoria, where a crowd of perhaps 6,000 well-wishers ('some 10,000', according to Perry) lay in wait. Somewhere in there was Suzanne Lenglen, the first lady of world tennis – and a Frenchwoman to boot. Perry's father had driven down to meet his son, too, along with some Brentham friends, and was surprised by the excitability of the crowd, which climbed over his car and 'bust all the glass'.

The players were escorted to dinner at the Savoy while the papers sang their praises. It was a famous victory, and, as Perry himself wrote, for a book published the following year: '1933 ought to be printed in letters of gold in the annals of British tennis.'

It was only the beginning. Less than a week after this heady success, Perry boarded a transatlantic liner for what was becoming an annual trip to America. This one ended even more gloriously than the others when Perry cruised his way to an epic US Open final against Jack Crawford, that year's Wimbledon champion. The Australian was a clear favourite, but Perry was no longer an upstart, and in the absence of a home contender a bustling crowd assembled to watch a British Empire showdown. Perry was actually confident about Crawford ('a perfect opponent for me') and put on quite a show, arriving for the final in a Rolls-Royce flanked by four motorcycle escorts. Crawford, if anything, was complacent – in one break he paused for a cigarette and chatted to his wife. But as the game went on Perry surprised him with his energy and zest. It wasn't even close: in the last two sets Perry dropped only one game.

While the London papers jumped for joy ('I am naturally very proud,' said his calm-as-usual father) Perry celebrated at a rooftop party surrounded by gorgeous girls and a Hawaiian band. But he had only just begun, and he knew it. He wasn't even planning to go home for a while yet: he was just 24 years old, and there was a great wide world to explore. First he intended to cross the Pacific and take on Crawford in his own back yard. The Australian Open would be the first big tournament of the New Year, and who was to say that 1934 might not prove even better than its predecessor.

The one shadow on the horizon was the constant murmuring about Perry's conduct. He had a waspish tongue and could be 'brutally sarcastic', according to Don Budge. Teddy Tinling, the tennis player turned dress designer, testified that he was 'never averse to using a caustic one-liner', and it was common knowledge that his catchphrase – he habitually applauded good shots by opponents with a sarcastic 'Verray clevah!' – drove people 'crazy'.[5] The papers had code words to describe his behaviour; he was 'exuberant' or 'volatile'; but America's Jack Kramer was happy to be more forthright in calling Perry 'an opportunist, a selfish and egotistical person'. Those famous books on gamesmanship by Stephen Potter lay 13 years in the future, but Perry seemed to have mastered the subject on his own.

After the US Open he travelled with Crawford to California for a spot of exhibition tennis, which he was coming to adore. After an enjoyable four-day train journey, the pair began to knock the ball to and fro in a light-hearted fashion, only to hear a familiar drawl coming from the sidelines: 'Well, Gentlemen, I think you could at least *try*.'

They turned, startled. It was Marlene Dietrich. Welcome to Hollywood.

---

[5] Henry Cotton became an object of interest for a strikingly similar phrase. When spectators put him off his swing by sniffing, coughing, moving, or breathing (it didn't take much) he would snap 'Very funny!' as he marched away in a huff.

CHAPTER EIGHT

1934

As 1934 dawned there was a tangible desire to put away the sackcloth and ashes at last. 'The year 1933 is going,' said the Archbishop of Canterbury in his New Year message. 'Let it go.' But in *his* New Year message the acting Prime Minister, Stanley Baldwin (Ramsay MacDonald was unwell[1]), put a braver face on things, declaring that 1933 had been 'the sunniest, driest and warmest in meteorological records', and that the country could afford to see the present as 'a time of ever-increasing hope'. The news from Germany was certainly gloomy – the Chancellor, Adolf Hitler, was making dark noises about the national *Kampf*, 600 newspapers had closed and 100 pastors had been arrested – but the people were determined to look on the bright side.

So, yes, Belgium was forming a corps of 2,000 men to patrol its eastern border. And, all right, the German skiing team *had* withdrawn from a winter sports meeting in Austria simply because it could not fly the swastika. But let's not jump to conclusions: these were skirmishes, minor clouds on a calm horizon. The final sunset of the year had been rosy, and there was no reason to think

---

[1] It was an unusual administration. Ramsay MacDonald had led Labour to victory in 1929, but in 1931 he agreed to lead a 'National Government' alongside Conservatives and Liberals. Some saw this as a brave response to the economic emergency, but a few Labour colleagues accused him of betrayal and expelled him from the party. No wonder he rambled in the Commons; no wonder his health failed.

it anything other than a good omen. Baldwin did his utmost to sound a reassuring note. Hitler, he was sure, had 'no other aim than to make Germany once again happy and free, no other aim than to restore honour'.

The newspapers also strove to promote an optimistic mood. Some brave soul had flown over the summit of Everest in a biplane, and taken actual photographs of the roof of the world – amazing! The flat-race jockey Gordon Richards had set a new record (259 winners) while the British Broadcasting Corporation was claiming six million listeners. There were bright spots all over. As if to prove it was the in-house journal of the elite, *The Times* reported that New Year's Day had been a fine one for the Belvoir ('Finding the first fox in a stick heap near Granby, hounds killed him in less than three minutes') and applauded the healthy turnout at the Old Boys' rugby match between Merchant Taylors' and Cranleigh ('Nearly all the old faces seemed to be there').

Fred Astaire was charming audiences at the picture houses in *The Gay Divorcee*, while a young actor named John Gielgud was lighting up the West End as Richard of Bordeaux. At the Savoy, on New Year's Eve, 1,500 diners toasted the midnight chimes at an Alaskan-themed dinner, complete with French can-can dancers and trumpeters from the Life Guards. Incongruous? Who cared? There wasn't a war on, you know.

It was a lively attempt to recreate the good old days, and the New Year Honours list gave colonial civil servants their turn in the limelight as if nothing about that world was changing: step forward this auditor in Bengal, bravo to that superintendent of police in Bangalore, well done that university vice-chancellor in Delhi. The National Society of Non-Smokers wished all its abstainer friends a happy 1934, while the classified adverts vibrated with people trying to nudge their way on in life – a father sought a boarding school 'with a practical bias' for a 14-year-old boy, a 'widely travelled' naval officer wanted a position in journalism, and a nursery governess with 'good needlework' was seeking a post, available immediately. This was also the beginning of the modern holiday: there were tempting posters for golf hotels on the Côte d'Azur and *pensions* in Zermatt, and the sailings from the major ports were listed in full: the *Olympic*, sister ship of the late *Titanic*, was departing from Southampton on the 3rd.

The biggest news story of all, though, in the early weeks of 1934, was the birth of the Loch Ness monster fairytale. Something rum had been spotted in 1933 by a water bailiff (shortly after the opening of a new road along the northern shore that year) and the *Inverness Courier* ran a nice sensation story about the beast that lurked in the depths. The *Aberdeen Courier* confirmed that it resembled a 'huge overgrown eel', while the sober *Dundee Courier* thought it might be a giant sturgeon. The *Daily Mail* sent a big-game hunter to investigate, and he duly spotted some hippo-like footprints in the mud which a scientific survey later suggested may have been made by an umbrella stand.

But there were more than enough sightings in 1934 to turn the monster into a craze: Nessie was seen diving, drifting, breaching, crossing a road or skimming across the Loch. There she blew, out in the mist; there she flew, racing across the Loch; there she was again, rushing out of the bracken or swimming hard, humps above the water. On 6 December the first photograph appeared (in the *Daily Express*) and in the early weeks of the New Year this was followed by more blurred images which gave rise to a widespread belief that there must be *something* down there. It was a good wheeze as far as tourism was concerned, and in the *Illustrated London News* G. K. Chesterton called the monster 'benevolent' for helping 'many poor journalists to place paragraphs here and there'. But the idea of an ancient beast in the depths proved durable. The world, in 1934, evidently felt like one in which myths and dragons truly might lurk.

The stars-to-be brought in the New Year thousands of miles apart. Verity was touring India, Cotton was in Belgium, Perry was in Australia and Dorothy Round was safely home in Worcester after an exciting autumn of tennis in America. After winning the Eastern Grass Courts Championship in New York she followed in Perry's footsteps to the West Coast, where she lost the final of the Pacific South West Ladies Singles. These were local rather than world championships, but she was clearly a coming woman.

In Calcutta, Hedley Verity was enjoying the fact that the previous day he had made 91 not out against an India XI. It was a year after Bodyline, and once again he was playing under Jardine as a trusted ally of the frosty captain. Always keen to broaden his horizons, he had spent the voyage east through the Mediterranean and Suez reading *Seven Pillars of Wisdom* by T. E. Lawrence. But he was also preparing himself mentally for the subcontinental wickets everyone said should suit him. Not that he had minded the surfaces down under: when all the sums were done, it wasn't Larwood and Voce who topped the averages on the Bodyline tour – it was Verity, with 44 wickets at 16.

Now, in India, he was at it again, taking 72 wickets on the hot, dry pitches, eight of them in Calcutta, where he extracted what *The Times* called 'a terrific amount of turn', and 11 in Madras.[2] 'No captain could have a greater asset,' Jardine said, repeating in public what he had told Verity's father, and this was a common view. Verity's room-mate, Charlie Barnett, agreed: 'I know of no other cricketer on whom one could rely whatever the state of the match. He really was a rock when the chips were down.'

The Test matches went well – two wins, one draw[3] – but a bigger event was looming: the arrival of the Australians that summer.

[2] In the second innings at Calcutta, in which Verity took four wickets (and scored 55) Jardine himself fielded at silly mid-off, so close to the batsman that he could have shaken hands. Even when the bowling was slow, he still knew how to intimidate.

[3] Though spoiled, from England's point of view, by the loss against a Vizianagaram XI in Benares – the first defeat for MCC in India for 31 years.

There was a school of thought that they should not even be sending a team after the Bodyline riot of the previous year. Those wounds were still raw; time had not yet healed all. But in the end the mutual desire to kiss and make up, not to mention the commercial dependence of two cricket boards on the enterprise, won the day. There was time for some diplomatic haggling, though. Australia demanded and received an assurance that Bodyline would not be permitted, and it was hardly a coincidence when it turned out that Jardine, Larwood and Voce, the men at the eye of the storm, would play no part in the rematch.

Jardine's case was interesting. After winning the Ashes thanks to Bodyline he now, with what Percy Fender called 'great dignity and magnificent disdain', declared himself unavailable. Naturally there was plenty of talk to the effect that the high-ups at Lord's had leaned on the skipper to suggest that, well, given the delicacy of the situation, old boy, the thing is, you see, we don't want any more *incidents*, do we, and what do you say, pastures new and all that, don't you know? Be a good fellow, what?

Some people were saddened by the news. Jardine may have been cordially loathed by his opponents, but he was loved by team-mates – even tough old professionals who might not have been expected to admire a southern public school type. Larwood was a devotee. The great Yorkshire batsman Herbert Sutcliffe, who scored 1,000 runs *every* season between the wars, began by finding him 'a queer devil', but ended up thinking him 'one of the greatest men I ever met ... as straight as they make 'em '. And Verity was happy to name his second son, born in 1933, Douglas – after the famous martinet.

None of these men was glad to see him go. And it did not make Larwood's problem any easier, either. The spring edition of *The Cricketer* felt that the home team's chances depended 'very largely' on the great fast bowler – he was still the fearsome spearhead of the attack. But as a sop to Australian sensitivities MCC asked him to apologise for what had happened down in

Adelaide, and when Larwood refused, on the grounds that he had bowled as instructed, no more and no less, the selectors left him out.

Larwood resented the implication that he was a loose cannon or lone gunman, and followed his captain into exile. So if the tense first act of Bodyline succeeded in hampering Australia's greatest batsman (Bradman averaged 'only' 50 per innings, half his usual tally), the second act, with nice symmetry, cut down England's greatest bowler.

It is not easy to grasp the impact these stories had at the time, because we can barely appreciate how little people knew. Very few cricket lovers had actually *seen* Bodyline, and since there were no television highlights or radio phone-ins to air its implications, it was shrouded in mystery. Larwood himself was reportedly paid five times his fee for that entire winter tour just to put on an exhibition of short stuff at Gamages, so that curious onlookers could at last see what all the fuss was about – an assignment he accepted with relish. He was still smarting at the lack of recognition he had won for driving England to that rare and prized 4-1 victory over Australia on their own soil.[4]

The upshot was that England were going into this series without the men who had made headlines in the previous one. And while cricket was a team sport, not a duel, there was no doubt that the absence of Larwood would put a greater burden on Verity. It was one he was now well equipped to shoulder. He had taken more than 160 wickets in a season every year since 1930, and in his last match-up with the great Don, in Adelaide, he had dismissed him twice. In the hard-to-please view of 1934 *Guide to the Tests*, he

---

[4] Several of the players shared this sense of grievance. Jack Fingleton, who faced Bodyline, had no doubt that it was a cruel, unsporting tactic, but Percy Fender thought the whole thing had been got up by 'irresponsible and sensation-seeking journalism'. Verity observed that so far as he could tell, Larwood did not bowl an out and out bouncer more than once every five or so overs – no fun, but hardly a vicious barrage.

'does not flight the ball quite as well as many of his kind', but his famous 10 for 10 was still 'the most remarkable piece of bowling on record'. In short, he was 'easily the best' spinner in England; and the nation was depending on him to a very great extent. As Jardine, now writing appraisals for the *Evening Standard*, put it, there were two 'key men'. One of them was Leyland; the other was his dear old pal Verity.

Most of the talk that spring, however, turned on Bradman. He was in ominous form. The *Guide to the Tests* called him 'the greatest run-getter in the history of the game', and predicted that he would give England's bowlers 'a thorough gruelling'.

You didn't have to be cricket-mad to see that Bradman was special. When he skipped down the steps at any cricket ground his manner – quick, alert, precise – generated a whiff of something unusual, and his assurance at the crease was striking even to those who did not know about the swirl of huge numbers that crested before him like a bow wave. He never rushed to the middle; he was always careful to accustom his eyes to the light. But on his good days you could see his cocky grin from the top of the stands. He became famous for this: that smile would make opposing bowlers want to knock his block off, but it filled his own team – and his fans – with sublime confidence.

On his previous tour of England he had smashed the batting records to smithereens, but in the earliest games of the 1934 season he was not his usual domineering self. He seemed jittery. There was talk he had been unwell on the long sea voyage,[5] and whispers that the nervous trauma of Bodyline had left scars. Maybe it was just a loss of form – such things do happen, even to giants. But it was not the ruthless Don of old who missed a

[5] Bradman hated sailing at the best of times, but this voyage was one of his worst. 'Jack Hobbs has the reputation of being a pretty bad sailor', he wrote in his memoir, *My Cricketing Life*, 'but if he is a worse one than I, then I am heartily sorry for him.'

straight ball from a hitherto unknown Cambridge University student named J. G. W. Davies in the match at Fenner's – a man who, as *The Cricketer* reported, 'did not pretend to be anything other than a change bowler'. Gasps echoed through the famous spires. 'To say that everyone was shocked is to put it mildly.'

In Jardine's absence the captaincy was offered to R. E. S. (Bob) Wyatt, who had scored an impressive 72 and 102 not out for MCC against the Australians in May.[6] He was an interesting choice, an amateur who was neither well-born nor well-to-do (his father was a schoolmaster). He had been a trainee at the Rover Company in Coventry, where he grew up, and when he scored his first fifty for Warwickshire in 1923 his fellow garage hands presented him with a fountain pen. He was the nearest thing to an anti-Jardine England could find: careful, not flamboyant, but solid enough to strike the selectors as a dependable sort of cove. He had captained England before, without much success, at The Oval in 1939, when Bradman scored 232, Australia 695 – and was widely blamed. But he had been Jardine's vice-captain on the Bodyline tour, and knew all about Verity: he himself had been one of Hedley's ten victims in that celebrated clean sweep against Warwickshire in 1931. He knew exactly what the man could do.

While the Australians set about finding their feet, so did Verity. He did not surpass himself when Yorkshire played MCC at Lord's, though he had Wyatt caught by Sutcliffe when the captain-to-be had made 132. But a week later he took 8 for 53 in the Roses match at Sheffield, and followed it with 8 for 68 against Northants in Bradford. The hot weather lured him into taking his sweater off – a rare sight. He was ready.

---

[6] This match achieved fame for another reason. Since the MCC XI included only one professional, and since amateurs and professionals had different entrances, spectators enjoyed the ludicrous sight of Patsy Hendren coming down the steps on his own.

Henry Cotton spent the early months of 1934 in humdrum style, nosing his Mercedes into the car park at Royal Waterloo Golf Club, giving lessons in the morning and then working on his game in the afternoon. In February Belgium grew funereal when King Albert I died in a mountaineering accident, falling 150 feet to his death while testing himself in the Ardennes. The British newspapers were full of the tragic tidings (royal disasters were front-page news in London), though they were comforted by the fact that the new king, Leopold, was virtually one of us – he was an Etonian, after all.

Cotton crossed the Channel in early spring to warm up for the Open. His form was sporadic – flashes of brilliance without the consistency he would need. In April he helped the Professionals beat the Amateurs at Royal Mid-Surrey, but after proving too strong in the pairs (with Alf Padgham, who had left Royal Ashdown Forest to become professional at Sundridge Park, and who was famous for his languid swing) he escaped with a half in the singles when Lancashire's Harry Bentley showed what the amateur spirit was about by conceding Cotton's four-footer on the 18th. The next day, in the Dunlop tournament, Cotton trailed home eight strokes behind Abe Mitchell after a curious display in which, according to *The Times*, he was visibly 'swinging too fast'. He finished a shot behind his brother Leslie, a rare event these days.

In May he went to Lancashire for the finals of the Southern Dunlop tournament in Southport, which he had won twice before. Though again he played 'shakily' in qualifying, he produced a new course record of 66 in the tournament proper; he missed an 18-inch putt on the tenth in the final round and ended up coming fourth, two shots behind Padgham.

He was still fighting a crusade both against the criticism of professional golf by many reporters, and the stuffy manners of old-time golf. Some of this was sartorial. In 1933 he complained that his brother had been told by 'a well-known London club' that he could not play in shirtsleeves and must don a jacket – and asked: 'what looks smarter than white plus fours, a sleeveless pullover and stockings to match, with coloured shoes – black or brown and white?' Today it might seem that he was simply swapping one dire uniform for another, but he felt himself to be taking a defiant stand.

In truth, golf was changing fast. At the end of March, splashed by the spring sunshine that fell on the pine woods of Georgia, a superlative new event, the 'Augusta National Invitation', was born. Augusta was a haven created by the architect Alister MacKenzie in association with Bobby Jones himself, out of gorgeous rolling woodland – it had once been an indigo plantation and a plant nursery. The holes had fragrant names like 'Flowering Peach' and 'White Dogwood', and Jones was proud to offer it to the United States Golf Association as a US Open venue. When the USGA declined, on the grounds that the baking southern sun would scorch the greens, he went ahead and organised a tournament of his own. He himself finished tenth in the first event, a long way behind Horton Smith, who snaked in a 20-foot birdie putt at the 17th hole to claim a purse worth $1,500. But his new event was widely felt to have been a success. Afterwards, it struck the management that there might be even more twists if they switched the two nines around; so in 1935 the front nine, with its picturesque par-5s, became the back nine … and the most famous finishing straight in golf was born.

Fred Perry's 1934 began in Australia. Fresh from landing his first title in New York, he crossed the Pacific to give the Melbourne crowd a glimpse of tennis's new big thing. There was plenty of on-board cricket on the voyage south and when he arrived he was greeted with firm reminders of the last load of English sportsmen who had come this way – the Bodyline bowlers. Playing practice matches in Sydney and Melbourne he was actually barracked by fans who had not forgiven Jardine, and when he made the mistake of wearing a fancy white tuxedo to a formal gala it was as if the overdressed English captain had come back to haunt the southern hemisphere, and there was much scoffing. 'We let it be known we had come to play tennis and not cricket,' said Perry. 'But our visit was apparently a little too near the period of acute feeling.'

Some aspects of tennis were still closely modelled on cricket: Perry actually played a 'Test' series against the home team – and won 4-1 (which didn't help). And then he made a further *faux pas* in Melbourne by remarking that he liked Aussies fine, frightfully good chaps, best people in the world and all that – and so they should be, they'd been picked by the best judges in England. That didn't go down well either.

Some of this friction continued into the Australian Open itself. Several newspapers noted that he was 'nettled' by the applause when he missed shots. 'Is this a cricket or a tennis match?' he spat at the umpire on one occasion. But he ripped through the knock-out rounds and soon found himself facing Jack Crawford once again, across the net at a major final, and this time with a noisy home crowd ranged against him.

In passing, we need to remind ourselves of the way tennis was played at this time. On the day before this Australian final, Perry played his singles semi-final *and* the doubles final. Both were close matches that went the full distance. So on the eve of a major final Perry was obliged to play ten sets of serious tennis, involving nearly a hundred games. If we feel that the athletic standard of tennis in 1934 falls short of what we expect today, we must concede that no modern player would consider such a heavy burden of play.

But this makes what happened the next day even more extraordinary, because after that sustained marathon Perry waltzed out and wiped the floor with Crawford, beating him in straight sets for the loss of only nine games. The *Sunday Sun and Guardian* reckoned that 'better tennis has never been seen in Australia', but Perry himself was cool. 'Put Jack and myself up against the world's top ten and Jack might get the better results,' he said. 'But Jack knows and I know that I have the type of game that must always worry him.' This was cocky, but shrewd. Crawford may indeed have won three of the previous year's majors, but he no longer looked sharp or strong enough to resist Perry when the mood was on him, and both players knew it.

At the moment of victory Perry hurdled the net in a premeditated and none too gallant gesture intended to rub the loser's face in things by demonstrating that he himself had plenty of energy left to burn. He remained oddly proud of this gambit. But in this case leaping in the air was hardly unreasonable: he had just won his second Grand Slam title in a row, and in great style. Back home the plaudits came thick and fast. A leading article in the *Manchester Guardian* saw him as a national saviour, and felt that his success 'should do much to explode the popular fallacy that England has degenerated athletically', while the *Daily Mail* called him 'the conquering hero of British tennis'.

There are no short cuts on the way back to Britain from Australia; all routes have to go the long way round. Perry, now the proud holder of two big titles, decided to break his journey in India and play some exhibition tennis with a new friend, the Maharajah of Cooch-Behar, in West Bengal. The Prince had been to Harrow and Cambridge, was tennis mad, and was wealthy to an extent that Perry had never imagined possible. When he was shown to his rooms in the vast palace, he asked after the Maharajah and was shocked to learn that the villa in which he stood was not actually the palace at all – merely a guest house. The real palace, a much grander affair, was over the way.

High society was Perry's new milieu, however. Back home he dined out with Bunny Austin and his wife at the Blue Train in Piccadilly, a fashionable nightspot popular with the smart set. They were just enjoying their dinner when Perry felt a hand on his shoulder. 'Don't get up, Mr Perry.' It was the Prince of Wales. He congratulated the lad from Ealing on his two great wins, and wished him all the best at Wimbledon.

In May Perry went to the Hard Court tournament at Bourne-mouth and, for the third time in six months, beat Jack Crawford in a significant final before going off to the French Open. Alas, we can't be *quite* sure what happened there, because there are conflicting accounts. According to Perry's autobiography, he 'strained' his ankle during his match against the Italian Giorgio De Stefani, conceded defeat and only agreed to continue (for the sake of the crowd) on condition that his opponent didn't run him around too much. The sneaky Italian reneged on this arrangement, forcing him into the corners and leaving Perry desperate for revenge – which he enjoyed when he faced De Stefani in Australia the following year and beat him 6-0, 6-0, 6-0. Thanks for coming.

Maybe it did happen like that. But just six months after the game itself Perry wrote (or at least put his name to) an article for the Melbourne *Herald* that took a different line. In this version, De Stefani was a 'perfect gentleman' whose consideration Perry would 'never forget'. He was fulsome. 'Giorgio was one of the first to help me up,' he wrote regarding the painful moment he tore his ankle. 'And when he saw I was determined to carry on he took good care not to place undue strain on my injured leg.'

Whatever the truth, the fact remained: Perry had a bad injury. With Wimbledon only weeks away, Jack Crawford itching for another crack at his nemesis, and the Davis Cup looming, things were not looking good. Crawford, who had come over with the Davis Cup team on the same boat as Australia's cricketers, had no intention of losing three in a row. And all the while, in SW19, the final preparations were under way.

The background noise in the early part of 1934 was the same topsy-turvy mix of gay diversions and hideous omens – the world flickered, as if in chiaroscuro, between radiant highlights and gaunt shadows. The leading newspapers were locked in an energetic circulation war, competing to slap colourful scandals on to the nation's breakfast tables. The popular prints were now *very* popular – with circulations running into the millions – and they loved to peddle sensational tales from the wilder shores of human interest. If there was one headline to which they aspired it might be this, from the *News of the World* in 1934: 'Illicit Love Ends in Tragedy'. The first generation of celebrities were 'fair game', and one woman named Jessie Matthews, a Pygmalion-style actress (the daughter of a costermonger, she became a star of the silver screen), was one of the first pin-ups to be hunted by the mass media when, after the end of her third marriage, her love letters to a married actor-director called Sonnie Hale led to a High Court Judge calling her 'odious'. The papers had a muck-raking field day.

But some of their stunts were more high minded. In one famous offer to readers, the *Daily Herald* gave its two million regulars the chance to buy the complete Dickens in a 16-volume set for a bargain-basement eleven shillings; and its competitors – the *Mail*, the *Express* and the *News Chronicle* – were so outraged they felt they had to offer a rival complete works for a shilling less. It was the scoop of the year. The summer issue of *The Dickensian* reckoned that some six million copies were circulated by this ruse.

And there was lots of other fun and games, too. Whisky exporters toasted the end of Prohibition in America; England's footballers beat Scotland 3-0 at Wembley; the Grand National produced a classic winner in Golden Miller (winner of the Cheltenham Gold Cup a few weeks earlier); the Varsity boat race set tongues wagging when *both* crews beat the 23-year-old record (Cambridge won, thanks to the power generated by an average per-man weight of 14 stones – Pathé called them 'a race of giants', though they were midgets by today's hulking standards). There were new Hobbs Gates at The Oval; three cute tiger cubs at Whipsnade Zoo; and a spectacular ocean liner, 'Hull No. 534' (later to be launched as the *Queen Mary*) was rising high above a Clyde shipyard.

The vogue for aerial photography meant that Britain's papers and magazines were vibrant with breathtaking scenery and wildlife snapped from the stunning new vantage point in the sky. A fabulous new world was put before the readers' eyes – flamingos on Kenyan lakes, glaciers in the Himalayas, tribal lands in Uganda, sweeping reaches of the Nile, Polar bears on Canadian ice floes, amazing visions of Jerusalem or ancient remains in the sands of Sumeria. A diamond nearly three inches long was discovered in Johannesburg and sold in London (allowing the lucky seller to splash out on a new Vauxhall). It is hard to recapture the mentality of Britishness at this time, when London seemed to rule half the world. In truth, some of the places depicted in all this vivid imagery were no longer colonies but free dominions; others were fighting for independence. After years of ignorance – few Britons could have found Hyderabad on a map – the media was kindling an affection for imperial flavours just when they were fast dissolving.

There was a flip side to all this levity. At the end of February, some 50,000 marchers from as far afield as Scotland converged on London's Hyde Park to protest in the drizzle against poverty and unemployment. One of the banners (from a Kirkaldy trade union branch) reflexively called for an end to 'hunger and war', as if they were synonymous. Protest marches such as this had become a regular feature of everyday life in Britain, and would continue to be until the great Jarrow crusade of 1936. But an increasing number of less needy citizens were using the roads to try out their new toy – the motor car – and they were not always careful. After a sudden jump in the number of fatal accidents, 1934 saw the introduction of an exam that had become popular on the Continent but until now had been thought to be most unBritish: the driving test.

There was even worse news overseas – most obviously from Germany. Thomas Cook was still buying space in newspapers to proclaim the beauties of the Teuton landscape – 'A land of infinite variety ... Nature's Holidayland'. But it was becoming harder to ignore or shrug aside the daily drip-drip of grim tidings from that part of the world. In March, only weeks before Perry went to Paris, 30,000 Nazi followers took a public oath to serve Hitler with 'unswerving loyalty and obedience'. And on the same day, in Potters Bar, Hertfordshire, a service of remembrance for those who died when two Zeppelins crashed in 1916 was disrupted when the German ambassador, invited to place a wreath, offered a Nazi salute. In recent weeks the Protestant churches in Germany had been subject to much harassment, and the Vicar of Potters Bar made himself a local hero by refusing to take further part in the proceedings. A few days later two storm troopers – all black jackets and swastika armbands – landed their plane in Croydon, just for the hell of it.

No one could say any more that people didn't know what was coming. A *Times* piece on anti-Semitism by 'a correspondent lately in Germany' triggered a hot rash of letters. The article quoted the now infamous Nazi newspaper *Der Stürmer* as urging readers to boycott all Jewish shops ('He who buys from a Jew is a traitor') and announcing, quite calmly, that 'our knowledge of the Jewish question has led us to the opinion that all Jews, in fact, should be castrated'. There were plenty of people in Britain who were not above bad-mouthing Jewishness over a pint or two – but this was too much. A stinging letter from Cosmo Cantuar (Cosmo Lang, Archbishop of Canterbury) said, on behalf of 'Christian public opinion', that *Der Stürmer* was spreading 'gruesome and disgusting' lies and legends, and was 'an odious incitement to religious bigotry'.

It certainly was. And a new translation titled *Germany Prepares for War* by Professor Ewald Banse did little to soothe the mood. 'The sword will come into its own again,' it proclaimed. 'The Third Reich can only be born in blood and iron.' Was the man serious? 'I cannot find a single suggestion,' said the review in the *Illustrated London News*, 'that international questions might be settled by peaceful means.' And there was one last piece of symbolism. While our own Prince of Wales was sipping champagne at Hunt Balls or letting fly off the first tee at St Andrews, the Kaiser's son was joining the National Socialist Motor Corps, and Hitler was being photographed on board a colossal new battleship, the *Deutschland*. Something unstoppable was building.

There was riotous unrest in Paris, and civil war in Austria. In the Saar, crude activists were doing their best to disrupt a plebiscite on whether to remain in French hands or be returned to Germany; and in Romania the Prime Minister was assassinated at a railway station by a hothead claiming to represent the 'Black Guard' – a name that couldn't but evoke the 'Black Hand' group behind the death of the old Archduke in Sarajevo.

Even the weather gods seemed to be grumbling. There was a horrendous earthquake in India, the Niagara Falls froze and water drained out of the Venetian canals, leaving architectural masterpieces and palazzos balanced over ditches of mud. This was the first time in the history of the world that news of such extraordinary events, from the furthest flung corners of the earth, could be delivered across Britain before breakfast. It was hard to keep a level head, hard not to feel that the apocalypse was at hand.

The same papers and bulletins were heavy with military imagery, too: naval exercises in Scapa Flow and the North Atlantic, icy waves crashing over grey decks and forward guns; submarines on the slipway in Barrow-in-Furness; HMS *Malaya* blasting its guns off Spithead, HMS *Sussex* and HMS *Revenge* tooting their way past Gibraltar. More than 400,000 visitors squeezed into the pavilions at the Aldershot Tattoo to watch battlefield re-enactments, and the Royal Tournament featured a blazing show of anti-aircraft defence, complete with sirens and searchlights performing a dreadful enactment of what the future might hold. The pictures from Moscow, meanwhile, showed march pasts grand enough to suggest a violent eruption of 'war-mindedness'. There had been acid whispers about deadly goings-on in Stalin's Soviet Union since January, when the London papers started listing the reasons why citizens were being 'purged'. Top of the list came 'Not showing enough Bolshevik zeal', closely followed by 'moral decay' and 'going bourgeois'. Even people who applauded the revolutionary ideals of Uncle Joe frowned. And now a would-be MP, Major Ralph Rayner, was watching the endless May Day parade and reporting that Stalin was 'openly and intensely preparing for war'.

Dear God. Anyone for tennis?

CHAPTER NINE

Magnus est Verity

On 1 June 1934, two men sat on a sunlit bench in London's Regent's Park. One was a tubby émigré academic of Czech extraction from Vienna named Arnold Deutsch, a cousin of Oscar Deutsch, the entertainment mogul who had carved his initials into a new cinema chain, Odeon. The other was a Cambridge graduate called Kim Philby, son of a notorious old Middle East hand from the Foreign Office. Deutsch doubled as a recruiting agent for the KGB, and this meeting would be the opening twist in one of Britain's most convoluted spy sagas. 'He was a marvellous man, simply marvellous,' Philby would say later. He himself was falling in love not just with the concept of a communist utopia, but with an exciting Viennese activist named Litzl Friedman – the two of them were newlyweds. Nudged by Deutsch, Philby agreed that he could better assist the cause by severing his own budding links with communist organisations and concentrate instead on posing as a clubbable member of the British establishment, which as a suave veteran of Westminster and Cambridge is exactly what he was.

It is easy now to see Philby as a straightforward traitor, but it requires no great effort to see what prompted him. Apart from the way egalitarian visions meshed with his own romantic impulse, there were plenty of reasons to find communism appealing, and he was by no means alone – lots of fashionable types were craving a crusade against fascism, what with the papers full of news about the tyrannies emerging in Italy and Germany. Only a month earlier (in April) Oswald Mosley had filled the Albert Hall with his own alarming brand of fascist theatricals, putting on a mini-Nuremberg of flags, black shirts, arc lights and trumpets. The coming show at Olympia was set to be even more provocative than usual. The *Daily Mail*, in its hearty way, was offering free tickets to readers who sent in endings to the phrase 'Why I like the Blackshirts …' And for at least six months in 1934, the paper formally backed the Blackshirts as the sound, unjustly maligned representatives of good old British common sense. Not that the *Daily Express* was more sensitive: in 1933 it published a front-page headline it would not be too keen to crow about in later years: 'Judea Declares War On Germany'.

In the event the 7 June rally at Olympia went off much as planned. A crowd of more than 10,000 squeezed into the hall to be dazzled by lights while Mosley stood on a high podium, beneath gigantic British flags, railing against the 'European ghettoes pouring their dregs into this country'. When hecklers raised their voices in protest (they knew what he was going to say and had been planning a scene) they were roughly thrown out by the dark-shirted stewards. A band played patriotic marches.

The rise of Mosley was matched by an equally vehement insistence on peace at any cost, and on principle. George Lansbury, leader of the Labour Party (and grandfather of the actress, Angela) proposed that the country 'close every recruiting station, disband the army and disarm the Air Force', and that his own party conference commit itself, like those famously unpatriotic Oxford students, 'to take no part in war'.[1] Naturally, not everyone agreed with such arguments: Winston Churchill insisted that war could not be avoided simply 'by dilating upon its horrors'.

---

[1] The Labour Party abandoned this policy in 1936, though the possibility remains that if Labour *had* won the 1933 General Election, Britain might not have built the Spitfires and Hurricanes on which it would soon depend. But it is easy to play what-if …

But as the summer breeze blew clouds over Regent's Park, the world hummed with contradictions. That morning's *Times* had been full of worried prose concerning the 'breakdown of capitalism' and the Disarmament Conference at Geneva, which was foundering on German intransigence and giving the future what Britain's negotiator, Anthony Eden, called 'a black outlook'. There was a piece on the upheaval in the Saar, too, with a telling map of the disputed Rhineland. It must have been tempting to be swayed by Arnold Deutsch's honeyed words, vibrant with that central European reverence for high culture, moral purity and sensual liberation.

Still, if Philby had glanced north he might have sensed a quieter sort of new world taking shape behind the trees, where workers were putting the finishing touches to an *avant-garde* pool for penguins at London Zoo, a swirl of white concrete and blue water – a geometric recreation of the Antarctic designed by a Russian émigré, Berthold Lubetkin. The pool was chic – the birds sunned themselves on the slipways like lazing supermodels (though in time this would turn out to be bad for their backs). And on the far side of those penguins, nestling beneath the elegant turrets of St John's Wood, lay a space closer to Philby's otherwise unpatriotic heart: the smooth green acres of Lord's cricket ground. In three weeks' time that famous field of dreams would play host to the second Test match, but this week Middlesex were playing (and losing to) Warwickshire.

Philby loved cricket. When the contents of his Moscow apartment were returned to Britain after his death in 1988 they included, among other things, a well-thumbed 1972 edition of *Wisden*. Nicholas Elliott, the MI6 chief who flew out to Beirut in 1963 to interrogate Philby about the suspicions regarding his behaviour – a tip-off that led Philby to defect at once to Moscow – later told the author John Le Carré: 'He knew cricket averages backwards and forwards. He could recite cricket till the cows come home.'

He would certainly have been aware of that summer's Ashes series – indeed, had probably seen the report in that day's *Times* describing a dinner thrown the previous night for the Australians during their match against Surrey. The Prince of Wales had sent a kind message, and the Archbishop of Canterbury made a few self-deprecating remarks about his own credentials (he had a top score of one). But the guest speaker was J. M. Barrie, the cricket-loving author of *Peter Pan*, and after talking down his own abilities ('How can I, a Scot, dare to talk about the game?') he admitted to a 'drawing' towards the Australians – 'especially their captain'. Cricket, he said, was 'an idea of the gods … a winged word' that stood for classic virtues: 'fortitude, fairness, an unconquerable gaiety of heart'. This surely entitled him to cheer the visitors.[2]

He concluded with some diplomatic remarks on 'the wisdom of forgetting'. It was a nice preface to the first encounter between the teams since the Bodyline tour.

As Philby sat in the park, a double-dealing worm stirring in his heart as he tiptoed towards treachery, Hedley Verity was himself on his way to Lord's. Fresh from those eight wickets in Yorkshire's victory over Northamptonshire, he was preparing to play the Trial match at MCC headquarters the following day (representing England against 'The Rest'). By now he was a family man with two young sons. But though he loved taking the family for picnics in the dales or the moors, or playing cricket on the beach at Scarborough (wearing a jacket and tie, naturally) his success as a Yorkshire and England regular meant that he was rarely at home these days. He had spent the last two winters abroad, in Australia and India, and his summers were now a protracted tour of county and Test grounds. He was part of a Yorkshire eleven that included some very famous names – he was teaching Len Hutton how to

---

[2] This was the second time Barrie had addressed the tourists. In 1926 he had spoken to them in similar vein, and two of the Australians, Charlie Macartney and Arthur Mailey, had returned the favour by playing for his gang of literary allsorts, the Allahakbarries (which translates roughly as 'God Help Us'). After the fourth Test match in 1934 he would write a letter to Woodfull congratulating him on a 'glorious victory'.

drive on the roads around Pudsey, and on rest days joined him for golf at Fulneck, by the Moravian church.

Lord's was changing. A neat square of formal lawn had been planted in a courtyard by the pavilion to honour the Kent and England luminary Lord Harris, who died in 1932 – the paving was cool York stone, and roses were already climbing the mustard-grey brick walls in a way that would rapidly make this an ideal spot for champagne parties and formal team photographs. A couple of days earlier the Committee meeting had expressed its satisfaction with both the extra lavatories and the new tall chairs in the Long Room, and agreed to let the England team use the amateurs' dressing-room (even the professionals). It approved the erection of refreshment tents on the practice ground, and, in an early assertion of media rights, insisted that flags be hung in certain areas to prevent the snatching of 'unauthorised photographs' from outside the ground.

There were a few more items on the agenda. A sculpture had been completed for the south-west corner – a Greek-style frieze depicted cricketing athletes beneath the jolly old Newbolt motto 'Play up, play up and play the game' (it is still there now, on the corner of Wellington Road facing Regent's Park). It had initially been proposed that Bill Woodfull, Australia's captain, be invited to unveil it, but in the end the Mayor of Marylebone presided at the ceremony. In a final detail, it was agreed that Mr J. M. Barrie be given a Rover Ticket for the game, along with the US polo team.

June was always a busy month in the sporting calendar, and 1934 was no exception. In tennis, Gottfried von Cramm was beating Crawford in the Paris final – the third loss in a row for 'Gentleman Jack'. In golf, there was a record entry (313) for the Open; Alf Padgham was winning the *Yorkshire Evening News* tournament; and the usual amateur events were going strong – the Sunningdale Foursomes, the Kent Championship, Press v Commons at Walton Heath. There was polo at Hurlingham, racing at Ascot, rowing at

Henley. And cricket was everywhere. Stan McCabe was spurring Australia to victory in the first Test at Trent Bridge – helped by the bowling of O'Reilly. Verity, unusually, had a meagre haul in that match, taking just one wicket in each innings.

The cultural scenery was bursting with life, too. The weather was glorious, so the bright mainstays of the English summer – Chelsea Flower Show, Trooping the Colour, Aldershot Tattoo – all went off with a fizz. And under the supervision of two German musicians, the conductor Fritz Busch and the director Carl Ebert (high-ranking refugees from Hitler, they had directed operas in Dresden and Berlin), a delightful new opera festival ('Mozart in Sussex') was popping up in the countryside near Lewes, at Glyndebourne. It bore very little resemblance to a working man's club. There was 'an excellent landing ground for aeroplanes' 100 yards from the opera stage, and the proprietors expected the audience to wear formal evening dress and be 'waited on by their own servants'. But the initial productions, *The Marriage of Figaro* and *Così fan tutte*, won admiring reviews – 'a fantastic idea!' trilled *The Times* – and were well received by almost everyone – not least thanks to the grand weather: the drought might have been awkward for golf courses, but it was perfect for *al fresco* concerts in the South Downs. A little touch of Salzburg in Sussex? Why ever not? It could hardly compensate for the loss of the renowned composers Delius, Elgar and Holst, all of whom had passed away in the early months of 1934. But it was better than nothing.

The weather remained consistently warm and sunny, and officious signs – 'Use Less Water' – appeared on public buildings and trams in a bid to fight the drought. The second half of May had been hot, and June looked set to be the same. It was no match for the blistering spell that was scouring America's Midwest into a dust bowl (the newspapers called it a 'black blizzard'), but by British standards a fortnight without precipitation struck people as a national emergency, and the suburbs were pockmarked with empty reservoirs and riverbeds. It was the driest spell for 80 years;

there was talk of sending up rockets with sand particles to shock the sky into releasing moisture.

And it was all set against a background of sharpening political unease. As the sun came out all across Britain, and public thoughts turned to holiday pleasures, Germany seemed to be spiralling ever more rapidly into some fearful abyss. The government was threatening to default on its national debts, Jewish businessmen were being attacked by Nazi Brown Shirts every day, and a rodent-faced 'doctor' named Goebbels was giving speeches in Warsaw about National Socialism and 'the position of the Jews'. Hitler and Mussolini were pictured shaking hands in Venice, with sunshine sparkling on the Grand Canal, even as various violent 'outrages' (bombs in restaurants and railway stations) were being committed by pro-German groups in Austria.

Along with continuing talk about the cruel famine in the Soviet Union, and news that Poland's Minister of the Interior had been assassinated by a Ukrainian nationalist as part of an argument in central Europe no one understood, this looked like textbook instability, and anyone reading the papers could be forgiven for thinking that the world was going over the edge. The phrase 'the next war' was becoming so common that some wanted it banned before it became a self-fulfilling prophecy. But what else could anyone say in the face of reports that told how, according to new Nazi rules, German parents could now expect to take charge of their beloved children only on Sundays – on Saturdays they belonged, and must be released, to the Hitler Youth movement?

According to the latest statements by the government, the economic outlook really was improving, but a new 'pilgrimage' was being organised by Britain's cathedrals to draw attention to the continuing anguish of the have-nots. The letters columns juddered with clashing views about the handling of hecklers at Oswald Mosley's rallies; there were Commons debates on the topic. The 760 policemen on duty at Olympia had for the most part collared protestors, and feelings were running high on both sides. Some said Mosley had 'modelled himself on dictators' and was 'out to destroy democracy' by using tactics 'utterly foreign to this country'; others felt that the attempt to shout him down was an infringement of liberty that 'cannot be tolerated'.

None of this could prevent London from grinding to a halt for the Epsom Derby on 6 June. It was many years since William Powell Frith had unveiled his famous painting of the scene (1858) which presented the race as a panoramic tableau of Victorian life, with aristocrats, bookies, jockeys, courtesans, gypsies, tricksters, acrobats and clowns rubbing shoulders on the same green hill. But the Derby hadn't changed greatly since those bawdy times: it was still a picturesque ragbag of English types having different sorts of fun. Some wore toppers and carried binoculars, others favoured trilbies or caps. It was a horse race, but also a funfair. A flamboyant West Indian named Ras Prince Monolulu sported a colourful feathered headdress, as if at a Caribbean carnival, before climbing on a box and yelling 'I gotta horse!' or 'Black man for luck!' at the grinning crowd.

In a feat of timetabling barely conceivable now, a 'special fast-electric train service' was put together to ferry passengers to the racecourse from the major London stations – Charing Cross, Holborn Viaduct, London Bridge, Victoria and Waterloo. Trains left London every five minutes; and the bus service from Morden, at the bottom end of the Northern Line, was running two buses per minute. Passengers emerged at three stations – Epsom, Epsom Downs and Tattenham Corner – and started walking into the course shortly after dawn. Thousands of cars and coaches were parked up by the rails, making an ersatz grandstand; and fleets of horse-drawn carriages nosed into the gaps. By lunch the population of a small city had pressed in – estimates varied from 250,000 (*Glasgow Bulletin*) to 500,000 (*New York Times*). For the first time, a super new auto-gyro plane was being used for traffic guidance, but it didn't seem to be making a great deal of difference. If you weren't fortunate enough to be part of the royal family's convoy of Rolls-Royces, you were almost certain to be stuck in a grinding queue.

The fine weather meant that the going was 'very hard', and for the traditional pre-race walk of the course officials put up signs asking strollers to 'spare the course', which was spangled with buttercups. But on the day itself there was sultry dampness in the air, and a hint of drizzle. Epsom began to resemble one of its thoroughbred racehorses: it steamed.

Around the world, in the far pavilions of Britain's sprawling overseas territories and beyond, people twiddled the dials on their radios and leaned forward to listen to the famous race;[3] the lucky ones cheered when Windsor Lad flashed past the post to win by a length and tie the course record. His owner, the Maharajah of Rajpipla, a friend of the Aga Khan and a well-known figure in racing circles (he was 'Good old Pip' to those who dropped in for tea and croquet at his riverside mansion near Windsor) led him in, clutching a grey top hat. He had, he said, 'realised my life's ambition'.

The Maharajah was soon sipping champagne with the King in the royal box, before going on to the Savoy to celebrate. The hotel cleared out a ballroom; lady guests were presented with purple and white orchids (to match his winning racing colours). At midnight an elephant lumbered around the room, also decked out in purple and cream.

It went down well in the subcontinent. 'Thousands cheer Good Old Pip', trilled the *Times of India*, and the *Bombay Sentinel* agreed: 'Maharajah of Rajpipla Wildly Cheered'. But the English summer soon took a nastier twist when, two weeks after the race, a brown canvas bag was opened at Brighton railway station to reveal the hacked-up remains of a female torso. That evening, a clerk at King's Cross opened another case and found two sawn-off legs. More bags were torn open, and the police were inundated

---

[3] The language of racing on the wireless in these early days was quaint, to say the least. 'He leads, he leads,' the commentator would declaim with operatic relish. 'Come then, gallant son ... Leap, brave heart ... Look, nothing can catch him now!'

with 6,000 letters (none helpful). The missing arms and head were never found, and a mystery was born. It became known as the Brighton Trunk Murders, and the papers loved it. It was just the kind of macabre incident that prompted Orwell (12 years later) to write his description of the perfect English murder – a gruesome riddle with which to beguile a rainy Sunday afternoon by the fire. But it was another reminder of the violent emotions that trembled beneath the surface of happier events.

Even this was not enough to knock cricket off the front page of the *News of the World* the weekend before Australia's appearance at Lord's. Lord Lionel Tennyson, grandson of the poet, ex-Hampshire cricketer and now a reporter, shook his head at the home side's chances. 'England have not won a Test match against Australia at Lord's since 1896. It looks extremely doubtful that they will lay the bogey in the present game.'[4]

Cricket wasn't the only way to take one's mind off the frightening state of world affairs. A nature-minded politician named Neville Chamberlain wrote to *The Times* that week to share the enticing fact that he had just spotted, in St James's Park, a grey wagtail.

The first day of the Lord's Test (Friday) dawned bright and windy. Strings of Union flags, emblems of Britain's great Empire, hung from the stands, shaking in the breeze like bunting, and the trees at the nursery end rustled as if at the approach of a storm.

The *Evening Standard* had a pair of cricketing giants to discuss the match on its front page. They had different approaches to the game. Douglas Jardine would 'applaud' if England set out to secure a draw, while C. B. Fry urged: 'Be bold. Play for a decision.'

---

[4] Tennyson, like so many figures in this story, had his own memories of the war, not all of them bitter. Serving with the Rifle Brigade in France, he was wounded three times – but achieved greater fame when he arrived at the Western Front armed with a case of champagne. 'I have never liked travelling light,' he wrote in his autobiography.

England won the toss and decided to bat, and when the opening pair nudged their way to 50 without loss it seemed a fair start. But then Herbert Sutcliffe was trapped lbw by Arthur Chipperfield, Walter Hammond spooned a return catch to the same bowler, Patsy Hendren nicked to slip, Cyril Walters fell 18 runs short of a hundred and the captain, Wyatt himself, was caught behind for 33. At 182 for 5 England were teetering. Maurice Leyland and the wicketkeeper, Les Ames, hung on, however, adding a hundred, and at close of play the scoreboard read 293 for 5 – an evenly balanced day.

Wyatt was playing with a broken thumb after being cracked on the glove by his own team-mate, the Essex opening bowler Ken Farnes, in the trial match; but he was determined not to let that stop him. He had to wear a metal thumb protector when he batted, and it flew off into the gully when he attempted a pull shot off Bill O'Reilly (the leg-spinner who would go on to top the first-class bowling averages that summer, with 109 wickets at an average of 17.04). But it was a very brave innings, and the time he spent at the crease was useful in another way. It allowed him to see that the pitch had a spiteful streak for spinners, and that Verity might well hold the key to this match.

On the second morning, a dull London Saturday, some 30,000 people crammed into Lord's – the gates were closed and large numbers were turned away. When play began first Leyland (with a fighting 109) and then Ames (with 120) turned a middling score into an imposing one, and when Verity, at number eight, chipped in with a handy 29, England posted 440. Of course, although in most circumstances this was a good total, it was not much more than the minimum needed with a fellow like Bradman around.

Australia made what *Wisden* called a 'splendid' beginning in reply. Woodfull and Brown posted 50 without loss and looked distinctly unfussed. But when Woodfull was out, Wyatt tossed the ball to Verity knowing that it was a significant point in the game. The man on his way out to the wicket was the little maestro himself. This was it.

Verity began in his customary tidy fashion, with two maidens, but Bradman was in one of his moods, and plundered three boundaries in his usual flamboyant style. The fielders barely had time to move as he rifled the ball into the gaps between them, and up in the press box Cardus writhed with pleasure. It was an innings of the rarest quality, he wrote – 'spirit lived in every stroke'. Afterwards he would maintain that it was 'far greater' even than the 304 the great man would go on to score at Leeds later in July. It was a perfect reminder of what The Don was all about, style and substance married in one artful demonstration. 'When Bradman was batting thousands of hearts were uplifted. The excitement throbbed. Perfect strangers spoke to one another.'

This was the party that Verity was supposed to be spoiling, and for a while the task looked beyond him. He probed away patiently, as ever, but wasn't able to make things 'happen', as the saying goes, until his 18th over. According to Bowes, it was classic Verity. Knowing that the standard Australian response to spin bowling was to move back and across the stumps and watch the ball like a hawk off the wicket, he left the leg side free and invited front-foot swishes across the line. Bradman, equally keen to wrong-foot bowlers, came waltzing down the wicket, trusting his eye – by no means a foolish idea; it rarely failed him – and started drilling the ball through that vacant leg side. He raced faultlessly on to 36. And he was overdue one of his giant scores.

Verity didn't panic. He kept his fielders where they were, leaving that inviting space on the on side, offering The Don more easy runs against the spin – and held the ball back. Bradman was too smart to fall for so obvious a trick right away, but it did give him pause. Should he take on the challenge and slam Verity through the leg side, or respect the delicate position of the game and think about safety first? Caught in two minds, he wafted at the ball without his usual conviction, and up it flew off the leading edge. When it fell into Verity's hands the crowd fell silent. Bradman out? Surely not. Then a growing rumble of applause began to ripple round the famous stands.

Across London, the afternoon newspaper billboards said simply: 'He's out!' – and everyone knew exactly what was meant. Indeed, something of the importance attached to the goings-on at Lord's can be deduced from the way the *Evening Standard*, which had the luck to be first with the news, gave over four of its first five pages to the event – even more than usual. Douglas Jardine contributed long, lavish columns of continuous present: 'Verity has changed ends … I still wish he'd try one over from over the wicket … Neither batsman is comfortable … A confident appeal is disallowed … Verity has introduced a silly mid-on … Chipperfield is using his feet well.'

But at this moment of high triumph Verity was his normal, undemonstrative self. Nothing in his demeanour suggested that he had just dismissed the world's best player – if anything he had the absent-minded air of a man queuing for a lawnmower part.

There were no further wickets that day, so when stumps were drawn Australia were 192 for 2, with one of the openers, Bill Brown, nudging his way to a polished century. Nothing was certain, but a betting man would have put at least the top floor of his house on a first-innings lead for Australia, and it looked as if England would have to roll their sleeves up just to stay in the game. But the following day was the rest day, and rain was falling steadily over south London. On Monday the air was damp and surly, and the sky was grey. It was the kind of weather that makes bowlers smile, and it made the wicket 'beautiful to bowl on', thought Cardus, 'if you happened to be left-handed and born in Yorkshire'. Verity looked out of his hotel window and saw water on the road. 'I shouldn't wonder if we don't have a bit of fun today,' he murmured.

In the event he only just made it to the ground in time. According to his team-mate, the Gloucestershire batsman Charlie Barnett, the car taking Verity to Lord's hit a black cat and precious minutes were spent trying to locate the owner. And the roads near St John's Wood were jammed with people, despite the glum weather. The pavement on Wellington Road was thick with men in jackets, ties and raincoats, all queuing for the turnstiles by a sign that read 'Play Not Guaranteed'.

The day began with an unconvincing stutter when bad light pushed the players back to the pavilion for a while. But things soon resumed, and when Verity came on to bowl the atmosphere crackled with electricity. He drifted to the wicket in his usual unhurried way – 'lightly and decisively', as his captain put it – and rolled over that famous left arm. And all at once the game took on a fresh complexion. 'As soon as we saw Hedley Verity bowling,' wrote the wicketkeeper, Ames, 'we realised we had a very real chance.' As always he was finding 'an impeccable length', but now there was something else – the ball was turning and lifting in a way no batsman in the world could enjoy. Hammond described the surface as 'sticky and breakable', and Verity's first ball made him grin. 'We knew that the Lord had delivered them into our hands.'

Wyatt had a significant part to play, too. He rose to the occasion, asking Bowes to rein back his normal aggressive style and slow down, concentrate on line and length, and simply seek to limit the Australian run scoring: the plan was to keep one end nice and quiet while Verity swung his gentle wrecking ball at the other.

Somehow, Brown and McCabe added 62 without any undue alarm, but when Brown nicked Bowes to the wicketkeeper shortly after bringing up his century the dam burst. In a tumble of wickets so sudden that it took everyone present by surprise, the batsmen came and went, falling like ninepins. All but one of the rest fell to Verity. It was like a poem.

Darling, trying to sweep, skied to fine leg; McCabe edged a lifter.

Bromley turned one to short leg's hands; Oldfield nicked to slip.

Grimmett fell to a thunderbolt from Bowes; O'Reilly and Wall trembled.

Out they marched, the baggy green caps, and back they traipsed. As Verity's Yorkshire team-mate Sutcliffe put it: 'When the rain had done his work, Verity was able to do *his* work, and that was the end of it.' But when the eighth wicket fell the game still hung in the balance. England were well on top, but Australia needed only 27 to avoid the follow-on (in those days the follow-on target was 150 runs); and this, on a damp wicket, might prove decisive. If England failed to knock over the two last batsmen they would have to bat on this pudding themselves – no simple task. And if, heaven forbid, they were to struggle as Australia were struggling, then the pendulum might swing. It would be tough to post a demanding target, and Bradman couldn't possibly fail twice ...

At this knife-edge moment there was a pause in the proceedings (this being cricket) so that the players could form up on the grass in front of the pavilion and shake hands with King George V. Many of the next day's papers loyally published photographs of this ceremony, on the obedient assumption that the actual game was of junior interest to this magical rite. But the lull between the two Australian innings gave both teams a chance to reflect. England were 1-0 down after Trent Bridge, and Bradman hadn't got going yet. This was their best, perhaps *only* chance to land a blow. Ames for one knew that if they faltered now 'Australia might very well have forced us into defeat', and no one needed reminding what it would mean to beat Australia without Jardine, Larwood, Voce ... or anything resembling short-pitched bowling. Verity's left arm was holding out the possibility of sporting salvation in more ways than could easily be counted.

The next hour would decide whether England could manage it. Wyatt stationed his fielders in a tight ring, took a deep breath and nodded at Verity to come in again.

The tailenders played, missed, pushed, missed, jabbed, missed and scurried a few singles. And then, in a flash, it was over. Verity pressed one down a little faster and it arrowed through O'Reilly's defences; a couple of balls later he trapped Wall lbw. Australia had fallen seven runs short, and would have to go through all this again.

In the excitement of the moment it was easy to miss the fact that no fewer than eight wickets had fallen for just 92 runs, and that Verity had taken six of them – for a miserly 37 runs – to go with his expert removal of Bradman on the Saturday. If he did nothing else in the match, it was a fabulous effort. But the job was only half done.

When the two teams walked out for the second innings Verity pushed his hands into his pockets to keep them warm. It was just past midsummer, the high noon of the cricket season, but he was wearing a long-sleeved sweater to keep out the chill. He looked calm, but then he always did. Nobody had any illusions about what lay ahead: the plan was for Verity to bowl as soon as possible, and keep going until he fell over. Farnes and Bowes opened the bowling, and won an unlooked-for bonus when Brown, the hero of the first innings with his century, top-edged one down to fine leg and was caught by Walters for two. In a surprising development, McCabe walked out instead of Bradman, a sign perhaps that the great man was not his usual super-confident self. The interval was imminent, and nothing of note happened until the players wandered off for lunch.

Up in the dining room Verity helped himself to an extra plateful of strawberries and cream, and prepared for a long afternoon. And when the teams came out again Verity replaced Farnes right away. The strategy was the same as in the first innings. 'My aim,' wrote Wyatt, 'was to block one end while Hedley got them out at the other.' Once again he asked Bowes to throttle back while his fellow Yorkshireman went to work. Everyone watching had more or less the same thought: *Here we go*.

It didn't take Verity long to make inroads this time: he was soon plucking Australian feathers like a fox in a chicken coop. McCabe was the first to go, popping the ball up for Hendren to take a smart diving catch. And though this only brought Bradman to the crease there was a strange, jumpy light in the man's eyes: that odd, dizzy manner was upon him again. His captain, Woodfull, begged him to be careful this time, but The Don felt that his first-innings dismissal had actually been caused by *too much* caution – 'In endeavouring to carry out his wishes I did restrain myself and, in so doing, held a shot against my better judgement.' He was damned if he was going to fall that way again.

Some bowlers are intimidating by virtue of the rush and menace they express in their run-ups and action. Facing Larwood, it was said, was like being charged by an angry wild animal. Verity was the opposite: measured, placid, expressionless. A mild body turn saw his left shoulder point at the batsman after releasing the ball, so he looked balanced – but hardly venomous. According to Hammond he was, even on this day, 'unsmiling' and 'unruffled'. Perhaps it was this remote, otherworldly quality that rattled Bradman, because he was flailing away at Verity like a cat pawing at a wasp.

As in the first innings, Verity left the leg side open, inviting Bradman to attack, and this time the Australian was determined not to be caught in two minds. He pushed, scrabbled and scampered his way to 13, edgy and dissatisfied all the while. And when Verity floated one at his leg stump he jumped out of his ground, dropped his shoulder and swung at the ball like a novice. The ball flashed high into the murky Lord's air over the middle of the wicket. Verity might have got under it himself; or Hammond could have run in from cover; but in the end it was Ames, the man with the gloves, who trotted forward and took the catch. Australia's chief and legendary hope was gone.

In Bowes's view it was 'one of the worst shots he ever played'; Wyatt judged it born of 'desperation'. A Press Association photographer caught the moment, so we can see Bradman just after he has clipped the ball up. The wicketkeeper, Ames, and the other fielders are gazing up, tense and hopeful, and we can almost feel, in black and white, the collective holding of breath as the ball began to fall. Thousands of spectators felt the same way. Jardine, in the *Evening Standard*, saw Hammond and Ames converging and believed that 'for a breathless moment a collision seemed inevitable'. And the *Daily Express* thought the suspense was even more prolonged. 'The ball was so long in the air,' ran its report, 'that the England selectors might almost have issued from the pavilion and been in time to go into committee as to whose catch it was.'

That is how long it felt as 30,000 spectators held their breath. A hush fell across Lord's, followed by a wild eruption of applause when Ames took the catch. Bradman stood slumped – 'exposed in momentary embarrassment', Cardus wrote, 'like a dejected schoolboy'. Hammond looked at Woodfull's face and saw a look 'so compounded of anger and disappointment and woe that I have never forgotten it'. Warner, watching from the pavilion, also felt the force of 'the look that Woodfull gave Bradman'.

It knocked the soul out of Australia's batting. Woodfull edged to a tumbling catch in the gully, and the rest collapsed like a row of dominoes. Hammond managed to bowl Darling, and Verity undid the rest. Chipperfield, Bromley, Oldfield, Grimmett – they came, they took guard, and back they went to the pavilion. When Clarrie (Clarence) Grimmett was out first ball it seemed that a hat-trick was on, but it was not to be.

The end came rapidly: Verity induced Tom Wall to dolly up a simple catch from what Jardine called a 'very innocent half-volley', and Hendren snaffled it at silly mid-off. It was ten to six. Verity had bowled virtually unchanged for more than five hours, and had taken 14 wickets in the day – bettering his remarkable 7 for 61 in the first innings with a superlative 8 for 43 in the second. After tea he snared 6 for just 15 runs.

As thousands of spectators raced across the pitch ('pell-mell') in what the *Daily Mail* called a 'frenzied dash for Verity', the man himself had to break his own stately trot and sprint for the safety of the pavilion. A police cordon materialised in front of the Lord's steps, but the swelling crowd pressed and jostled in as close as they could. It had been nearly 40 years since anything like this had happened on this famous green patch of St John's Wood grass; no one could be blamed for wanting to enjoy it.

Wisden, restrained as ever, allowed merely that Verity was 'the chief factor' in the game, and there were a few other wise old birds reluctant to get carried away. 'The toss won the match,' said Warner in the *Telegraph*, surprisingly reluctant to give Verity anything like the credit he deserved while referring to Bradman's swipe as 'a most unguarded stroke at a critical time'. *The Times* was equally dusty, agreeing with Bowes that it may have been 'the worst shot he [Bradman] has ever made in his life'. Robertson-Glasgow was another who thought the game had been decided by 'Verity and sawdust'. Revered voices such as these prided themselves on being hard to impress, and tended to see their role as erudite judges of batsmanship, not bowling. But most onlookers were happy to salute a heroic effort. Fender called that bowling spell 'a wonderful exhibition of stamina'; and Verity's old skipper, Jardine, said that 'for clear thinking and execution it may stand alone for all time'. He sent two messages to the England dressing-room to show he was in earnest. 'What a great bowler Verity is,' he concluded. 'Every day of the week, to every batsman, on every sort of wicket.'

That day's captain agreed whole-heartedly with his predecessor. 'I cannot fully extend my gratitude to Verity,' Wyatt told reporters, 'for his wonderful performance.' Another great old spinner, Bernard Bosanquet (once the Huguenot-descended inventor of the googly, now cricket correspondent of the *Daily Mail*) observed simply that 'the win was Verity's, and Verity's alone'. Even the *Daily Worker*, the official organ of the trade unions, with a hammer and sickle on its masthead, felt obliged to mention the feat. It didn't usually cover sport, unless some Russian weightlifter set a new world record, and certainly wasn't interested in golf or tennis – but the front page on 26 June carried a modest item ('England win the Test') which was given even higher billing than the 'Soviet air heroes' who were about to arrive for an official ten-day visit.

Picking through the small print of the game, some noticed that one of the key moments had arrived on day two, when England's ninth wicket fell. There was a suggestion at this time that England, with the score on 410 and the last man, Bowes, unlikely to last long, might as well declare, but Wyatt chose to bat on, and Bowes and Verity enjoyed a 30-run partnership that proved absolutely decisive; without those extra runs England would certainly not have been able to enforce the follow on, and Verity would not have taken all those wickets in a day. Such is history; such is cricket; such is life.

In 1934 there were no thoughts of a formal post-match ceremony, with handshakes from beaming sponsors and anodyne words from the winning captain (we're delighted with the way we executed our skills, and thanks to the fans for their great support, etc). Ames, Leyland and Wyatt came on to the balcony to wave at the happy spectators filling the outfield as far back as the wicket, and the tall figure of Verity – well, it *might* have been him; in the bustle of the moment it was difficult for people to be sure – appeared for a second in the tall windows of the dressing-room. Wyatt cupped his hands round his mouth and yelled a few words (no microphones in those days) which nobody could hear, and that was that. Verity's team-mates entreated him to add a word or two, but he waved them away. It was not his style. His usual habit was to find a quiet seat in the changing-room where he could brood on the day, reflecting on what he might have done better. In a typical moment of fellow feeling he confided to a reporter his sadness that Jardine wasn't playing; his old pal would surely have enjoyed this.

Not everything about the moment of victory was clear at the time. It was only later, for instance, that Hendren gave his version of the winning moment. A keen souvenir hunter, he had his heart set on one of the stumps, but when it fell to him to take the winning catch his chance went with it: by the time he turned round, the stumps had all vanished. He looked down at the ball in his hands – that at least was better than nothing. But after a moment he shook his head, realising that he couldn't keep it.

'Here, Hedley,' he said, handing it over. 'I think this is yours.'

The 14-wicket haul wasn't quite Verity's best-ever day: the previous summer he had taken 17 Essex wickets for 91 runs, also in one day. That put him alongside the great and tetchy S. F. Barnes, who had once taken 17 wickets against South Africa. But only one other man had pulled off anything like this Lord's effort in an England shirt, and that was Wilfred Rhodes, with 15 against Australia at Melbourne in 1904 (for 20 more runs). As luck would have it, Rhodes had come to Lord's to see Verity; he was now the cricket coach at Harrow School, and lived not far away. He pushed through the throng to be among the first to slap his protégé on the back, and according to Ames, who saw the two famous Yorkshire spinners locked in a delighted handshake (real men didn't hug), he gave every appearance of being 'the happiest man on the ground'.

Rhodes was still savouring the glow of it all when he told a journalist that Verity's had been 'a magnificent piece of bowling ... and he wasn't lucky, either'. Some match reports contradicted this by suggesting that 'England had all the luck' and that the weather gods had been on Verity's side. But though 'the clouds in their courses gave him just the kind of conditions he liked best', there was no arguing with the fact that Verity had set 'a record unapproachable in any Test match under English skies'.

When it was all over, the large crowd at Lord's, and the much larger crowd reading the next day's papers, were left with an imperishable vision of a historic day's play. The leader of the orchestra, Neville Cardus, resorted to martial imagery, claiming that England's 'artillery' had laid down a 'barrage of fast bowling' in an 'action' led by 'Bombardier Bowes'. But he ended by paying tribute to the man of the hour, Hedley Verity, in the poetical style that was by now synonymous with his view of cricket: 'The Gods of the game, who sit up aloft and watch, will remember the loveliness of it all, the style, the poise on light toes, the swing of the arm from noon to evening.'

At the picture houses, a Pathé newsreel entitled 'England's victory' projected the highlights on to the silver screen. Here came the jaunty band music and packed stands ... there went the King, shaking hands with the teams ... here came the Australians, facing 'hot work' ... there went Verity, easing into his action off that nine-stride run. And down went the wickets – going, going, gone. When the last one fell the narrator went for a pulpit tone: 'Thus ended the second Test match. Verity's match.'

It was official, and other newspapers passed the news around the country like flares lit from beacons. 'Amazing Feat', said the *Yorkshire Evening Post*. 'Verity Makes History', declared the *Dundee Courier*; 'Remarkable Test win', wrote the *Western Morning Post*. Hundreds of others joined the chorus, lyrical in their praise. 'I can only tell you', said the *Sunderland Daily Echo*, 'that we looked for a wicket with every ball, and in one over of immortal memory we saw him take three wickets.' The reporter for the *Evening Telegraph* (Jack Hobbs, no less) was quick to frame a properly historic response: 'This Test will always be known as Verity's Test', he wrote. 'Where England would have been without him I cannot even think.'

If these sound like over-excited reactions to one simple win, it is worth remembering what happened next: England did not beat Australia again at Lord's for the entirety of the 20th century. Not until Andrew Strauss's victory in 2009 was the old ghost laid to rest. And a lesser-known record came to an end four years later, when Graeme Swann became the first English spinner since Verity to take five Australian wickets in an innings on the famous ground. Does that put Verity's 15-wicket haul into perspective? It ought to. And we need to resist the modern reflex urging us to believe that things were easier back then. Two of Verity's scalps belonged to the best batsman of all time, by far. As Hammond insisted in his memoir: 'It was a Test performance that I do not expect to see repeated in my lifetime.' He spoke too soon – he himself lived to see Jim Laker's even more amazing 19-wicket haul at Old Trafford in 1956 – but the point was fair. In 1934, no one could easily imagine Verity's effort ever being bettered.

In his twilight years Bob Wyatt could often be seen in Paul Getty's box at Lord's – sometimes acting as host in Getty's absence – and not minding *too* much if England failed to win, aware that he was the last captain to have done so in this sacred place.

It was, in other words, quite a bit more than an ordinary victory.

The *Yorkshire Evening Post*, in Leeds, was able to send a reporter out to Rawdon in pursuit of the family's reaction. Some of the London papers picked up on his findings. Verity's wife and children, it transpired, had been following the action from their front room. 'I listened on the wireless,' said Kathleen. 'That was quite enough for me.' Her sons, Wilfred (four) and Douglas (one) were on her lap, and the older one 'wriggled' whenever he heard his father's name – which made for quite a lot of wriggling. The other Mrs Verity, Hedley's mother, was sufficiently overwhelmed to add that she always found watching the game hard. 'There's only one thing I can't stand about cricket,' she said: 'seeing catches dropped off his bowling. That really makes me mad.'

In all the excitement – the welter of congratulatory calls, telegrams and personal visits – the family actually forgot to send a message of its own. But it didn't matter. 'He'll know all right just how we feel,' said his father. As usual, he refused to over-react, pointing out that this was only the beginning of Hedley's story – 'My son is still learning, you know.' He then headed east, in his capacity as Rawdon's Urban District Councillor, to a conference in Whitby. When the meeting began he was asked to rise to his feet to acknowledge the cheering that broke out as people realised just who was in their midst. He did so, according to the *Yorkshire Evening Post*, with 'no more than a smile'. Then it was back to drainage systems and postal rates. Like son, like father.

CHAPTER TEN

Cotton Picking Good

An editorial in *The Times* on 26 June rendered Verity's great day in classical terms by announcing *Magnus est Verity, et praevaluit* – Great is Verity, and he has prevailed. But there was a plentiful supply of other news that morning, not least the fact that in the first qualifying round for the Open Championship at Royal St George's, England's Henry Cotton had played some equally historic golf, and was leading by three strokes.

If we think that sports news of this sort was of secondary importance so far as the public was concerned, we may have to think again. Even *The Times*, the paper favoured by the men who ran the country, placed sport before the other news. Its famous front page was still a dense collage of small advertisements and classified notices about jobs, hotels, shipping and so forth, but after that it was sport first, other news second.

The public mood was still divided and uncertain. Since 1 July was the anniversary of the Somme, London was vibrant with memorials to the fallen, while in Paris there were torchlit parades beneath the Arc de Triomphe to mark 20 years since the summer of 1914. There was a hint in both countries that something essential – a martial spirit – had been lost since then. In June 1934 Marshal Pétain made a speech at the Verdun Monument that paid tribute to 'the virtues of our race' while expressing sorrow at the way the Verdun dead were no longer seen as heroes or saviours, but as victims of a tragedy. In Britain pacifist ideas were equally strong. Kingsley Martin, editor of the *New Statesman*, called war 'a product of ignorance and idealism', and Bertrand Russell argued that patriotic fervour meant little more than 'a willingness to kill and be killed for trivial reasons'. All talk of resistance, ran the line, was a provocation.

But Henry Cotton's eye might have been caught by something else. On 18 June, three days after the anniversary of the Battle of Waterloo, the mighty clash that still haunted the muddy corner of Europe where Cotton now lived, the 4th Duke of Wellington passed away. He was 85, so it was no shock, but it was a sad day. The late Duke had been a keen patron of the battlefield memorials and people in Belgium, so although he was buried at Stratfield Saye, the Hampshire residence built by the Iron Duke himself, he was much mourned in the countryside south of Brussels, too.

It was often said at this time that Wellington's great victory had been won on the playing fields of Eton – and this seemed to confirm the popular connection between sport and war in the public imagination. It was a doubtful version of the truth, though, one of those common misconceptions that survive only because they *seem* apt. In Ralph Nevill's 1911 history of Eton the Duke merely observed, passing a cricket match at the school years later, 'there goes the stuff that won Waterloo'. It was a kindly analogy, nothing more. In truth there was no sport at Eton in Napoleonic times; the only useful skill a boy might have acquired was the strength to survive bullying.[1]

A lot of British people might have seen Waterloo as a long way from home, but Cotton wasn't one of them. As the crow flies, Waterloo was a good deal closer to Royal St George's, the golf links at Sandwich in Kent, than Bournemouth or Birmingham. It didn't take long to drive his flashy red Mercedes to Boulogne, hop

[1]   In contrast, there is not much doubt that when Wellington became Chancellor of Oxford University in 1834, he most certainly owed *that* to the battlefield at Waterloo.

on a car ferry across the Channel and motor up the coast to the
hotel where he and 'Toots' were staying.

Sandwich was an evocative place, a harbour that was one of
the original Cinque Ports along the English Channel; it had been
thriving since the Crusades. It was here, in 1255, that the first
elephant seen in England (a gift to Henry III) disembarked. A few
miles south of the medieval town was a village called Ham; not
surprisingly, the road sign that said 'Ham Sandwich' was stolen
so often the local council gave up replacing it.

Cotton was in low spirits. He had played well in Dunlop-
Southport in Lancashire, in May, and had worked hard back in
Belgium, but he wasn't hitting the ball well in practice, and things
didn't improve during a woeful dress rehearsal on the Saturday.
He had brought four sets of clubs, he told his friend Henry
Longhurst (or perhaps three – accounts vary), but he 'couldn't
hit his hat with any of them'. What else could he do, though, but
soldier on? 'I might as well play, now I am here,' he groaned.

Royal St George's was an odd place, a slice of windswept
'Scotland-sur-mer' situated within convenient reach of London.
The brainchild of some well-connected golfers from Wimbledon,
who wanted a place in the country and scouted out this bleak stretch
of sandy coast with golf in mind, it was already a much-loved locale.
Cunningly laid out so that the holes ran in different directions,
finding a fresh angle for the wind each time, its rumpled fairways
presented a challenge even to the world's best golfers. Harry Vardon
had been calling it the finest course in the world for three decades.

It is possible that Cotton's pre-tournament incompetence has
been overstated – not least by himself. Walter Hagen's old caddie,
Ernest Hargreaves, arrived in Sandwich that weekend looking for
work. Cotton already had someone on his bag, a local man called
Ernest Butler, who knew the greens, but Hargreaves watched him
long enough to feel (and later write) that he was hitting the ball
extremely sweetly. Either way, the day before the event Cotton
couldn't see the point of fretting over his swing, so he caddied for
'Toots' instead. It was a wise decision. It can't have been easy, for

a man whose lifelong pursuit of a perfect golf game was based on a profound faith in practice, practice and yet more practice, to put away his clubs at such a time, but – such are the vagaries of golf – it worked a treat. On the Monday morning he went out for his first qualifying round (everyone had to play the pre-qualifying tournament in those days – golf was no respecter of fame) and four hours later was putting the finishing touches to a freakish score of 66, two strokes better than the record on these famous links.

Both *The Times* and the *Daily Telegraph* reached for the same phrase in describing his golf as 'flawless to the point of tedium'. But it wasn't true: Cotton had actually leaked a shot or two. Three putts grazed the hole without falling, so with a touch more luck he could have gone even lower. In all he used his putter 33 times, a frankly modest effort. With better form on the greens, who knows what score he might have secured? But there was no arguing with the awesome power of his driving. The *Telegraph* reported that he had struck the ball well over 300 yards 'on several occasions', an enormous achievement with the clubs and balls available at the time – and no mean feat even today, with a gleaming set of brilliantly tooled, titanium-charged modern weapons.

On the 370-yard second hole his drive left him needing no more than a 'tiny chip'; his approach to the 238-yard second (with a spoon, an ancient three-wood) landed 15 feet from the pin; and he reached the 520-yard 14th (named 'Suez' after the watery trench across the fairway) in two. And this on a course slowed by rain – the same rain that had spiced up the Lord's pitch for Verity – dulled by what *The Times* called 'a strong growth of grass', and dead into what knowing onlookers were calling a 'light wind'.

All in all it was, wrote the same paper, 'such golf as had never been seen on the links'. This was not a matter of opinion; it was right there on the scorecard. But the bald number didn't tell the whole story. Big-driving modern players can often attack the green with lofted clubs – six or seven irons. Cotton frequently found himself playing spoons or two-irons at distant flagsticks. But still he kept trickling the ball close.

Though a keen cricket fan who would have been as pleased as anyone by what Verity was doing at Lord's that day, Cotton was an early starter, so was striding down the 18th long before the Australian openers clattered down the pavilion steps for their second innings. Whatever it was that inspired him that day, it wasn't the Ashes. But there was no debating the fact that it had been, as Longhurst wrote, 'one of the greatest rounds ever played'. The *Telegraph* called it 'a record-smashing achievement immaculate in its execution'. And it was easy to forget, with headlines such as these flying around, that the Open proper hadn't started yet: this was only the first of two qualifying days.

Cotton didn't take it easy the following morning, at Deal, but he knew he could relax. His 75 was not a distinguished effort, but it was workmanlike, and it meant that only one man, the Englishman Bert Gadd, pipped him in the qualifying rounds. The *Daily Express* was thrilled. 'The Union Jack floats over the Royal St George's clubhouse,' it said. 'For the first time in 11 years we are unashamedly proud to look at it.'

Cotton himself was happy to share the credit for this promising start with his caddie, Ernest Butler. Butler supplemented his work as a club carrier at Royal St George's by doing odd jobs in the Sandwich area. The two had met when Cotton spent a week playing and practising on the Royal St George's links early in the year; Butler's local knowledge and 'uncanny' ability to read the hidden borrows on these large, undulating greens were obvious, so Cotton wasted no time in recruiting him for Open week. He did not regret it. 'So often did he pick out the correct line,' wrote Cotton in *This Game of Golf*, 'which I at the time doubted and yet which proved correct, that I left the decisions to him.' A caddie who can read these subtle breaks was worth a couple of strokes a day – or eight in the course of the tournament, a winning margin.

On the first day of the championship itself, there was a breeze from the south-east and rain in the air. But Cotton was no longer someone setting forth in a spirit of hit and hope. After his play on

Monday he was one of the favourites, even though Gene Sarazen, most people's tip to win the claret jug, was telling reporters with a chuckle that while Cotton's round had been 'spectacular', it was of no great relevance. By Wednesday morning, when the real game began, it would have been 'wiped from the slate'.

The first tee at Royal St George's is unusual in that it sits a hundred yards from the clubhouse in a featureless expanse of windswept grass. It is not possible to see the rough outline of the challenge ahead; when the course is empty it is not even obvious which direction a golfer should face – there are no trees to frame the view and organise a golfer's sense of direction. There is something lunar and otherworldly about it. Even when the first fairway is spotted, rising barrel-straight up a gentle incline, it is hard to see what lies beyond the waving grass on the ridge up there. It is not quite a blind shot, but no one could call it clear-sighted. In the distance are some deep, dark gashes that must be bunkers, while the waving grass on the right seems to beckon the newcomer. It would feel like the middle of nowhere if it weren't for the starter's hut, a little thatched cottage which, in the absence of any other landmark, is usually called 'iconic'.

The clubhouse is a low, homely affair – a gabled Edwardian villa that looks a bit like a country hotel and a bit like a prep school. In spirit it resembles a snug mountain base camp, a cosy nook from which intrepid souls might set out into the wilds, returning many hours later, bedraggled, aching for a hot bath and a drink. Bernard Darwin was unrestrained in extolling its beauties – the sun glittering on the sea (on those rare days when it does shine), the white cliffs of Pegwell Bay, the larks ascendant on a summer breeze. It was, he wrote of these green ridges and swales, a place of 'sandhills and solitude – as nearly my idea of heaven as is to be attained on any earthly links'.

This year's championship would be the fifth on this austere terrain since J. H. Taylor's inaugural win in 1894, a decade before Cotton was born. Since then, both Vardon and Hagen had won twice – it was clearly the kind of links on which cream rose to the top.

Cotton's playing partner, the slender Frenchman Marcel Dallemagne, came from Paris, though his name suggested German roots. There was a buzz of anticipation in the gallery at the first tee, and when Cotton ripped a drive up the broad fairway, clean as a blade splitting a log, there was a throaty cheer. 'He's off,' wrote *The Times*, as if watching a horse exploding away. As it happened, Dallemagne holed a birdie putt on this opening hole, but this might have been the best thing that could have happened: it focused Cotton's mind. On the second he crashed the ball over the dog-leg some 370 yards away. A chip and a putt later he was under par himself. And he also managed to save par at the third, where, after reaching the green with his 'spade-mashie' (the period equivalent of a modern six-iron) he had to hole a snaking eight-footer.

When you stand on the fourth tee the way ahead is blocked by two towering bunkers which obscure the fairway. The one on the left is deep enough, a treacherous pit with a vertical face made out of railway sleepers – but it is dwarfed by the one on the right, which is the height of a house. Only experts can hoist the ball forward from these great sand traps; weekend players have to come out backwards, turning a long, 415-yard par-4 into an absolute monster. But they present no obstacle to above-average players, and by now Cotton was a long way above average. He cleared the sand by miles, middled a 'spoon' on to the raised, sloping green, and enjoyed another comfortable two-putt. When he walked to the fifth hole, which turned left and wriggled downhill towards the sea, with the Guilford Hotel rising on his right above the beach, he was, in the curious vocabulary of the time, four-under bogey – bogey being the score a 'good amateur' was expected to match. Not bad.

From then on Cotton and Dallemagne matched one another blow for blow, ding for dong: when Cotton chipped in for a birdie at the fifth, the Frenchman holed a ludicrous putt. Cotton reached the turn in 31, Dallemagne in 33, and both then carried on in the same vein. 'Nothing whatever happened,' sighed Darwin, 'except the obvious and perfect thing … Every approach putt was laid

stock, stone dead.' It was a procession – fairway, green, hole …
fairway, green, hole – all described by *The Times* as 'wholly
magnificent'. The *Daily Mail*, never a showcase for the virtues of
understatement, went further: 'His golf was as near to perfection
as human achievement can make it.'

No one had a better view of all this than Ernest Hargreaves. He
had been on Walter Hagen's bag when the Haig beat Cotton in the
1929 Open at Muirfield, so Cotton was keen to make use of him if
he could (since he shared a name with Cotton's actual bag-carrier,
it would drive home the importance of having two Ernests). He
hired him as a 'forecaddie' to wait in the fairway and spot his ball
as it landed, and since he poured every drive down the dead centre
of the fairway no one ever had an easier job. At the second hole
the ball soared so high over Hargreaves's head – he had positioned
himself for a good, not a supercharged, shot – that he never saw
it land; but it was safe enough up by the green. Sitting in the bar
of the Admiral Owen pub that night, just behind the hotel where
Cotton and 'Toots' were staying, it struck Hargreaves that, if he
had been a betting man, he could have done a lot worse than put a
few bob on his new employer to win this thing.

Cotton finished with a 67 to stand in the lead by three shots;
Dallemagne, after a fine round of his own, was four back.
Actually, Cotton hadn't played *quite* as brilliantly as in Monday's
qualifying round, but this time he knocked in some long putts to
secure a score. Sixty-seven was the lowest ever total in an Open,
matching Hagen's score at Muirfield in 1929 – an effort Cotton
could remember all too clearly, since he himself played with
Hagen that day, and had been pictured walking off the final green
with him, all smiles.

Waiting to tee off on the second day, Cotton chatted to three
of golf's greatest names – J. H. Taylor, James Braid and Ted Ray.
They urged him to keep attacking: it was far too early to think of
defending his first-round lead. Cotton took them at their word,
starting 4-3-3-4, to be two under par on the fifth. Soon afterwards,
on the high mounds above the sixth green, he spotted an even more

famous golfer, possibly the grandest of them all: Harry Vardon. Vardon was (not counting the Scottish founders of the game, Old Tom Morris and his son 'Young Tom') the greatest golfer the world had yet seen, and like Cotton he was staying at the Guilford Hotel, not far from this famous hole (known as 'Maiden'). In fact he had been down to play this Open himself, at the age of 64, but wasn't in good health, and on doctor's advice withdrew. But he liked to stand on the hillock above the green and watch the field go by. When Cotton arrived he raised a hand and waved at Vardon's 'staunch' presence (a 'most unusual gesture' for him, according to Hargreaves). But they exchanged no words. Vardon knew better than to distract a man with a putter in his hand and an Open to win.

There was just one lapse. At the eighth (a 183-yard par-3 that is now a twisting par-4) Cotton tried to clear the bunker with his two-iron ('to make sure of pitching well up the green') and pushed it – an occupational hazard when you take too much club. The ball sank into the soft sand just below the steep front lip, chest-high. It was tempting to take a penalty drop, but Cotton aimed sideways, played what 'I immodestly consider one of the greatest shots ever', somehow dug it out to the edge of the green, made his bogey four and, in Hargreaves's words (he was the first who peered into that bunker and saw Cotton's plugged lie) 'permitted himself a broad smile of relief'.

He drove on through the back nine, taking only 32 shots. It wasn't all plain sailing – he had to save himself from sand at the 12th, and holed a ten-footer at 'Suez' to cling on to par. But there was magic in the air: there wouldn't be a single five on his card.

The closing holes at Royal St George's are notorious: no one had made three threes, ever. But Cotton nearly hit the pin from the tee at the par-3 16th (where Thomas Bjørn took three strokes in a greenside bunker to throw away the 2003 Open). At the 17th – a tricky proposition, with a long carry to a humped fairway, then a tough approach to a raised green – he knocked the ball close again and made a ten-footer. And the final hole is more obliging, with a broad green landing strip spread out in front of faraway cross bunkers. There are some tricky slopes on the green, but when you are only six feet away they don't matter much, and Cotton rapped home his third birdie putt in a row. He had shot 65 – another record![2]

The two-iron he played into that 18th green was rated by Hargreaves 'the finest I had ever seen'. Fiercely struck up the right-hand side of the target, it veered in towards the flag 'like a homing pigeon' before landing softly on the firm bright green.

At the completion of this amazing hat-trick, Cotton permitted himself a rare smile. It was, wrote the *Manchester Guardian*, 'as if the Sphinx herself had opened her lips'. The spectators took this as their cue to let themselves go. Women shrieked and yelled, while 'elderly colonels and crusted golfers clapped their neighbours on the back and invited them to long and expensive drinks'. It was a rare and thrilling moment, one that surely signalled that magical thing: 'the resurrection of British supremacy'.

In truth it hardly felt real; it seemed to break the usual boundaries of the game. 'No one knew whether to laugh or cry,' wrote Darwin. The *Manchester Guardian* called it 'a Mozartean round … golf as might have been played on greens and fairways of asphodel'. Henry Longhurst picked up the phone to the *Evening Standard* and gasped: 'Words almost fail me. I am convinced that Cotton is the greatest golfer alive today.' And a cartoon in the *Daily Mail* by Tom Webster ('The Miracle Man!') depicted the swishing hero putting into a hole the size of a cave, with the caption: 'To Cotton this Championship course at Sandwich is just one great big hole'. His play, continued Webster in another drawing, was 'not only unbelievable but shouldn't be allowed'.

His partner for the first two days, Dallemagne, broke into immaculate English to sum up how it had been to see such play up close: 'Marvellous, marvellous, marvellous!'

---

[2] Quite a few players have subsequently matched this famous score, not least Thomas Bjørn himself, who made a 65 in 2011 to banish – too late! – the memory of his 2003 disaster.

Cotton himself was nonplussed – 'I don't know how I did it'. In fact he still felt he had played better on the Monday, and would insist to the end of his days that the 66 in qualifying was his best ball-striking of the week – indeed, the 'most perfect' 18 holes of his golfing life. But on that Thursday he had a belting hot putter – he used it only 28 times, five fewer times than in qualifying. His 65 meant he had set a course record for the second time in three rounds, and established a two-round Open mark that would not be surpassed until Nick Faldo started 66-64 at Muirfield in 1992. It was the kind of display that brooked no argument from anyone: an authentically fabulous effort.

It meant, apart from anything else, that he was an amazing *nine* strokes clear of the field: the championship was as good as his. At least one rival – Densmore Shute, the US Open champion and nearest American challenger – declared as much. 'What have I to say of Cotton's golf?' he asked, rhetorically. 'Just nothing! It is so phenomenal it does not admit of speech.' Over on the Royal St George's putting green another of the Americans, Macdonald Smith, said he was wasting his time – the thing he should be practising was holing out from the fairway. And when Gene Sarazen heard the news he grimaced, then smiled. 'What is this?' he said. 'I need a 57 to tie?'

'Such perfection almost bordered on monotony,' thought the *Daily Sketch*, but most reports were more excitable. 'The whole story is that of T. H. Cotton,' wrote *The Times*, 'and for him at the moment superlatives are futile.' J. H. Taylor followed his every step and wrote, in the *News of the World*, that it was 'the most wonderful golf ever played … the strokes that were not faultless can be counted on the fingers of one hand.' The *Telegraph* almost broke into tears, too. 'I have seen the wonder round of golf,' its correspondent wrote, 'the one of which I have been dreaming since I began to play many years ago.' Such a tremor was forgivable. The correspondent's name was George Greenwood, who, a decade earlier, at Alleyn's, had supervised young Henry's first ever golf lesson.

It is often said that you can't win an Open in the early rounds – only lose one. Until the finale you are simply playing yourself into position to challenge down the closing stretch. This is a distinctly modern way of thinking; in Cotton's day no one bothered to deploy such terms. If they had, Cotton was contradicting them, because this second round surely settled the fate of the Open. At the halfway point (the final 36 holes would all be played in one day to allow the professionals to return to their clubs for the weekend) everyone else was playing for second place – and knew it. The fat lady had long since sung – she had her feet up and was sipping tea in the dressing-room.

The last two rounds (on the Friday) were thus in one sense an anticlimax: the outcome was a foregone conclusion. But the prospect of a home-grown winner rippled around the Home Counties, thanks to newspaper stands and the new wireless sets, and thousands cancelled their plans, climbed into cars and headed for the seaside. 'A journey that takes in the ordinary way five minutes,' wrote the *Daily Mail*, 'lasted an hour.' Some 3,000–4,000 spectators lined the first fairway, and hundreds of cars filled the nearby fields like beetles. Cinema vans added to the *mise-en-scène* by mounting cameras on the roof, sending tangles of wires snaking across and around the first tee.

Off the golfers went, in pairs, and it was fortunate that the rules had recently changed. A few years earlier, thanks to the convention by which only those players within 14 strokes of the lead played the final two rounds, there would have been only *five* golfers left to tee it up – so gargantuan was Cotton's lead. But now there was a full field.

It was Cotton the crowd had come to see, though; and they had come prepared, as if for dinner. Their costumes, wrote one eyewitness, 'would have done justice to Ascot'.

Under dark skies and a gusty breeze Cotton played fine golf ('unruffled and apparently untired', according to the *Manchester Guardian*), bagging a 72 to extend his lead to ten shots. It was impressive, but … yawn. Did he know, asked a reporter as he strode off, that he had just broken no fewer than five Open records? 'I shall not be content until I have broken six.' He survived a downpour (ground staff sponged puddles off greens) and there was even a hailstorm – 'Gee,' said Sarazen, holding up a lump of ice, 'you could fix a highball with one of these.' But nothing worried Cotton until lunch.

Not much tastes better than a near-impregnable lead, but something happened on this occasion that disagreed with Cotton. As he waited in the starter's tent for the afternoon round – and there was a delay while stewards called the oversized crowd to order – Cotton's always delicate stomach seized up with nerves and began to cramp; he felt feverish and went green. He hooked the first drive, took three more to reach the green, and only a brave ten-footer stopped him from starting with a double bogey. He hooked his next two drives as well, missed par, and lurched to the turn in 40, nine more than he made on the first day. At the fifth he hit his approach into a crater; at the sixth he missed a tiddler, and at the seventh he three-putted. Suddenly, his lead halved.

It was one way to lend drama to an otherwise predictable afternoon. And things took an even more theatrical turn when he began the back nine with three bogies. Every shot went left and low. After a week in which he seemed to be walking on air, nonchalantly flicking the ball wherever he pleased, the golfing gods seemed to be having their fun at last. Memories of the previous year's Open at St Andrews flooded back. This time a year ago, Cotton had begun the last round with a share of the lead, but shot a disastrous 79 to finish miles adrift of Densmore Shute, who went on to win in a playoff.

He was being followed by a gallery of 600 people in stout coats and hats, among them his old mentor, J. H. Taylor, who had cast his expert eye over the 14-year-old Cotton all those years before, and now was pressing through the dunes to cheer him on. As his boy froze, he was beside himself. 'He *must* get his left arm up!' he muttered. According to Bernard Darwin, also clambering over the hillocks to watch this awful collapse, Taylor was 'almost frantic ... in a greater state of tension than any of us'. After spending three rounds with his neck craned as Cotton's ball flew high and far up the fairway, Ernest Hargreaves had to do some actual ball-spotting as his man muffed a dozen tee shots in a row: 'for thirteen holes he hit scarcely a shot off the middle of the club.'

It was an astonishing turnaround. And it wasn't made any easier by the size of the crowd that had converged on the links and was chatting, clicking early cameras and even – horror of horrors – *running* around the course. Several times Cotton's partner, Reg Whitcombe, held up his hand to try to quieten the 'stupid gallery disturbances' that were chasing them around. At one point Cotton himself looked up at some know-all telling him what he should do, and snapped: 'Will you *please* leave it to me.'

But on the par-5 13th the mist parted and a ray of light shone through. Cotton hit a good drive, found the greenside bunker with his second (no bad thing on a long hole) and blasted it out to within seven feet of the hole. A birdie putt at last! He made it, and the tension eased. But as he left the green he told 'Toots' that his legs were shaking. 'I can't go on,' he said. Her reply is not recorded, but according to 'Laddie' Lucas, leading amateur in the 1935 Open, 'she must have said something pretty severe'.

The birdie 'seemed to cheer me up', Cotton wrote later. His game jolted back into the brilliant groove of the previous few days, and when he birdied the 14th, 'Suez', where many a fine round had been sunk – he could see blue sky at last. He cruised the last few holes, all fairways and greens, and strolled down the 18th in holiday mood. When he missed a three-foot putt at the last it was that rare thing: a laughing matter. He had won the Open by five clear shots. 'So, with cheering and laughter,' said *The Times*, 'ended a round that must have seemed to Cotton the longest he has ever played.'

The crowd surrounded him in a sea of hats and smiles, hoisted him shoulder high and carted him to the clubhouse, 'Toots'

marching alongside. J. H. Taylor was near enough to ask him a
few questions for the *News of the World* (which now claimed an
enormous circulation in excess of three million) and was handed
some surprising answers. 'I was nearly beaten by indigestion,'
Cotton told him. Confident of victory, he told reporters that he
had eaten beef with spaghetti at lunch, and then gulped down a
merry bowl of ice cream – and paid a bitter price for breaking his
usual strict rules on such things.[3] 'Every time I pivoted I felt the
effect. It was like a knife sticking into my body.'

Reg Whitcombe, his partner, shook his head with a rueful
smile.

'You pivoted well enough, Henry,' he said.

How long had he been training for this championship, someone
asked.

'Since I was eleven.'

Since Cotton's own coat was in his car, miles away, he borrowed
a fetching brown camel number from Henry Longhurst, and
draped it over his plus fours and patterned V-neck to accept the
trophy and pose for the cameras. In the photographs we can see
him cradling the old jug, beaming fondly as though at a new-born
child. 'I do feel that our golf has been put back to the top again,'
he said, raising his voice. 'And that's the thing that really pleases
me more than anything else. It may do something to destroy the
impression in America that British golfers do not count very
much.' Who needed media-training experts? Cotton already
knew what to say at a time like this.

Longhurst was soon busy at the typewriter for the *Evening
Standard* and the *Sunday Times*, telling the world that 'the tide
of British golf has turned at last', and that it was a moral as well

---

[3] Fourteen years later, in *This Game of Golf* (1948), he would reject stories
about this spaghetti and ice-cream lunch, insisting that 'at such an important
moment I would be most unlikely to break my rules'. But it was widely
reported in the papers at the time, and J. H. Taylor was no scurrilous gossip-
merchant, but a senior champion of golf.

as athletic victory – 'the worthy result of long hours of practice'. He was fortunate to accompany Cotton back to the Guilford Hotel, the grand Edwardian pile on the edge of Sandwich Bay, a few hundred yards south of the third green, where the new champion was staying. The hotel was part of a complex that had been created (back in 1903) on land owned by Lord Guilford, one of the descendants of the original Lord North, Earl of Sandwich, Prime Minister in the late 18th century. A special narrow-gauge railway had been constructed along the shore from the mouth of the River Stour, to haul materials to the building which was soon looming over the beach in a tumble of turrets, arches and gables. It dominated the links and on a fine day, from an upstairs room, you could see France. In 1913 George Bernard Shaw had tried to woo the actress Mrs Patrick Campbell here, arguing that if they had children it might be an ideal combination – her beauty, his brains; she feared the opposite and rejected him. He didn't take it too badly: in 1914 he invented Eliza Doolittle in *Pygmalion* for her.

The hotel no longer stands, but it was to here that Cotton and Longhurst repaired that night. They sat in Cotton's bedroom, surrounded by 'sheaves' of telex messages and cablegrams, to chew over what had just happened. 'I attribute my success,' said the Open champion, shrugging off Longhurst's coat and kicking away his shoes, 'to one man – a French doctor.' He went on to amplify on the health problems from which he had long been suffering, and which had nearly wrecked his day. And he did not fail to grasp J. H. Taylor's point that the real culprit was pressure. 'The strain of a modern golf championship is terrible,' he admitted. 'I suppose it is a matter of nerves attacking one in one's weakest spot' – in his case, the stomach. In the old days he used to lose seven pounds in the course of a tournament and today, after that ill-advised lunch, he felt 'seasick'.

He picked up one of the messages that lay piled up on his bed – the one offering him $5,000 to go and play in America for a while – and told Longhurst that there was 'not a word of truth' in the stories that he might say yes. His contract with Royal

Waterloo stipulated that he would remain there for six months after the Open, so that was that.

Other papers were happy simply to bang the victory drum roll. 'There were years that were Jones's and years that were Hagen's,' cried the *Manchester Guardian*, 'and in between there was a Barnes or a Sarazen.' Aware of Cotton's roots in the North-West, the paper felt obliged to note that 'the Cheshire-born golfer had put British golf firmly on the map'. And it noticed, too, the historic link with Belgium: 'It gives Waterloo an association with another notable British victory.' The *Field* took a similar line: 'Cotton has killed the American bogey.' And so did the *Observer*: 'Since the Great War, American players have annexed [the Open] with such ease as to suggest they were involved in a kind of picnic.' Not any more. Henry Cotton had 'stepped into the ring' and shown everyone that Britain could still claim to be the home of golf.

No one was more pleased than J. H. Taylor. Before the event he had tipped Padgham to win, but in the *News of the World* he indulged himself with a rare show of pleasure and pride. Until now he had been modest, in public, about his own influence on Cotton's early career, but at last, bursting with pride in his former protégé, he came clean. 'I was instrumental in helping Cotton decide on golf as his profession,' he wrote, casting his mind back to the way a pushy engineer from somewhere up north had come to Royal Mid-Surrey and asked him take a close look at his two teenaged sons. 'I am glad that the advice I gave his father some years ago has been thoroughly justified.'

Another man who was still smiling the next morning was Henry Longhurst. So far as he could tell, 'every newspaper in the world' was printing the picture of Cotton at the moment of victory, which meant that 'millions of people' must have been sharing an identical thought: 'What a beautiful coat he's wearing.' Since the coat was his own, borrowed on the spur of the moment, he had earned the right to this sly in-joke.

The morning after the night before, alongside a jubilant match report ('All's Well that Ends Well') *The Times*, the *Evening Standard* and several other newspapers published a display advertisement for Dunlop, whose ball Cotton, along with the second- and third-placed golfers, had used. The illustration was a facsimile of a note in which Cotton said that the ball helped 'very considerably ... its colossal length and accuracy are marvellous'. He signed off with a flourish, giving as his address the Guildford (sic) Hotel.

One of the other guests in the hotel was Harry Vardon, who had not been on the links that day. The master had suffered his first bout of tuberculosis back in 1903, and had never truly got over it; it shadowed him for the rest of his days. That morning's attack meant that even the short stroll to his spot by the sixth green was beyond him, but Cotton took the claret jug up to Vardon's room to show him what he had done. Vardon looked at his own name, engraved six times into the antique silver. Not much was said; nothing needed saying. Vardon's keen old eyes filled, and so did Cotton's. It was one of those moments.

That notice in the newspapers was the beginning of a historic relationship. In honour of the record-breaking second round Dunlop launched a new ball named the Dunlop 65, which went on to dominate the golfing world for decades. The champion was paid £150 a year to promote it, an arrangement that was now routine – Vardon himself had sold his name to an 1899 gutta-percha Spalding ball known as the 'Vardon Flyer'. In due course Cotton would earn £40,000 from this, a tidy sum; but by modern standards he may have sold himself short. Years later he called it 'the worst deal I ever made'.

The iconic Dunlop 65, with its echo of Cotton's great round, is only a memory now; the company website fails even to mention how it came into being. But of all the ways in which that famous ball influenced the game of golf, few can match the starring role it played in a bravura piece of fictional action. The tense playoff between James Bond and Auric Goldfinger, in which Bond outwits the arch-fiend, is played on links ('Royal St Mark's') that are a barely disguised portrait of Royal St George's. Ian Fleming was a keen member of the club and, in the year of his death, the captain-elect. The description of the course in *Goldfinger* – the stretch of 'shaven seaside turf' that leads to the first tee – is clearly the Sandwich links, and the caddie master, Alfred Blacking, is a none too subtle version of the real-life Albert Whiting. Fleming himself was staying at the Guilford Hotel when he suffered his fatal heart attack in 1964. And the ball at the centre of the decisive dispute between Bond and Goldfinger is – as if in a coded tribute to Cotton – none other than a Dunlop 65.

Eulogies to Cotton hummed in from around the world. *Golfing Magazine* reported that he had 'eclipsed anything that has ever been seen since golf began'. J. H. Taylor's piece for the *News of the World* was titled: 'How Cotton Smashed the Records'. And Longhurst waxed lyrical in the *Sunday Times*. 'There is no one alive,' he said, 'who could have been less than eight shots behind Cotton after his first three rounds.' Though he stumbled at the end it had still been an amazing week: 'the finest exhibition of the game as it should be played that has ever been seen'.

The *Observer* spoke for many in seeing it chiefly as a victory over America, and, as is often the way, resorted to the language of combat to make the point. 'Cotton has put so effective a spoke in the enemy's wheel that I doubt whether he will recover from the shock for many years to come.' A rather more magnanimous word came from Bobby Jones, who said: 'It is difficult to conceive of the superb play by which he achieved his victory. I well remember the Sandwich course. I could never break 70. I wish I had been there – but against that kind of golf maybe it is just as well I am safely at home.'

CHAPTER ELEVEN

Silence in Court

On the Wednesday after Australia's defeat at Lord's, the very day that Cotton was putting together his fabulous first round at Sandwich, several Australian players went to Wimbledon to cheer on Jack Crawford, with whom they had become friendly on the voyage over. But even though Bradman, Brown, Chipperfield and Kippax sat on Centre Court in suits, ties, overcoats and hats to ward off the dismal Pommie weather, it wasn't enough to ward off the virus ripping through the championships. The *Daily Sketch* was calling it a 'mystery illness'; the *Evening Standard* preferred 'summer flu'. It was left to the *Birmingham Post* to come up with 'Wimbledon throat'. It was an epidemic. The *Evening Standard* asked an 'eminent doctor' what was going on, and learned that it was a form of 'follicular tonsillitis' brought on by the hot dusty weather. An ambulance station was set up to provide 'gargles and treatments'. Permanganate of potash, mixed with salt and bicarbonate of soda, was warmly recommended.

It was a nasty ailment: in Chipperfield's case it was being described (in the Australian papers) as a 'violent bilious attack'. As if being laid low by Verity wasn't sickening enough. The cricketers headed north to Manchester for the third Test in a fragile state; Bradman, confined to his bed, was obliged to rely on a substitute fielder.

Wimbledon had been getting ready for weeks. There was a new stand over Courts 2 and 3; tall chairs (six feet high) had been installed to give the umpires a better view; an invasion of leatherjackets (the grub of the daddy-longlegs) had been repelled, and a lot of work had been done on the grass to protect it from drought. For the first time ever, a firm of bookmakers was being allowed to operate in the sacred precincts, and in an even more controversial breakthrough, lady players were permitted to wear shorts. One LTA official thought this made for 'a disgusting sight', and didn't care who knew it; but the players themselves were enthusiastic: they were athletes, not models.

When the seedings were announced, Perry stood at the foot of the draw as the number two seed. The favourite was last year's champion, Jack Crawford, and it didn't matter that Perry had just beaten him twice in a row: Wimbledon saw other championships as of no great significance compared to itself. And there was another reason: Perry was carrying an injury. It was only a few weeks earlier, in the quarter-final in Paris that he had twisted his ankle in a way that left him 'crying out in pain'. It made headlines in Australia, where hopes were high for a Crawford double. But Perry had made a decent recovery after hopping home on one leg and a stick, and, a week before Wimbledon, played a set or two with Dan Maskell (the Davis Cup coach, later the voice of the BBC), who reported that the great white hope was playing 'absolutely tip-top tennis'. In Maskell's view, the injured ankle would play no great part – in fact he reckoned that he had given Perry a workout every bit as stern as anything he might encounter in the tournament itself.

So far as the public was concerned Perry had a big chance. Sir Francis Gordon Lowe, the Baronet who wrote on tennis for the *News of the World*, felt that he was good for a semi-final, at least, while Helen Wills Moody saw him as the man everyone had to beat. 'Ask the question this year,' wrote Stanley Doust (ex-captain of Australia's Davis Cup team) in the *Daily Mail*, 'and nine out of ten people will answer: Perry, of course!' The *Sunday Times* concurred. Under the headline 'Perry Can Win', it advised that Perry was 'one of the greatest all court players England has produced'. All he had to do was curb his 'natural impetuosity', and anything was possible.

Dorothy Round was more than entitled to fancy her chances, too. She had lost the final the previous year, to Helen Wills Moody, but the champion was absent this year, and, in reaching the final, Round had done well enough to be hailed as 'every inch a world player' by the *Sydney Morning Herald*. By now she was a public figure: as far back as 1932 she had delivered a speech on the importance of church in the lives of the young people to a Methodist congregation of 10,000 at the Albert Hall. Her rasping forehand was a formidable weapon, but it was widely felt that her Sabbatarian refusal to play on Sundays gave her a spiritual head start: the *Daily Telegraph* said that 'the moral advantage was hers'. Chosen to play for England against France in 1933, she noticed that the final matches were due to be played on the Sunday, and took her usual stand. The tickets had already been sold, and there was a flurry of administrative vexation ... but she stood firm, and the games were duly played on the Monday.

The first day was grey and sultry, with rain threatening, but a record crowd of 33,000 jostled into the arena to watch play commence on the flawless, billiard-table courts. Perry was coming into Wimbledon on the verge of a mighty treble, after his marvellous victories in America and Australia. And these days he was a perfectionist who left nothing to chance. He wouldn't even drive a car, on the grounds that it might affect his vision and focal range, and he kept his right hand stuck in his pocket to avoid shaking hands with strangers and risking a strain. Some players liked a massage before games, but Perry saw relaxation as the enemy, preferring to remain tense and wound up. And he never watched games that preceded his own, fearing they would distract him from the task in hand. At the All England Club he would sometimes while away the hours before his matches on the putting green at Wimbledon Park, just across the road.

His first match pitched him against Raymond Tucky, the sort of opponent he liked: a Public Schools champion, a Cambridge Blue and a Lieutenant in the Royal Engineers. He was the kind of chap Wimbledon liked, too – indeed, the members knew him well, because his mother had won the doubles back in 1913. But the public was here to see Perry, and he showed little mercy, winning the third (last) set 6-0. The *Morning Post* thought it a 'patchy display' marred by some 'foozled volleys', but it wasn't close.

The second round saw him taking on another of Wimbledon's favoured sons. The child of a wealthy family in Philadelphia, Dick Williams was a melodramatic story in his own right. As a boy he had survived the sinking of the *Titanic* (his father was not so lucky) and had gone on to captain the US Davis Cup team. At 43, however, he was two decades slower than the Englishman, and it showed: Perry lost only four games. He was 'never in difficulty', according to *The Times*, but for once he didn't rub it in. It was a one-sided but good-humoured game ('a smiling encounter') played in friendly spirit. The *Daily Telegraph*, quoting Alexander Pope, said the players seemed eager 'to make men happy and keep them so'. It was just as well: the air above Wimbledon was still grey and oozing water, with veils of drizzle drifting across the court.

The great drought had broken at last. On both the Wednesday and the Thursday play was suspended from time to time – all 'most unsummerlike', sighed the *Telegraph*. Worse, it was 'inimical to fluent footwork'. And the bad weather had another effect, promoting the outbreak of coughing and spluttering that was cutting a swathe through both players and spectators. Four of Thursday's matches had to be postponed because of sickness in the changing-room; more were abandoned when 20 umpires reported sick. It didn't discourage the crowd, though. On that Thursday, with Perry set to play Menzel, there was, noted *The Times*, 'neither a seat nor standing room to spare'.

This third-round match was Perry's first real test since it brought him up against Menzel, a giant with a kick on his serve 'as big as a house', in Perry's description. And he came from a part of the world – Czechoslovakia – that brought to mind a vanished empire, the great, gilded Austro-Hungarian dynasty that had sunk with the First World War. Czechoslovakia was a young country – only 16 years old – and no one yet knew what to make of it.

In the early exchanges, Perry, nervous about his ankle, played within himself and lost the set to love – a shock to the system. The crowd was tense, and the mood seemed to paralyse the English star: he could do nothing to counter Menzel's juddering serve. Up in the stands his doctor, Hugh Dempster, saw him moving gingerly and sent down a note: 'Either you go for the wide ones or I pull you off the court.' Perry hadn't realised how much he was holding back (the next day's papers would say he came 'perilously close' to losing) so this woke him up. He gave himself a talking to and fought his way back into the game. As Menzel tired in the latter stages, worn out by his own big serve, Perry clicked himself into a new gear and waltzed away with the fifth set.

At the weekend the now-traditional queue began to form along the undulating road outside the main entrance. As usual, the All England Club was holding back tickets for sale on the day, and this year people seemed to be especially willing to camp out all night in the hope of grabbing one. They brought coats, umbrellas, cushions and flasks of tea, and settled in for an all-night picnic, with card games on upturned boxes and pipe smoke in the air. By breakfast there were hundreds of them jostling in the road outside the entrance (in an orderly and polite English fashion, of course).

But by this time the weather had changed. The sun was beating down again, and there was no need for waterproofs – in fact there were dozens of fainting cases. It was the day after Cotton's great victory in Kent, so the papers were already shrill with good news. And King George V and Queen Mary were due at Wimbledon, so all was right with the world. Perry's opponent was Adrian Quist, a fine young Australian who, though a smart prospect, was not nearly so daunting as Menzel. Some pundits were still tempted to nit-pick when it came to Perry's style: *The Times* was not impressed by his constant preference for passing shots, arguing that while they *looked* smart, the lob had 'always been recognised as a sound reply to the advancing volleyer'. But no one could argue with the result. Perry swatted Quist aside as if he were an irritating insect.

If *The Times* also noticed 'a strange lack of excitement in the crowded galleries', this was not to do with an overt lack of enthusiasm for Perry, but down to the fact that there was so little drama or suspense to quicken the pulse. There was something rather cold and relentless about such one-sided tennis. But not all the papers were frosty: in the *Sunday Times* Quist was 'outclassed … made to look like a plucky novice', while Perry's form made him 'in the opinion of many, the best player in the world'. Don't speak too soon and all that, they seemed to be saying, but our man was playing 'well-nigh perfect' tennis. Better still, he was part of a wonderful double, since Henry Cotton had just given the nation an Open champion after a similar wait. 'Britain's Great Day At Golf And Tennis' sighed the *Daily Mail*, and many other journals did the same.

Some observers, however, refused to be impressed. A letter in the *Morning Post* on the Monday railed against the behaviour of one 'prominent' player, and there wasn't much doubt whom it had in mind. The letter was published in a ruled box in the centre of the page, beneath a picture of Perry playing Quist, and the headline was pointed – 'Manners On The Court'. The writer claimed to have been 'astonished' to see a 'caper of exultation' from this player. He was 'dumbfounded' by such 'antics', which left him 'unable to applaud', and thought that 'many people would rather see our players defeated than that any of them should let down the one-time tradition of British sportsmanship'.

With Bodyline so fresh in the memory, it is not surprising that the author was so keen to promote the 'one-time tradition' of British fair play. The high-minded, may-the-best-man-win culture still had traction, however gravely and often it was breached. And while we can suspect that this Corinthian reflex was widely dishonoured even in its prime (W. G. Grace himself was famous for his combative approach to the rules) it is possible that there *was* something new in the air. In sports like golf and tennis, the win-at-all-costs attitude was still a novelty; even cricket, which had embraced professionals for decades, continued to be dominated by amateur ways of thinking – too much so for some tastes. In being keener to win than to make friends, Perry, like Cotton, Hagen and quite a few others, was challenging the comfortable status quo. The balance between his approach and the amateur path was shifting fast, and not everyone liked it.

As it happens, Perry was by no means alone in wearing his feelings on his sleeve. The impeccably schooled Bunny Austin, in the course of losing to America's Frank Shields, committed a far worse breach of etiquette when he actually kicked his racket into the crowd, an unthinkably ill-tempered gesture for which he apologised in the *Evening News*. 'I am more upset about that than I am about my defeat,' he said.

Perry's next opponent was George Lott, an American Davis Cupper and doubles specialist who had won the US Championship four times, on No. 1 Court. With a semi-final spot up for grabs, both players fought like lions. Lott had beaten De Stefani in the previous round, depriving Perry of the chance to gain revenge for that incident in Paris – and proved a difficult opponent, volleying his way to victory in the second set to square things up. And the next two sets were tight as well. In winning them both – 7-5 and 10-8 – Perry showed a level of endurance and patience many people thought he did not possess. 'I don't think I have ever played better,' he said – and he wasn't being falsely modest. His game, his fitness, his speed and his appetite for victory were propelling him to a new level – he was now more than a match for anyone. And aside from that first-set hurricane kicked up by Menzel, he hadn't really been stretched yet. Things, thought *The Times*, were looking 'decidedly interesting'.

On semi-finals day the midsummer air turned tropical. A cloudless sky parked itself over south London, and a sweltering sun sizzled over the courts. A *News Chronicle* cartoon depicted the players as melting, like figures in a Dalí painting, above the caption: 'We would have drawn more, but the heat became so intense we went up in spontaneous combustion.' The Australian cricketers, happier under a sun-kissed sky, came back to watch Crawford's semi-final, and were given lunch by the Committee. The public gates, meanwhile, had to be pushed shut on yet another capacity crowd. 'Elbow to elbow,' said the *Evening Standard*, 'stood a mass of expectant people.'

Perry had always found Sidney Wood a tricky proposition – he had lost in the semi-finals to him back in 1931, a tournament Wood went on to win when Shields defaulted in the final with an injured ankle. The American had a nonchalant manner that seemed to rile Perry – *he* wanted to be the coolest cat out there. But on the morning of this new game Perry delivered a generous assessment of his opponent in the *Evening News*, admitting that 'when Sidney is in full cry there is very little to be done about it' and reminding readers that Wood had given the author 'a severe trouncing' back in 1932.

Once again the crowd was quiet – 'strangely subdued', in the words of *The Times* – on this occasion thanks to the 'air of tension and anxiety' created by the rare hope of a British finalist. Crawford was first on court, making short work of Shields to reach his second consecutive final. And though he was not in his usual elegant form – he had been struggling since the quarters with 'Wimbledon throat' (and it might not have helped that he was a devoted smoker) – he marched safely on. Could Perry join him?

For four closely fought sets of staccato rallies he fought with 'calm deliberation' as the match teetered to and from. Neither man could gain the upper hand for long. When it went to a fifth set the crowd, seeing Perry beginning to totter as Wood sauntered to the net and polished off his volleys, found its voice at last, cheering every home point. And at 4-3 in the decider Perry went for broke, landing what *The Times* called 'two of the most glorious passing shots of the day'. He was serving for the match now, and though the *coup de grâce* came with a net cord, no one cared.

He was in the final.

It was very good news for the touts. Four tickets for the final, with a face value of two pounds, could now be sold for twenty. And Perry's win was a job-creation scheme in other ways. A long queue was already snaking back along Church Road, complete with the usual camping stools, mattresses made from cardboard and newspaper, draughts boards, brollies and cigarettes. Among the throng moved Sergeant J. B. Hamilton, proud holder of the Victoria Cross he had won at Ypres. For a small consideration he was willing to act as a 'seat-keeper' should anyone wish to leave the queue for any reason.

The day of the final, Friday, was another scorcher, with not a cloud in sight; it was easily hot enough to drive away the memory of that dull first week. As the sun warmed the tennis precincts, half a dozen workmen pushed a fat iron roller across the gleaming turf. In the sunlight the famous grass looked bare, but the staff were busy making sure that it had the fresh, sappy bounce that made lawn tennis such a fast and appealing spectator sport. It was, said the *Guardian*, 'a very dream of an afternoon'.

Some 20-odd photographers took their places at the front of the stands, crouched in front of row upon row of people fanning themselves with newspapers, creating a shimmer of expectation. Back then, most papers were restrained when it came to discussing events that had not yet taken place – they were there to report events, not promote them, contenting themselves with the line that F. J. Perry and J. H. Crawford would contest the 'Gentleman's Singles final' that day, after the mixed. But the *Manchester Guardian* thought the players well matched – Crawford offering 'flint to Perry's steel' – and while it reserved its most lyrical phrases for the Englishman ('How swift in action, how dazzling at the net …') it overlooked the fact that Australia was now an independent dominion and recorded its pleasure that Crawford's presence meant there were 'no foreigners in the final'.

Both men wore long trousers, and Crawford wore long sleeves as well. It was rather racy of Perry to bare his bronzed forearms, and it was clear that he intended to press his old enemy from the word go. He took Crawford to three deuces in a hard-fought first game, and the Australian needed a trio of aces to save three game points. Perry responded by racing through his own service game, winning it to love; and then he set about Crawford's serve again. He looked dangerously purposeful, all business. But Crawford was not the champion for nothing. He was winning the longer rallies – no easy task against Perry – and it looked as though his superior experience would tell when he broke serve in the fourth game for a 3-1 lead. The crowd leaned forward.

Far from unsettling Perry, the setback seemed to galvanise him. He broke back at once, thanks to some stinging passing shots, and went on to win his own serve to love. The set was all square at 3-3. The next game, known to some as the 'vital seventh', was indeed decisive. Crawford tried to take the initiative by advancing to the net, but Perry cracked a couple of backhands past him to reach 15-40. Crawford fought his way back to deuce, but then staggered. Two quick mistakes later, the Australian was 3-4 down and looking, according to the *Guardian*, thoughtful.

This time Perry drove home his advantage, battering Crawford's serve to win another game to love: Crawford fell tamely in the end, with a double fault, to lose the set 6-3. F. J. Perry, of Stockport and England, had won five straight games in what seemed like the blink of an eye.

It was a tremendous start, but both players knew that it was only the beginning. Perry marched past the umpire's chair – no breaks for towels, drinks and a sit-down in this austere age – and prepared to serve again. Crawford readied himself. A modern player in his position might go for a 'comfort break' at a time like this, or send for a physio. That wasn't the done thing in 1934. With no time to regain his balance, Crawford back-pedalled like a boxer as the second set flashed past him in a blur of aces, returns, drives, volleys and smashes. Crawford had no answer to any of it. In a fiery blizzard of what the LTA called 'world-beating tennis, such as has never before been seen from Perry', the boy from Ealing seized the second set 6-0, dropping eight points. 'The Australian had no adequate weapon,' reported the LTA, 'to check Perry's onslaught.'

All Perry could say later was that 'during that wonderful 20 minutes I could do nothing wrong'. He knew that the trick with Crawford was to 'run him about a little', so when he saw backhands coming high over the net ('volleyable') he blitzed them. Crawford was somewhat 'below his best' – it was no secret that he had succumbed to the flu – but a final was no place to make allowances, and chivalry had never been Perry's strong suit anyway.[1] On his own admission he 'didn't smile once' as he belted the ball at the corners. 'I don't think I have ever played better,' he told the *Manchester Guardian*, 'and I don't think I ever will.' This was exactly what he had said after his game against Menzel, but he really had raised his game again. In his 1936 memoir he insisted: 'I never played better tennis than I did against Jack Crawford in that final.'

There was no resting between sets either, but somehow, without a break, Crawford was able to fight back and make a better fist of things as the match continued. He found the range with a few passing shots, chased and scrabbled, changed the rhythm of the game with lobs, and managed to break Perry's serve to take a 5-4 lead when a forehand hit the top of the net and fell kindly. The crowd rose in applause; the English public liked players who battled when they were down, and also liked close matches – some of them had been queueing half the night and wanted more than three quick sets for their pains. But the public display of sympathetic affection for Crawford roused Perry to angry new heights, and a series of raking drives brought him to match point.

The end was a damp squib. Having stumbled to love-40 on his own serve, Crawford foot-faulted and miscued to hand the title to

[1] He even made a point, when volleying, of playing the ball directly in front of his own body, so the ball would be hard to see against the sight-screen of his white shirt.

the man who was now, beyond question, the world's best player. He gave what Perry called a 'scornful little bow' to the line judge, and that was that. The winner did a trim cartwheel and leapt over the net, feet together like a long-jumper, to shake hands with the loser.[2] And for the first time in a quarter of a century Britain had a home champion.

In truth, the ending was of little consequence – the jig had been up for a while. It was Perry's third victory in a row over Crawford in a major final, and the pundits were hard put to think of a single thing the Australian could have done to prevent it. In the view of the LTA journal, the crowd, too, was 'momentarily dumbfounded', so the joy of a home win was tinged with a palpable sense of anticlimax. It had taken only 72 minutes; it was almost too easy. 'No final rally,' sighed the *Telegraph*, 'no breathless suspense, no deafening clamour.' After a few moments, however, it began to dawn on the crowd that something historic had just been decided, and the spectators began to roar out their approval: 'All the pent-up feeling broke loose,' reported the LTA journal. As he left the court, Perry was 'rapturously cheered'.

He was soon telling reporters what it felt like. 'What I have done today means more to me from a patriotic sense than as a personal success,' he said. 'Now for the Davis Cup ...' For his part, Crawford lived up to his 'Gentleman Jack' sobriquet by insisting that Perry was 'tireless ... like streak lightning. There was no holding him.' He even added that 'England could not have found a better sporting champion'.

Plenty of onlookers echoed that view. Helen Wills Moody spoke for many when she wrote, in the *Daily Mail* the next morning, that Perry was 'without doubt ... the best singles player in the world today'.

---

[2] This bravura vault over the net was no whim. It was a Perry trademark, designed to show beaten opponents that he was still full of zest – 'one of my methods of injecting a little gamesmanship,' he wrote. To his critics, it smacked rather of 'rubbing it in'.

The *Telegraph* joined the charge – 'Tennis Title Home after 25 Years' – in tones that echoed up and down Fleet Street. 'Britain's Comeback After 25 Years,' smiled the *Daily Sketch*. The *Observer* ('Perry Puts Britain On Top Once More') added that Perry 'was heartily applauded, and should have been applauded even more heartily'. The *Daily Mirror* gave over its entire front page to the story, beneath the banner headline: 'Perry World Tennis Champion'. It also featured a picture of the champ being carried down the stone steps of Ealing Town Hall – 'Shoulder High in Triumph' – in front of a massive crowd of local supporters, including a sprinkling of smiling bobbies and, somewhere in there, his own father. The Mayor and Mayoress were present, too; it was a fully-fledged street party. A tired looking Perry did his best to wave and smile. 'It was sheer luck,' he shrugged. 'I happened to hit the lines, and he happened to hit the net.' When asked what his plans were he shrugged: 'I want to relax by playing golf.'

'I firmly believe,' wrote Gordon Lowe in the *News of the World*, 'no Englishman previously has produced such remarkable tennis.' The *Mirror* proudly called Perry 'a Middlesex club player', as if that added lustre to the achievement (in truth, it was journalistic code for his being an ordinary sort of chap) and hailed 'a brand of play unprecedented in its mastery and precision'. Noting that his 12-game hot streak in the middle of the match was a new Wimbledon record, the paper felt that such a show of superiority, 'against a man of Crawford's class', was truly extraordinary. This was pretty much the unanimous view. Perry hadn't just won; he had made history. *The Times*, while sparing a thought for 'so likeable a loser',[3] felt 'no one was prepared for the brilliance of Perry's game'; it was 'tennis that only wizards play … he could put neither foot nor racket wrong'.

---

[3] This chivalrous tone was appreciated on the other side of the world. In Tasmania, the *Advocate* was able to console readers that the mood was 'very subdued … owing to the tragic ending to the match, and also to the great popularity of Crawford'.

In a peevish aside it did mention that he had played with 'almost American intensity', as if this were a black mark, but for the most part the top people's paper lavished praise on its new hero. His victory, ran the editorial, would 'delight the great body of tennis players in this country, and the general public too. And it will give British players a better conceit of themselves.' Cotton's feat was not forgotten. He and Perry were 'destroying the legend of American invincibility'.

Typically, *The Times* also took the opportunity to bang an old drum and hope that, in slaying their respective dragons, Perry and Cotton would silence the 'ultra-patriots' who had become obsessed with winning these trophies for King and Country. 'A game is a game,' it reminded its readers. 'If sport ceases to be followed in a sporting spirit, then it will be high time to put a stop to international competitions altogether.' It was a slightly distorted way to celebrate winning – to be gladdened by the way it might put an end to the boring obsession with winning – but that was how things were.

The LTA tried not to be 'ultra' about anything, but it, too, was proud of what Perry had done, and happy to use his success as a riposte to the moaners who liked belittling home talent. His victory was a bold reply to 'the pessimists who have for so long bewailed British decadence in lawn tennis', it declared. Perry had put a much-needed boot into 'the legend of overseas invincibility'. In a serious aside it acknowledged that his rise was 'meteoric', was delighted to report that Crawford had been 'outplayed in every department' and held up its own hand: 'Frankly, many of us had not believed that Perry had such tennis in him. On Friday he never put a foot wrong.'

The LTA journal's best comment on the match, however, came from a Cambridge Blue who happened to have taken his stopwatch to the final. He had timed the entire match, and thought his fellow LTA members might be interested to know that the first game took 86 seconds, the second 70, the third 215, and so on. It was all neatly lined up and set down. The longest game was five minutes seven seconds; the shortest 40 seconds. The writer repeated his hope that this would prove gripping and signed off, sincerely … H. M. Abrahams. Readers could only gasp. Harold Abrahams was a luminous star, the 100-metre gold medallist at the 1924 Olympics (the legendary sprint in *Chariots of Fire*). So it didn't matter that the time it took to play tennis was of no importance. Harold Abrahams was a man for whom the stopwatch was the highest arbiter of athletic endeavour – perhaps its only true measure. The thought of him sitting through the final, clicking and unclicking the watch in his lap, was a treat in itself.

CHAPTER TWELVE

The Champion's Tale

The story of the 1934 Wimbledon final has a curious ending. It should have been the crowning moment of Fred Perry's life so far, but the next hour was numbing. There was no formal presentation of the trophy in these polite days – players simply gathered up their gear and walked off. So within minutes Perry was soaking in a bath in the dressing-room, letting the significance of his achievement sink in. That's when he heard a voice that turned the hot water icy. He knew it well: it was Brame Hillyard, of the All England Club's Committee. Back in 1930, in the second round (on Court 10, if memory served) Perry had marked the fact that Hillyard was the first man to wear shorts at the All England Club by beating him in straight sets. Now the same man had come to present Perry with a club tie – in this hallowed heart of the amateur game there was no prize money beyond a notional £10 for expenses. The occasion called for a symbolic something, though, and Hillyard had brought chilled champagne.

Perry froze when he heard Hillyard greeting Crawford. 'Congratulations,' he told the Australian. 'This was one day when the best man didn't win.' In Perry's absence he handed the bottle to the loser, draped the winner's tie over the back of a chair, and left.

It was a situation that might have sat better in a West End farce. Perry jumped out of the bathtub, wrapped a towel around his waist and marched out to find Crawford with the champagne bottle that was rightfully his. It was baffling: he had a distinct memory of having thrashed Gentleman Jack a minute earlier. Now, in his moment of glory, this ...

'I don't think I've ever been so angry in my life,' he said later.

He knew he was not the kind of fellow the upper-class All England types thought of as a champion – and Hillyard was certainly part of the club's inner circle: his father had been Secretary of the All England Club for years, and played a leading role in the creation of the new Centre Court. Perry was, as we have seen, not that sort of chap. But he never expected his victory to be greeted with a shoulder quite this cold. It left him 'almost in tears'. Somehow he managed to hide his feelings and share a glass of fizz with Crawford (though in truth he was not a habitual drinker) but inside he was seething. 'My paranoia about the old-school-tie brigade surfaced with a vengeance.'

Modern players face a barrage of interviews, ice baths and massages at times like this, but Perry was under no such pressure. He summoned the Secretary of the Lawn Tennis Association, Anthony Sabelli, and declared squarely that if he did not receive a full apology from Hillyard he would withdraw from Britain's Davis Cup match against the United States, which was only three weeks away. Then he raced off to celebrate.

As he reached the centre of London, driving his own car – no fleet of limousines in those days – his spirits rose when he saw, on every news-stand placard, a single word.

Fred!

It was true. He really had done it.

Then it was away to the bright lights for the kind of party London was becoming famous for. The harsh consequences of economic misery were, as always, not evenly experienced: it was all right for some. The notorious 'hard-faced men' had done all right in the war, and others were now determined to enjoy life to the full, too. The flapper-era fun of the twenties had given way to a louche age of jazz-age cocktails and nightclubs. Gentlemen in black tie and ladies in ball gowns glided through the palaces of Mayfair and Westminster, with the first generation of press

photographers waiting to pop flashbulbs in their pretty faces. It
was a swell place for a celebration such as this.

The dinner reservation was – where else? – at the Savoy Hotel,
the scene, only weeks earlier, of the post-Derby mêlée, elephant
and all. And his date was Henry Cotton, the only man in the
entire country who knew how Perry felt, having just reclaimed
for Britain another prize thought to be beyond the reach of home-
grown players. Cotton was an inch closer to the establishment
than Perry (the papers called him 'the public school golfer') but
he, too, was brash, pushy, and not always a popular figure in his
own sport. He was a touch too single-minded and ambitious – not
quite a gentleman, what?

Another compelling fact about Cotton, so far as Perry
was concerned, was that he was a professional in a game run
by amateurs, and thus came up against many of the same
strictures Perry himself chafed against. After his treatment on
this momentous day Perry was tempted, in a rush of hang-it-all
excitement, to sign up as a professional, take the money and run as
far and as hard as he could; but the thought of having to miss out
on Wimbledon and the Davis Cup was a tough one – these were
big events to skip. In turning pro, Cotton may have had to avoid
clubhouses, but he never had to contemplate missing the Open.

But all that could wait. Tonight was for clinking glasses, patting
one another on the back, scanning the menu and toasting the fact
that Henry Cotton had – by just a few days – 'pipped me in our
personal rivalry about who would win the big prize'. The two of
them had a long-standing bet (£10) on which of them would be
the first to lay this bogey, and Cotton had won – just. It would be
Perry's pleasure to pay up.

The hotel insisted on footing the bill – it was fun, this winning
lark – and even gave them a pair of tickets for the neighbouring
theatre (the Savoy was famous as the home of D'Oyly Carte's
Gilbert and Sullivan productions). The production that night was
a historical saga, *Clive of India*, described on the posters as 'A
Play of Youth, Adventure and Romance'. By the time they fell

out into the Strand, just round the corner from the Cenotaph, the pale memorial to the fallen of the Great War built by Lutyens in Whitehall in 1920, Perry was exhausted. He had to get to Eastbourne, he said. He was expected to join the Davis Cup team in Sussex.

Perry's own autobiography described the remainder of that hectic night in lively detail, and his account of what transpired has been repeated in almost everything ever written about his life. So this is not a new story. But it still has the power to twitch hairs on the back of one's neck. The top-hatted doorman of the Savoy had seen plenty of gentlemen in Perry's tipsy condition, and it was clear that he could not possibly drive to Sussex.[1] He gamely volunteered to take the wheel himself, an offer that was gratefully accepted. When they arrived it was starting to get light, and all Perry wanted to do was tumble into bed. But there was a policeman waiting for him, with interesting news.

Had Sir forgotten? His appointment at Wimbledon later that day? The Mixed Doubles final ... surely it hadn't slipped his mind. The King was looking forward to it.

This time there was a police escort to clear the route into London, and as they neared Wimbledon they found roads covered with sand to create a clean surface for the royal party. Large crowds lined the route, hoping for a glimpse of them. Perry stared out, amazed, and doffed his hat – 'the least I could do, in the circumstances'.

His father brought fresh clothes for the presentation ceremony, but first Perry had to clean up. He jumped through a bath, shaved 'at breakneck speed' and rushed up to the royal box to meet Their Majesties. It had been an unusual night and he was, he had to

---

[1] The evening of his Wimbledon triumph was one of the few occasions when Perry drank. His father was an 'ardent' temperance activist, and Perry abstained, too, most of the time – 'my ambition was to be the fittest man in my sport, and you can't be that if you are burning the candle at both ends'. In Paris he went by the nickname 'Monsieur Lemonade'.

admit, 'swaying a bit'. Showing great consideration, the King urged him to sit down.

While all this was going on, Dorothy Round was writing her own name into tennis history. She was playing another American, Helen Jacobs, a pioneer of the 'bare leg craze' (though Round had experimented with shorts, today she was wearing a split skirt – 'because it was my fancy to do so'). And for the second day running the stands were packed in the hope of another home triumph. By now Round's backhand was 'the best of any woman now playing' (*Manchester Guardian*) – so, if anything, she was the favourite. A buzzing audience, many of them women, had been queuing outside for the best part of 24 hours to see history being made on the Centre Court – it had been eight long years since an English woman held the title, and much longer since Britain had both crowns at once – for *that* one had to return all the way to the year of Perry's birth, 1909.

It was a hard fight. Round won the first set decisively (only two games went to deuce) but Jacobs took the second 5-7 as Round's usually reliable forehand began to wobble. At last the crowd had something to push them to the edge of their seats. In an early instance of what would soon become routine, some wag yelled, 'Come on, Dorothy!' at a tense moment, with Jacobs holding two match points. Round battled back to win a final set that included what the *Sunday Times* called 'some of the finest tennis ever seen in a women's final'. When Round won she ran to the net and burst into tears. 'I am too happy to speak,' she said. 'It is wonderful.' The crowd 'rose as one and cheered and cheered', said the newspapers, and the King and Queen clapped and grinned along with the rest of them. Her parents had come up from Dudley and felt weak. 'I would not go through this again for £50,' groaned her father.

It was, shouted the *News of the World*, 'the greatest double event there has ever been in English sport'. Should anyone be wondering when Britain repeated this double, the answer is … never: 1934 remains the last time that this sort of lightning struck twice.

Round didn't have time to change before being hustled up to the royal box to meet the King, the Queen and the new men's champion, F. J. Perry. In Perry's account, they all chatted for a few moments; then it was time to get down to business in the Mixed Doubles. But Round was still shaking with excitement after winning her final. If Perry was feeling a tad morning-after-the-night-before, he was better off than his partner. She was drained. The thrill of victory was giving way to an attack of the shivers.

'I don't know what I'm going to do,' she whispered. 'I don't know how I'm going to hit a single solitary ball. I scarcely know where I am.'

The newly crowned men's champion took confident charge. 'Fine,' he said. 'Stay in the tramlines as much as possible, and I'll do the rest.'

He was as good as his word. Somehow, the two of them 'hung in there' and managed to win the match and the title.

All of this is narrated in solemn detail in *Fred Perry: An Autobiography*, which was written in association with (another way of saying 'by') Ronald Atkin, the *Observer*'s tennis correspondent.[2] A very remarkable story it is too. Sadly, it is not true. The record books are clear: this is not what happened. Perry and Round did indeed meet the King and Queen in the royal box, and the ceremony was faithfully recorded in the LTA journal and many other newspapers. The Monday morning *Times* printed a photograph of them beside the monarch, who was decked out in summer togs: bow tie and straw hat. According to the *Daily Telegraph* ('A Perfect Day for English Sport') Perry was very much present to watch Miss Round's 'almost perfect all-court game'.

The King and Queen were marking their 41st wedding anniversary of the day before with a nice afternoon at the tennis, and a pair of British winners made a very fine gift.

---

[2] Not surprisingly, the story is repeated, with a hint that it might be somewhat too good to be true, in Jon Henderson's biography of Perry, *The Last Champion: The Life of Fred Perry* (2009).

But here is the thing. Only one of the champions was due back on court, and it wasn't Perry. He wasn't even *in* the doubles. He and Round did win the Mixed in 1935 *and* 1936, but on this occasion, the 1934 championships, they did not even enter. This was Round's day, not his; *she* was the one destined to make the headlines this time. Not long after leaving the royal box she was marching back out on Centre Court with Ryuki Miki, of Japan.

The crowd was in a 'festive mood' (*The Times*) and, though if anything they had a softer spot for the all-British team, Bunny Austin and Dorothy Shepherd-Barron, there were plenty of happy cheers when Round and Miki fought back from a set down to win the title. And when Round herself emerged from the clubhouse at the end of it all a gaggle of well-wishers was waiting to give her a full-throated send-off. A few jumped on the running board of her car as she motored away. She was never much of a one for the high life. As a *Sydney Morning Herald* reporter wrote, 'Her favourite drink is lemonade, and I doubt if she has so much as tried a cigarette.' But tonight was special: it was the Wimbledon dinner at the Savoy, and she was one of the guests of honour.

The following week's *Illustrated London News* carried several pictures of all this, including one of an elegantly dressed Perry 'giving a hint' to Round up in the royal box, with the unambiguous caption: 'Their Majesties saw the final of the Women's Singles, and afterwards received both Mr Perry and Miss Round. Miss Round added to her laurels on the same day by winning the Mixed Doubles, partnered by R. Miki.'

Round celebrated her victory with a brief caravanning holiday in Wales before going home for a civic reception in Dudley.[3]

---

[3] Four years later, in 1937, in another memorable double, Round won Wimbledon again in June and was married that September. As the newsreels put it, Miss Round became Mrs Little. Thousands of fans gathered outside the church in Dudley to shower the happy couple with confetti. It was the end of a fine tennis career, but Mrs Round Little did go on to be President of the Worcestershire LTA, and wrote a book, *Tennis for Girls*, which the *Dictionary of National Biography* called 'cheerful and sensible'.

Tennis, she told reporters, was 'a gift not to be used for selfish ends'; so she was happy to hear that a 'cot for afflicted children' was being named after her. The newspapers were equally careful not to go overboard about the result of the final: *The Times* called it 'wretched luck' for Jacobs. But most people – certainly those who were there to see it – were too busy celebrating to care much about Jacobs – indeed, *The Times* went on to add, 'Wimbledon has not heard a mightier shout for many a day.'

The *Evening News*, more simply, called it 'Britain's Greatest Wimbledon'. It only added to the sense of sporting magic dust in the air that, on the very same day, in the third Ashes Test in Manchester, England had amassed a stunning 627 for 9, with Verity making a more than useful 60. Was it possible that we had those dashed Australians on the run again? '1934 is certainly England's vintage year,' sang the *Manchester Guardian*. 'Our long sojourn in the shadows makes it a trifle difficult to get used to the high light.' The *Sunday Times* summed up the mood with a crowing leader entitled: 'Britain's Brilliant Day of Sport'. Apart from all these head-spinning triumphs in cricket, golf and tennis, records were tumbling at Henley – and the sun was still blazing. All things considered, it seemed beyond doubt that the events of the last few days would 'definitely restore England to world leadership in sport'.

It seems a touch ungallant of Perry to have misremembered all this. Had he been the least uncertain, he need only have turned to his own book, *Perry on Tennis*, published in 1936. There, only two years after the events in question, he had his facts lined up. 'The day after my own final I was able to watch Miss Round,' he wrote, 'whose strokes are just perfection, beating Miss Jacobs … She and I had the supreme honour of receiving the congratulations of the late King George.'

So he did at least *watch* her final. And it is not as if he didn't know Miss Round. She and her partner, Ryuki Miki, had once beaten F. J. Perry and Miss Heeley, a Midlands club mate of Round's, in a Mixed Doubles tournament held at Cromer, in Norfolk, back in

1932. Perry and Round had also lost on the very same day in the US Championships at Forest Hills in 1933 (she in the Singles, he in the Doubles). He had written warmly about her in his newspaper column (while also praising Jacobs, the 'girl from sunny California with the never-say-die spirit'). It is hard to believe he could have forgotten what she did that day, yet somehow the passing of years saw the whole thing slip his mind.

On one level we can understand it. Perry's autobiography was published in 1984, half a century after that glorious double triumph. It is certainly possible that, over the years, the details became confused in his memory – indeed, which of us, in all honesty, can recall with anything like clarity what we were doing 50 years ago? Things do grow misty over time; they cross wires with other years, become anecdotes, and in decades of retelling gain a few flourishes. Perry did win this thing three times, after all.

But there is another, more delicate level to contemplate. As even his biographer, Jon Henderson, remarks, Perry was an 'inveterate yarner' of tales who 'could dress up any story', and now that we pause to think about it, with doubt in our mind, there is indeed something faintly greedy and blustering in the account. Quite a few of those 'details' don't scan. To discover, soon after sunrise in Eastbourne, that one is required in SW19 at lunchtime may be inconvenient, but it does not honestly call for a tense, police-escorted dash. Wimbledon was only a few hours away, even given the 1934 speed limit of 30mph and the absence of anything resembling a modern motorway.

Questions like these bring other problems to the surface. That jolly dinner with Henry Cotton, the two champions slapping one another on the back and going to the theatre ... it sounds like good fun, but there is a possibility that this never happened either. Cotton never mentions it in *his* memoirs – an unlikely omission, since he was not averse to dropping names. And half a dozen newspapers place Perry instead (with photographs to prove it) at that civic reception in Ealing Town Hall – quite a big and lively affair. The front-page picture in the *Daily Mirror* had not been ambiguous: Perry was being saluted by a cheering crowd of well-wishers, including his own father and tennis fans from the neighbourhood, and was being carried head high back to his car on the shoulders of the Brentham players among whom he had learned the game.

Is it possible that Perry's memory missed a gear over this, too? On the Saturday night after Round's victory, there really *was* a banquet at the Savoy, and very grand it was. But it was the official LTA dinner, not a cosy *tête-à-tête* between two stars.[4]

Perry and Round, the Singles champions, walked into the room 'amidst prolonged acclamation' from hundreds of guests in white tie and ball gowns, all seated at tables decorated with flowers in the colours of the LTA: red, blue and yellow. As guests of honour they were escorted to the top table by the President of the LTA, Sir Samuel Hoare, and his wife, Maud. Hoare was no functionary. A Harrow and Oxford man, he had spent the First World War in British Intelligence – indeed, had recruited an Italian socialist by the name of Benito Mussolini to the Allied cause (not the proudest line on his CV, but an arresting one).[5] A Lieutenant Colonel, he had been Secretary of State for Air and now, in 1934, was Secretary of State for India. In recent times he had held fraught meetings with Gandhi, discussing how India might leave the Empire. But that evening he was calling for a simple sporting toast – 'The new Champions!'

His speech began by praising grand occasions such as this. 'If I am asked to describe a typical event in the public life of

---

[4] It is possible that Cotton was at this dinner, but not likely. The LTA journal listed dozens of now-forgotten members of the great and good as VIP guests, and would scarcely have omitted the new Open champion had anyone thought to invite him.

[5] Just a year later, in 1935, Sir Samuel Hoare, by then Foreign Secretary, was one of the authors of the Hoare–Laval Pact, which offered Italy a free hand in Ethiopia and ignited the public uproar that led to his resignation. He went on to become one of the senior British figures urging conciliation, not conflict, with Adolf Hitler.

Great Britain,' he said, 'I would without hesitation select one of our great sporting events – Aintree, Wembley, the Derby, a Test match ... and Wimbledon.' He went on to praise the way the velvety grass of the All England Club turned brown in the sun as the tournament progressed, and the handsome crowd who savoured the tennis like 'epicures' at a garden party before the final 'spectacular contests'. He ended with a bold plea – 'Long may Wimbledon so continue' – and paid warm tribute to Perry's 'physical fitness, his dash and his energy'. Congratulations on a 'brilliant and remarkable victory' ... everyone present was immensely proud.

Perry himself received a 'great reception' when he rose to reply. He made a witty show of thanking the flu outbreak that had laid low so many of his rivals; then he tipped his hat to Crawford, hoping that when it was *his* turn to lose this great title he would do so as gracefully as had the Australian. And he closed on a sycophantic note. Now the laurels were home, he felt sure the All England Club could hold them 'as long as they [the All England Club] had Sir Samuel Hoare as President'.

The Times called this 'an excellent speech', and it was followed by a cabaret by the Western Brothers. Perry was a great fan of dance music ('there is hardly a tune I don't know') which was just as well, because, as tradition demanded (and still demands), the winners were expected to lead the parade. Perry took to the floor with Round, and the victorious pair spun through the perfumed night wearing what the *Evening News* called 'a smile of mutual triumph'. Their footwork, noted its correspondent, was 'perfect'.

Once again we have to ask: is it possible that Perry could have forgotten such a magical evening? If he really did meet Cotton at the Savoy on the Friday night after his win, is it credible that the grand banquet the following night could have faded from his mind? And this was no ordinary dinner, but an extremely formal bash for over 300 upmarket guests. It does seem true that he left Wimbledon quietly – the *Telegraph* said that he 'disappeared' with mysterious speed – 'to the disappointment of many fans, who wanted to shake his hand or get his autograph'. As for the rest ... well, it is hard to accept that it left the champion with only a dim memory of how his week ended.

In this light we have to entertain at least the suspicion that the tale of the Wimbledon official insulting Perry as he lay in his bathtub may also be – ahem – a notch too good to be true. *This was one occasion when the best man didn't win.* People have enjoyed repeating the anecdote ever since – it fits so neatly with the image (by no means a false one) of Wimbledon as an upper-class enclave.[6] America's *Esquire* was happy to call Wimbledon the most toffee-nosed place in sport (it had evidently not been to Augusta) and in 2013 the *BBC History Magazine* declared Perry 'a sporting outcast in his homeland'. Even a publication as august as the *Dictionary of National Biography* said that Perry winning Wimbledon was 'like a mongrel winning Crufts'.

Yet even as he retells the tale in *The Last Champion*, Jon Henderson concedes that it might have been 'closer to the truth in essence than detail'. It seems that Hillyard, the author of the famous jibe, actually thought highly of Perry: in February 1934 he wrote in the *Morning Post* that Perry was 'a very fine player with every chance of becoming Wimbledon champion'. People usually like seeing their own predictions come true: he is not *very* likely to have bad-mouthed the man of the moment. If he did say anything mean about Perry, it is much more likely that it was just courteous small talk – a word of consolation to the loser – which sounded much worse when overheard.

Most telling of all, the episode is not so much as mentioned in Perry's 1936 account of his win over Crawford, written while

---

[6] Most of the obituaries after his death in 1984 repeated it. Perry was 'born the wrong side of the net', according to the *Observer*; to *Esquire* he was 'a poor boy without a Varsity background' trying to make his way at 'the most snobbish centre of sport in the world'; the BBC had him as 'the icon and the outcast'; the *Independent* ('Why tennis establishment shunned Fred Perry'), the *Daily Mail* ('a sorry tale') and almost every other significant recorder of these events has fallen in with this version.

it was fresh in the memory. 'I left the court scarcely knowing whether it was Christmas or Stow-on-the-Wold,' he wrote. 'And he and I pledged each other's health in the dressing room.' Not a hint here about the ugly put-down. And while it is possible that tact stayed his hand, that discretion struck Perry as the better part of candour, this was 1936, when he was on the brink of emigrating. It wasn't the worst time for an indignant parting shot, if one was really called for.[7]

There is one more detail. At the Savoy dinner there was a special tribute to 'Mr A. H. Sabelli' (the hapless official summoned by Perry to apologise) for all the hard work he had put into the championships. Perry knew Sabelli quite well, as it happened; he had played golf with him and Dan Maskell in Paris during the 1933 Davis Cup trip. This public tribute – *another slap in the face!* – would surely have stuck in his craw enough to be worth mentioning, or at least remembering. His own father was at this dinner, too (the *Sunday Times* printed pretty much the entire guest list in its society column) – it is most unlikely that *he* would have let his son forget about such an evening.

There are other accounts of what happened in the moments after the final. According to the *Daily Mail*, the very first person to congratulate Perry as he left the court was none other than 'Mr A. H. Sabelli, Secretary of the LTA'. In this report, written that very evening, 'the two men embraced, and Perry in his excitement kissed Mr Sabelli'.

Not much sign of the icy betrayal that Perry narrated there. And the *Evening Standard* reporter, Bruce Harris, was able to go further. 'In the dressing room,' he wrote, having been fortunate

---

[7] Interestingly, the 1936 work is a happier volume than its successor; more relaxed, less anxious to score points. 'No one can win Wimbledon without luck,' it says. 'This year it was my turn to have a full share of it.' Of the final he wrote: 'Do not expect me to tell you what happened ... Everything went right for me, everything went wrong for him.' And Crawford? 'He congratulated me cordially – he is that sort of fellow.'

enough to witness the gleeful scene for himself, Perry was 'heartily congratulated by officials and players.' Putting his success down to pure luck ('I got him on an off day') he put a kindly arm round Crawford's shoulder.

'Let's have a drink, Jack.'

'Make it a *big* drink.'

The Australian was as generous in defeat as Perry was magnanimous in victory. 'Don't believe what he said about luck,' he told reporters. 'He played better than I did.'

It seems a shame that Perry edited this sportsmanlike scene into something so prickly and self-righteous. Perhaps it suited his self-image to cast himself as the gifted outsider spurned by the establishment (and there was some truth in that, no question). If that lavish dinner at the Savoy, in which he was so extravagantly saluted by the tennis elite, did slip his mind, maybe it was because it clashed with his sense of himself as a man jilted by the 'old school brigade'. In truth, and without wanting it to appear as though we are ganging up, he was not *quite* the wrong-side-of-the-tracks rebel he sometimes seemed. Although his father was indeed on the Labour side, hardly aligned with the conservative culture of Wimbledon tennis, he *was* an MP, and it did mean that the young Fred sometimes went for lunch in the Palace of Westminster, where he was feted by a wide range of VIPs as a coming thing. He may not have been an Eton and Balliol man, but there *are* regions further removed from the tracks than this.

None of this is intended to cast aspersions on Perry, whose great achievement speaks for itself. But it does remind us to be somewhat wary when it comes to making any too firm judgements about the past. History is not what happened – it is what we remember happening, or wish to think happened; it is how we choose to recall the past, not the past itself. And we all know how unreliable memories are, even happy ones.

CHAPTER THIRTEEN

After-effects

In May 1934 the government asked Lord Selsdon to lead an inquiry into the possibility of setting up a new public television service. His report was delivered the following January, and in due course it became the White Paper on which the BBC was built. As a postscript to his declaration that the corporation's mission was to inform, educate and entertain, Lord Reith urged that when it came to major sports events it should in effect allow the public to be present at the 'functions and ceremonials upon which national sentiment is consecrated'. The religious flavour of this remark was telling – sporting occasions were indeed a form of public communion, a secular sort of mass.

In time a set of such occasions would be ring-fenced as sacrosanct so far as national broadcasting was concerned, and while there is no way of proving it, we can at least speculate that one reason why the Lord's Test, the Open and Wimbledon became so central a part of the national 'crown jewels' was thanks to the prominent part they happened to play in this glorious summer of 1934. There are no documents revealing that Lord Selsdon was inspired by Verity, Cotton, Perry or Round, but it was certainly a good time for cricket, tennis and golf to be advancing their claims.

If Bradman had been dropped, if Cotton's stomach had turned, if Perry had twisted his ankle, if Round had faltered ... who knows what might have happened then? All three sports were starting to feel like overseas possessions; they might not have seemed so replete with 'national sentiment' if they had not been recaptured in those exhilarating three weeks. It may even be an indirect consequence of 1934 that Wimbledon, the Open and the Lord's Test became, along with Trooping the Colour, Bonfire Night, Carols from King's, Remembrance Sunday and the Queen's Speech (which Reith himself inaugurated in 1932), fixtures in the furniture of the national mind.

Such was the thunderclap of euphoria surrounding these heady days that Winston Churchill, a week after Perry's victory, was clutching his head in the *Daily Mail* at the way the country seemed to have given itself over to a bread-and-circuses dream. 'I look with wonder upon the thoughtless crowds disporting themselves in the summer sunshine,' he said. 'All the while, across the North Sea, a terrible process is astir. Germany is arming.'[1] He might not have been consciously thinking of Kipling's dig at the sports-mad citizenry of 1902 – 'the flannelled fools at the wicket … the muddied oafs in the goals' – who didn't seem to be giving a fig about the Boer War. But he was making much the same point. It didn't stop him setting off for a three-week holiday in the South of France with his son and a box of watercolours. But he was indeed being kept awake by the spectre of a re-arming Germany, and found it hard to fathom how others could snooze so contentedly. Maybe he was reminded of Field Marshal Roberts's cry of August 1914: 'This is no time for games. We are engaged on a life and death struggle.' Or perhaps he was mindful of that powerful W. G. Grace letter to *The Sportsman*, which called for cricket to lay down its bat and take up arms instead.

Either way, he was no longer a voice in the wilderness. In the middle of Wimbledon, as Perry prepared for his quarter-final

---

[1] Churchill was no sports enthusiast, but his popular put-down of golf – a matter of knocking balls at holes 'with weapons singularly ill-adapted for the purpose', was borrowed from Horace Hutchinson, who said, in *Lessons from Great Golfers* (1924), that it was a question of 'putting little balls into little holes with instruments very ill-adapted for the purpose'. But maybe *he* got it from *Punch*, which spoke in 1892 about trying to hole a very small ball using 'engines singularly ill-adapted for the purpose'.

against Lott, and Cotton adjusted to life as the Open champion, events in Germany took a new and awful twist. In an orchestrated attack, Adolf Hitler assassinated hundreds of his rivals (the final body count would be over a thousand) in a move to consolidate his power over the Nazi Party. Some British onlookers cheered. The *Daily Mail* accepted the line that this was 'nipping treason in the bud' and said: 'Herr Adolf Hitler, the German Chancellor, has saved his country.' And the *Telegraph* felt the Führer had cleared out 'a dangerous nest of conspirators'. But others were shocked: *The Times* saw it as 'Herr Hitler's Coup'. The details were not clear – Hitler himself was calling it a 'purification'; others ran with 'purge' – but it was patently a brazen spree, with no respect for judicial nicety. It was not yet called 'the Night of the Long Knives', but, as new details came out, the language intensified. In *The Times* Germany was using 'medieval methods … persecution … suppression of all freedom … a plague of spies and informers … intense propaganda … the glorification of force and violence'. Up to now *The Times* had been polite about Hitler's desire to rebuild a wounded nation's pride. But this latest incident was too much. 'Germany,' railed a resounding leader, 'has ceased for a time to be a modern European country.'

This news came on the very day – 1 July – that Britain was commemorating the first day of the Somme. Many minds must have flown back to what France's Marshal Foch had said in the days after Versailles. 'This is no peace,' he fumed. 'It's an Armistice for twenty years.' A simple calculation was enough to confirm that 15 of those years had already flown by: could a resumption of hostilities really be so close? In 1933 H. G. Wells, in *The Shape of Things to Come*, echoed Foch by predicting war in 1940, while the BBC was running a series of radio talks on the subject, and newspapers were providing daily hints that time was running out. Britain's progressive thinkers were especially excited, believing the death of capitalism to be imminent: the June issue of *The Communist Review* warned that we were 'On the Eve of a New World War'. No one could say they hadn't been warned. The clouds on the horizon were piling up fast, and three weeks later, on 20 July, the government authorised the formation of 41 new RAF squadrons over the next five years. The initiative was opposed by both the Labour and the Liberal parties, but this was where the Battle of Britain truly began.

H. G. Wells chose this jumpy moment to travel to Moscow to interview Stalin for a *New Statesman* pamphlet due to be published in October. Like many British thinkers he still believed in the idea of an idealistic new dawn in the east, but his words sound somewhat comical now. The Soviet leader, he reported, struck him as 'fair, candid and honest'. He himself had only just arrived, he gushed, but he was already *most* impressed by 'the happy faces of healthy men and women' he had been shown, and sensed that 'something very considerable is being done here'. He was right, though not perhaps in the way he thought: several million Ukrainians were being liquidated even as he spoke, and it is hard not to imagine Stalin's smile as he listened to this famous writer (whom, given half a chance, he would probably have been happy to execute as a degenerate liberal) falling so politely for the hook, the sinker and the whole Soviet line. But Wells and many others really did believe, with reason, that the capitalist system was juddering on its last legs, and that Hitler was the chief threat to international stability. That is why he still felt able to tell Stalin that of *course* the British people agreed with his stated view that 'the system based on private profit is breaking down' – without feeling a cold blast of Siberian wind on his neck.

It was hard for a right-minded person *not* to take such a view after the decade of crash and slump that was only now passing. It was no mere coincidence that a new board game was being hatched at just this time: *Monopoly*. Invented in Atlantic City, New Jersey, in Depression-torn America, its original intention was not to promote property trading but the opposite: to expose the evils of monopoly capitalism by demonstrating that an unregulated free-for-all would end up with one person owning all the property – and all the money, too. This aspect of the game has been misunderstood ever since. Hitler's Germany banned it on the grounds that it boosted 'Jewish speculation', and, when it came to Britain in 1936, it was enjoyed not by anti-capitalists but by those who thought that on the whole it *would* be rather spiffing to own a slice of Park Lane, Pall Mall or Bond Street.

Back at home the heatwave returned. Newspapers and magazines ran guides to refreshing pools and ponds alongside pictures of desiccated rivers and dead lakes. If only the Loch Ness monster had been lurking in an English reservoir – it would have been having a beer with *Daily Mail* reporters by now. But it was good news for the annual boating party at Henley, which enjoyed (said the *Illustrated London News*) 'the most perfect weather that has been experienced in many a decade'. Up and down the land there were signs that Britain was recovering its verve. July saw the opening of a new tunnel under the Mersey in Liverpool, the largest underwater construction in the world. And imposing new libraries (this was a time when a new library still seemed to signify civilisation and progress) were springing up in Sheffield and Manchester.

The launching of the *Queen Mary* (by the Queen, naturally) provided an awesome spectacle for the thousands who gathered on the slipway on the Clyde. She was vast; the ballroom alone was big enough to house the fleet that carried Columbus across the Atlantic in 1492. And new top speeds were being attained all the time, on sea, air and land. In November, the *Flying Scotsman* became the first steam train to reach 100mph.

Sport continued to apply a glow of warming mood music. The Empire Games were held that August, mainly at White City, in a second edition of what would eventually become the Commonwealth Games. Initial plans for Johannesburg to host the Games faltered over concerns regarding South Africa's intransigent attitude to its non-white population, and as part of the fair-minded rubric implied by the switch of venue, the London games became the first to include women. A new stadium, Wembley Arena, was built, and 40,000 pigeons were released when the athletes paraded around in pursuit, as Pathé News put it, of 'nothing more than honour and glory'.

Britain came top of the medals table by a mile, winning 29 golds (six in the boxing ring). It didn't matter, in this context, that the home nations did not even enter the second football World Cup, which was won by Italy – in Italy. The view in Britain was that the Home Internationals offered a sterner test, but it did mean that few noticed the way the winning Italian team – urged on by Mussolini – came back from 0-1 down to win the final at the 'Stadium of the National Fascist Party' in Rome; nor did anyone greatly care that Italy were crowned champions with three players who had represented Argentina in 1930, on the sketchy grounds that they had some sort of Italian ancestry.

The story that gripped Britain most eagerly in the back half of 1934 concerned the America's Cup. The British yacht, *Endeavour*, was seeking to win the oldest trophy in sport (founded 1851), and its owner and skipper was Tommy Sopwith, a man whose own life story was one of those amazing sagas in which this period specialised. In an incredible accident, as a ten-year-old boy he had killed his own father when the gun on his lap went off at a shooting party in Scotland. As a grown-up he was also drawn to high-risk pursuits such as motorcycling and aviation, and won a gold medal for ice hockey at the first European championships in 1910. In June 1912 he set up a new aircraft company, named it after himself, and started turning out the most famous plane – the Sopwith Camel – of the Great War: he would end up manufacturing 6,000 of them.

Some people called this profiteering, and he was taxed to bankruptcy when the war ended. But he soon set up a new firm, named after his designer, Harry Hawker, and made himself a second fortune. It meant he was able, in 1934, to play with yachts like other supremely wealthy men. *Endeavour* was something new, an elegant design built in Gosport, Hampshire, with a steel hull, sails made from Sudanese and Egyptian cotton, a steel mast and a radical new spinnaker. Everyone agreed on one thing: she was a beauty.

She sailed – quite literally – through qualifying rounds in the waters off Harwich, Southend, Lymington, Falmouth, Torquay and the Isle of Wight. And the coming challenge to America was looking all shipshape and Bristol fashion until the middle of July, a week after Wimbledon, when a pay dispute with the professional sailors meant the entire crew had to be replaced. Still, when she left Portsmouth *Endeavour* was given a rousing send-off by both the Royal Yacht and a passing warship.

The final was held at Newport, Rhode Island, against a vaunted American, *Rainbow*. After one false start, the race began in earnest on 15 September. *Endeavour* won the first two runs over the 30-mile course, but lost the next four. The decisive tie was the fourth, when a protest from *Endeavour*, claiming that *Rainbow* had taken its water unfairly, was dismissed on the technical (some said questionable) grounds that Sopwith hadn't raised the protest flag correctly. The incident decided the fate of the trophy, but perhaps more importantly gave rise to a legendary headline in the *New York Journal*: 'Britannia Rules the Waves, But The New York Yacht Club Waives The Rules.'

The celebratory atmosphere surrounding all this was muted, in August, by the 20th anniversary of the Great War. Most publications ran souvenir issues: the *Illustrated London News* printed a five-page special on 'war fever' in Germany, and it was impossible to miss the hint – coinciding as it did with the awful murder in Vienna of Austria's Chancellor Dollfuss – that something similar was on the rise again. The belfry at Ypres might have been rebuilt, but memories of that inferno had not faded. And the Nazi rallies in Nuremberg in September, immense Wagnerian pageants over which the Führer presided like a commanding officer, looked very like the preliminaries in some terrible new struggle. 'They are blind,' yelled Germany's new dictator, 'who imagine that our regime can be destroyed.' It was all very well to applaud John Gielgud's 'lucid and penetrating' Hamlet in the West End. There were other games afoot.[2]

For Hedley Verity, the second half of 1934 did not live up to the first. The endless grind of English cricket was good at keeping a fellow's feet on the ground. The day after the Lord's Test Verity and Bowes simply said their goodbyes and went to Northampton for a county match. As it happened they were granted one taste of celebrity: there was a game going on when they arrived to drop their bags, with a few spectators sprinkled around, and when the England pair walked in everyone, players included, stopped what they were doing, rose to their feet, and gave them a fervent round of applause.

But the rest of the summer was all downhill from England's point of view. Bradman came back from his poor showing at Lord's to dominate utterly the last two Tests. It says something about his position in the game that a series in which he scored 304 and 244 could be described by *Wisden* as something of a disappointment. He was, the Almanack felt, in a 'curious' mood; though he remained 'amazingly brilliant', his form on the whole had been 'less than normal' – indeed, in a very strongly worded judgement, at times he seemed to have 'lost control of himself'.

None of this was apparent in the last Test at the Oval, where his first-innings 244 set up the win that gave Australia the Ashes. As if to prove that the cricketing gods mete out their rewards in arbitrary dollops, Verity took nought for 123. The King sent the victors a sporting telegram, congratulating them on a 'brilliant display' which would be 'remembered for ever'. So when the final tally was done, it turned out that in the course of the summer Bradman had scored 758 runs at 94.75. This made his stark failure

---

[2] Unity Mitford, in Munich, was so caught up in 'the Night of the Long Knives' drama that she felt compelled to write to her sister Diana: 'I am so *terribly* sorry for the Fuhrer...the whole thing is so dreadful.'

at Lord's, when Verity dismissed him twice for 49, all the more remarkable.

The Don wasn't the kind of man to forget or forgive a day like that, so it was not a shock when he played Yorkshire in front of 12,000 people and rattled up 140 between lunch and tea – an effervescent display even by his unique standards. He followed it up by going on the attack against a Leveson-Gower XI in Scarborough, scoring 132 in an hour and half – including 19 off one over by Verity.

'I enjoyed myself,' he said after that. But nothing could dim the shining memory of Verity's marvellous spell at Lord's, and in later years Bradman would pay plenty of tributes to it. 'I could never claim to have completely mastered Hedley's strategy,' he would say. 'It was never static or mechanical.' And he would admit that there had always been something mysterious about the man. 'With Hedley I am never sure,' he said, in a rare puzzled moment. 'You see, there's no breaking point with him.'

It had never looked like being a quiet summer, and when Australia faced Nottingham in August, Bodyline reared its unpleasant head again. Voce hurled down bumpers with four short legs, just like the old days, and it worked: he took 8-66. Australia fumed, refusing to take the field next day if Voce was playing. Naturally the Nottinghamshire Committee couldn't *possibly* be seen to bow before such blackmail, but as luck would have it Voce developed a mystery 'illness' overnight, something to do with his shins, and was unable to take any further part in the game. Later, the Committee made a clean breast of things, admitting that Nottinghamshire had indeed been guilty of 'direct attack' bowling (they could not do otherwise, since the umpires found the accusation to be 'fully proved'), but emphasising that this ran counter to the club's expressly stated principles. The captain was sacked, and an apology sent to MCC.

Actually, the most embarrassing aspect of the incident was the boorish behaviour of the crowd, which directed a 'storm of booing' at the hapless Australians. It was this that led *Wisden*, in its summary of the season, to describe it as an 'unpleasant' one – marred by behaviour that was 'utterly foreign to the great traditions of the game'.

Bradman's own breaking point was tested severely in September when, after his great innings at The Oval, he collapsed with appendicitis at the hotel in Portland Place. One of Australia's most celebrated surgeons, Sir Douglas Shields, was able to perform an emergency operation in nearby Park Lane, in his private clinic, but by the time he cut out The Don's appendix it was gangrenous and the prognosis was touch and go. People began to say he had been ill all year – some said he looked 20 years older than his age. Since this was not the era of 24-hour rolling news there were no satellite vans outside, but word soon spread, especially when the call went out for blood donors. The rush to help the great batsman was so great that the hospital was overwhelmed; dozens of cricket-loving passers-by dropped in to roll up their sleeves and do their bit.

The papers were full of the story, and a long queue of dignitaries – Pelham Warner, Jack Hobbs and many others – came to pay their respects. The King and Queen sent a telegram conveying their good wishes. 'I want to know everything,' said the King, as if to an old pal, insisting that regular updates be transmitted to Balmoral. And J. M. Barrie stopped by to lend the stricken cricketer some happy thoughts.[3]

Bradman's room soon looked like a brimming florist's parlour. When he revived he told a reporter from the *Adelaide Mail* that it had been 'a rough time' and 'a near thing', but that he was feeling 'pretty fair'. Invited to comment on reports that he had decided never to play in England again, he said he was 'too sick to make statements about statements he has never made'. The P&O Line kindly gave Bradman's wife a free ticket to England,

---

[3] Bradman never forget Barrie's kindly visit. In 1950, when Barrie wrote a book about his own cricketing life, The Don happily agreed to provide an introduction.

so she raced across Australia on the express from Adelaide ('pale but cheerful', according to the *Adelaide News*) before catching the steamer from Fremantle. It was not fast enough to reach Bradman in his hour of need, but she did make it in time to join him on a recuperative holiday in the South of France.

The following year Verity proved that 1934 was no accident by bagging 200 wickets for Yorkshire and England, making him the toast of domestic cricket. But he did not have everything his own way. When Yorkshire played South Africa he was whacked to all corners by Jock Cameron (30 off a single over) in a barrage that inspired a nice legend; halfway through the over the wicketkeeper, Arthur Wood, called: 'You've got him in two minds, Hedley. He doesn't know whether to hit you for four or six.'

Through all of these ups and downs Verity remained both a professional to his gifted fingertips and the very model of a gentleman – he was single-handedly proving that the two were absolutely not incompatible. According to Norman Yardley he was 'modest, thoughtful, greatest in the crisis, a man who never did a bad turn to anyone on the field, and who was liked and trusted by everyone'. Verity himself tended to see bowling as a question of temperament and character, not technique, though this involved taking his own high, deceptively easy action for granted. When asked to advise youngsters he tended to emphasise the importance of a 'stout heart' and a clear head: 'Don't get despondent when the luck of the game is against you,' he would say. His father, too, liked to attribute his son's success to hard work. 'Over and over again,' he wrote, 'he told beginners that only by perseverance could they be successful.'

On days off he wasn't hoofing it up in nightclubs; he played games of cricket on the windswept beaches of North Yorkshire with his children (Hedley in his Sunday best, as usual), drove the family up into the high dales and moors, or went to the rugby in Leeds. 'He was a lovely, warm, happy dad,' remembered his son Douglas, decades later. 'He was always laughing, and made everything seem so interesting. I remember going to the 1938 Headingley Test with him. He took me into the England dressing-room, and had me demonstrating my forward defensive shot to everyone.'

Henry Cotton's victory at Royal St George's made *him* famous, too. Back in 1925 the President of the English Golf Union, Sir Ernest Holderness, had ventured the opinion that even the Open champion (Jim Barnes, that year) could 'pass unnoticed' through Charing Cross station. Cotton was changing all that. And it wasn't just thanks to his brilliant golf. His dandyish ways were catching the eye of the emerging media; news cameras had been on the links to record his every move, while Bernard Darwin gave nightly summaries on BBC radio. The audience who had not been there to see it now vastly exceeded the one that had actually traipsed over the dunes in his wake.

Exhausted, Cotton skipped the Open de France, which he had planned to play in after Royal St George's, in favour of a celebratory dinner at the Savoy and a break. And he offended Selsdon Park Golf Club in Surrey when, having agreed to take part in an exhibition match (with Sarazen and others) on the Sunday after the Open, he withdrew, claiming he was 'too tired'. Two thousand people turned up to see him, and when he wasn't there the club had no option but to offer them a refund. It says something about the nature of British life at that time that only two people accepted this offer.

But when he returned to Waterloo the members did him proud. They had showered him with telegrams in Sandwich, and now they welcomed him with an arch of raised golf clubs on the steps of the clubhouse. At dinner they gave him a gold cigarette case – a fine gesture, if a surprising one to give a zealous non-smoker. Best of all, as a 'mark of esteem' for what he had achieved, they granted him his dearest wish and made him an honorary member. His new-found status in Britain had dissolved most of the reasons that had brought him to Belgium in the first place, though, so after winning the Belgian Open on Waterloo's own fairways in August 1934 (sneaking past Percy Alliss in the final round) he began to think about leaving. Once he had honoured his six-month contract it would be fun to move on, not least to be part of the Ryder Cup again – he was still not eligible to play in 1935, even though the USGA wrote a formal letter saying that for their part they would be quite happy to waive this obstacle and welcome him as an opponent. So Cotton was out because he worked at Waterloo, while Sidney Brews of Blackheath was in, even though he was South African.

The claret jug was useful for opening doors with the great and good, however, and it wasn't long before Lord Rosebery was asking him to help put Ashridge Golf Club (a new course in a deer park near Berkhamsted) on the map. It was a good time to leave Waterloo, as chance would have it: the club would soon be in direct line of the German advance on Paris. He and 'Toots' built a house near Ashridge, named it Shangri-La, and turned it into the most palatial home a British professional golfer had ever lived in. He even hired his old forecaddie, Ernest Hargreaves, as a valet. These were still the days when newspapers were full of applicants for such positions: excellent gentleman's gentleman, hardworking, reliable on both table and door, solid references. Years later, Hargreaves wrote a memoir that gave readers an unusual glimpse into Cotton's private life. By now 'Toots' was an intimidating mistress who insisted that the various cars be washed after each outing, no matter how brief, insisted that he shine his shoes with automobile polish, rejected her daily lapel flower (white orchids and camellias from the greenhouse) if it had the least blemish, and endured no nonsense from the staff – one German cook, two Austrian maids. Cotton referred to her simply as 'Madam'.

His work at Ashridge began in January 1937, and he was soon teaching the golfers of Cambridge University, some of whom had visited him at Waterloo. In Belgium he had built an unusual covered shed as an all-weather practice area, with balls hit not into a net but out across a roomy range, so their flight could be properly studied. He did the same in Berkhamsted. But just as his triumph in Kent had triggered some sour behind-the-hand comments to the effect that he hadn't beaten many golfers of note – it *was* a weak field, as it happened – now, at Ashridge, he was also failing to impress the membership, partly because he declined to play with them as much as they expected and hoped, and partly thanks to his unusual and lucrative way of giving lessons. On a typical day he would teach three students in the morning (for £5 a head), then give them lunch at Shangri-La (greatly to the irritation of the club's own dining room) before playing and beating them for £10 a head in the afternoon. Not a bad day's work.

No one could find any weakness in the field that went to Carnoustie for the 1937 Open, however, because the entire US Ryder Cup team was there – Byron Nelson, Gene Sarazen, Sam Snead and all. The weather was so bad the shops ran out of umbrellas. Cotton stayed in touch for three bedraggled rounds and then, in the fourth, completed the front nine in 35 strokes – a near-miracle on this sodden beast of a course, with no roll on the fairways and puddles on the greens. At the 18th, holding the lead, he tried to fly a two-iron over the famous burn … only to catch the right-hand bunker. But a solid chip and two putts were enough to make sure no one would be able to catch him.

As a double Open champion he wasn't ready to rest on his laurels. Aside from the prize money, he could now charge £200 a day for exhibitions, £10 for lessons, fat fees for newspaper work and other appearances, and tidy sums for endorsements (clubs, balls, gloves and much else). He even put on a show at the Coliseum in London's West End, hitting luminous balls across a darkened stage. The following summer he toured Europe in a chauffeured car, winning the Belgian, German and Czechoslovakian Opens (at the last of which, in Marienbad, he was watched by a new friend: Rudyard Kipling). None of these could claim to be major competitions – he merely needed to beat a few well-born chaps from embassies and the odd local hero. But he was blazing enough of a trail to make him one of the founders of what would become the European tour.

The day after Wimbledon, still basking in thoughts of the various ways in which his victory would transform his life, Fred Perry received an interesting telegram from an ex-baseball player called Bill O'Brien, who in partnership with the US tennis star Bill Tilden had (since 1926) been staging lucrative tennis matches across America. It had now turned into a fully-fledged travelling circus, and Tilden aimed to recruit at least one hot amateur each year to refresh his squad and stop the format from becoming stale. In 1934 he signed up two, Ellsworth Vines and Henri Cochet, and now he had his sights fixed on Perry. The man had won three majors, was brash, brilliant and handsome. The telegram offered him $25,000 to quit amateur tennis.[4]

The English newspapers had been twittering about this awful possibility all summer: it was no secret that Perry was tempted. The *Telegraph* expressed dismay at the way these hucksterish promoters were bidding for England's brightest new star, in terms that suggested the man's soul hung in the balance, while others were quick to depict it as a vulgar assault on British probity. But no one could overlook the grand disparity behind all this. Winning Wimbledon was glorious, to be sure, but it would not make Perry rich. And no one could play for long at his high level while holding down a job elsewhere. Various strategies were

---

[4] This sum needs putting into context. There were roughly five dollars to the pound in 1934, so this was only £5,000 – but since a mansion on a Surrey golf course at that time cost around half that (yet would be worth a couple of million today) we can really imagine this windfall as being worth around £4 million in new money. Not bad.

explored – one involved 'selling' Perry a valuable mansion for a knock-down price – but professional tennis, however tacky, held out the promise of serious wealth, and as the *Manchester Guardian* put it, Perry could 'not be blamed if he were to help himself to some of it while the going is good'.

Some of the photographs of Perry taken the day after Wimbledon show the corner of that telegram poking out of his suit pocket. It must have been burning a hole in the lining. But despite his claim that the locker-room insult made him want to grab the first decent offer that came along, he paused. Britain's defence of the Davis Cup was imminent, and he was not quite finished with Wimbledon either.

On 26 July he relaxed by playing golf with Austin at Woodcote Park; two days later his autobiography came out (in one way fun, in another ridiculous, since the biggest story of his life was not part of it); and two days after that he was beating Sydney Wood all over again in the Davis Cup – at Wimbledon, of all places – en route to another heady triumph. After winning in 1933 Britain did not have to play any qualifying rounds and passed straight into the final against America. And when Perry beat Wood on the Saturday and then Shields on the Sunday the Cup was safe.

Once again there were mutterings about Perry's over-combative approach, the way he jerked his racket in annoyance when he lost a point, for example, or the unfeigned pleasure he took in his own flukes. But he was a proven champion now, and most observers were happy to take a mild line even on this point. 'It is the devil in Perry,' argued the *Star*, 'which makes him one of the finest fighters in the game.'

In August it was announced that he intended to marry a film actress and singer, Mary Lawson, with whom he had been 'friends' (according to the gossip column in the *Star*) for 'a few weeks'. This made headlines in far off Tuscaloosa – Perry was a citizen of the world. The couple had pledged their troth in one of Europe's most giddily romantic locations – King's

Cross station ... But while the affair fizzled out even before the wedding vows, as Perry began to move in faster company, the topic of his turning professional refused to go away. That autumn, when he embarked on the defence of his US and Australian titles, he told reporters: 'I must consider my future livelihood', and added: 'If I turn professional I shall not return to England.' In New York he went even further, telling one interviewer that he was 'tired of tennis, hang it. I like golf and I intend to master it.' And out in California he met the tennis-loving comedian Harpo Marx, who advised him bluntly: 'You can't buy groceries with glory.'[5]

He did nothing rash, however. In 1935 he accepted a post with Slazenger and said that from now on tennis was merely a pastime. 'A man must have a hobby,' he told the *Evening News*, 'and mine will be tennis ... I shall be a businessman, with black coat and trousers and that sort of thing.' He fooled no one. When he took the French Open in 1935 (the first Briton to do so) along with a second Wimbledon crown, he made himself the most famous man in tennis. When he won Wimbledon again in 1936, and a third US Open, too, it seemed that there were no more amateur peaks to climb. He might have been wrong about this. Two of the players whom Perry beat in his last Wimbledon, Don Budge and Gottfried von Cramm, would go on to contest one of the most celebrated matches of all time just one year later. Billed as Freedom versus Fascism, their 1937 Davis Cup clash involved five brilliant, see-sawing sets, and suggested, on the contrary, that there was still glory to be had in the amateur game.

His left-leaning father, Sam Perry, still pleaded with him not to step away from all this glory, and Sir Samuel Hoare, who had sat beside him at that LTA dinner in 1934, rang him in Hollywood

---

[5] Even without prize money, it wasn't *that* bad being an amateur. When Perry played in the 1933 Davis Cup in Paris, for example, he stayed at the Crillon, a terrific hotel, and played golf at St Cloud, a very grand establishment, home of the French Open.

in an attempt to dissuade him. Perry ignored them both. 'There is nothing more for me to win,' he said in 1936. 'Why should I put myself up as a target? Tournament tennis is hard work, with nothing to gain and everything to lose.' Why indeed? The truth was that he was weary of top-flight tennis. When he let slip again that he was 'bored' it was seized on as a scandalous form of conceit, but it was a real burden being the world number one. When Britain faced USA in the 1935 Davis Cup a commentator wrote: 'Perry is good for his two singles matches before he starts.' From Perry's point of view it was a lose-lose – failure earned him reprimands, while success won no more than a shrug. As he put it: 'I had had tennis up to my brim.'

He finally 'swapped glory for gold', in the words of the *Philadelphia Inquirer*, in the autumn of 1936. He would earn £100,000, it was said, for five and a half months' tennis – a princely sum for a boy from such ordinary beginnings. But by now he had a keen taste for glamorous black-tie society. In 1935 he fell for a Hollywood star, Helen Vinson, and this time did tie the knot – spontaneously, after a grand night out. Though the marriage didn't last long, it was a vivid entrée into smart American circles. With his regular opponent Ellsworth Vines, Perry bought a stake in the Beverly Hills Tennis Club, a fashionable hang-out for the movie crowd, paid some pretty starlets to adorn the swimming pool, and enjoyed the social whirl – at the launch he played tennis with Charlie Chaplin against Vines and Groucho Marx. Errol Flynn, Merle Oberon, David Niven and other big-screen names were regulars. He dallied with Marlene Dietrich, became firm friends with Bette Davis, went to the *most* amusing parties, darling, and entered into two more marriages. Wimbledon's loss was the gossip columns' gain.

When the news came through that he was leaving both these shores and the good old amateur game, Sir Samuel Hoare sent a horrified telegram – 'Why did you do it?' But he put things more gracefully when he informed the House of Commons what had happened. 'Whether his decision is right or wrong,' he said, 'is not for us to say. But it is for us to thank him for his services ... and give him our best wishes for the future.'[6]

Of all the questions asked of these champions of 1934, the most common is the most unanswerable: how good were they? But though there is no authoritative or reliable way of comparing sports at different times, there is no great harm in having a guess.

In Cotton's case there are measurable yardsticks. The tees he played from at Royal St George's are nearly identical to those in use today for club players and visitors, the best of whom could not come close to Cotton's score – even with the assistance of the brilliantly tooled, precision-forged modern clubs that have 'revolutionised' the game. Cotton's total was only seven shots worse than the winning score notched by Darren Clarke in 2011 (admittedly in wet weather, on a course lengthened to compensate for the power of modern equipment). And his two-round, halfway score was seven shots *better* than the one achieved by Sandy Lyle on his way to victory in 1985, on a course only 100 yards longer than the 1934 design. If Cotton had played in the 2011 Open (from the old tees, with his usual out-of-date clubs and balls) his score, even including that final-round horror show, would have placed him 9= (along with Sergio García). He would have beaten Rory McIlroy and Adam Scott by *five* clear shots.

If this challenges the common assumption that golf has 'progressed' or 'advanced' since those days, we should not be too put out. In truth, the average handicap of recreational golfers has barely moved in the last few generations, despite the famous changes in the quality of clubs and balls. This is because the

---

[6] Though the tense distinction between amateurs and professionals has dissolved, we can still see its silhouette in the way we entrust the highest positions in the land to elected politicians with little direct knowledge of their fields – as if their professional expertise were suspect or dubious. One might even suggest, in a playful way, that this derives from nothing more than a historic preference for the good old amateur way.

underlying trigonometry of the game – player, stick, ball, flag, cup – has not altered one iota. It is likely that if an avatar of the 1934 Henry Cotton appeared today, and was handed a spanking new set of Mizunos, he could more than hold his own.

It might not be possible to say the same about Perry and Round, because lawn tennis really *has* moved on. When we watch Perry and Crawford on the bustling old black and white newsreel, or Round delivering her well-ordered instruction on Pathé, it seems a pale shadow of the strenuous tussles we now take for granted. In her long skirt Round looks more like a nurse than a tennis star, and Perry and Crawford both wore antique cricket whites in their final – long trousers and well-tailored shirts. We can see that Perry was a lithe and rangy athlete, quick when he had to be, but they all appear, if we are honest, to be knocking up, patting decorous serves at one another with both feet courteously grounded. They actually *walk* through some rallies, stroking the ball back and forth like good-natured guests at a Gloucestershire tea party.

Some of this is down to the conditions governing the game: the rules stated that one foot must remain grounded during the service action, so the super-athletic modern serve was out of the question. But it is hard to avoid the stark conclusion that neither Perry nor Crawford would take even one game off Roger Federer. Modern tennis bears little resemblance to the one played in those days: it would take years for Round to adjust to the power of Serena Williams's serve. While the dimensions of the court have not changed, and the scoring system remains the same, the game itself has speeded up. Tall athletes throwing and screaming their way through the ball, both feet in the air, pounding it over the net – no one could contemplate such tennis in 1934.

Cricket stands somewhere between these two extremes. It may well be that in modern times the *average* level has risen – the weakest player in today's county game might be fitter and faster than the weakest inter-war hanger-on. But there isn't a batsman alive who would relish facing Larwood in his prime, and Verity would surely breeze into the England team now. As for Bradman, he might just feel that after surviving Bodyline en route to a Test average of nearly 100 he was up to the challenge of facing Ben Stokes.

There can be no firm conclusion to such musings. There must have been plenty of old-timers who looked at Cotton and thought he was all show, not a patch on old Ted Ray – now *he* could hit a golf ball. Ageing cricket fans must have shaken their heads at Verity, saying that Hirst or Barnes would never have been seen *dead* bowling rubbish like that. In truth, even Verity might be taken aback by the power-hitting of the modern crash-bang-wallop merchants, just as Bradman would have to adjust to the new cricket landscape (he never played India or the West Indies). But sometimes we must suspend our ingrained belief that things always get better. Not all wine improves with age.

One thing we can say for certain – perhaps the only meaningful yardstick – is that all of the 1934 title winners rose far above their contemporaries. They beat all their rivals, which was the highest they could aspire to, and no small thing. But we can notice that one of the ways they achieved this was by disobeying the prevailing orthodoxies. Generalisations are blunt instruments, but a surprising number of the best-ever do turn out to have been unorthodox, scornful of the usual dogmas, negligent of the accepted methods and usual wisdom. All developed techniques that gave them an edge over their more ordinary peers.

In Verity's case this was accidental: he was simply taller than most spinners; in team photographs he towered over his colleagues, even the fearsome pacemen (at 5ft 8in, Larwood was much shorter). A tall finger spinner went against the grain – men like Verity were expected to deliver the ball with speed – but the extra bounce it gave him made him an awkward proposition, especially hard to play off the front foot.

For Cotton the novelty, as we have seen, came down to the way he used his hands and wrists. The authorities were unanimous: the right hand must be quiet. James Braid, in *Advanced Golf* (1908), was all for a 'whip-like snap' through the ball, but saw a loose right hand as the cause of hooks. He had teed it up with W. G. Grace, and frowned at the cricketer's wrist move: 'It is difficult to become a first-class golfer when the driving is done this way.' Harry Vardon, in *How to Play Golf* (1912), was even more emphatic. The hook to the left was 'the most frequent of faults', and caused by 'turning the right hand over at the moment of impact … in no circumstances should the right hand be the dominant partner'. And Abe Mitchell, whom Cotton admired above all other golfers, agreed. In *Essentials of Golf* (1927) he declared that 'the left hand must lead the club into the ball … care must be taken not to attempt this movement with the right wrist'.

Cotton rejected every last scrap of this advice. He felt sure that his own right hand – the stronger one – was a resource, not a handicap. It went against what these teachers said, but so what? So he scrubbed away at those hickory shafts, and made a point of swishing a club one-handed through wet grass as if there was no tomorrow, to strengthen this grip of his. Combined with his other keen conviction – a braced left side – these exercises allowed him to create a new kind of golf swing which could, with what one observer later called 'a terrific flash of the hands', fire the ball 300 yards up a fairway, time after time after time – an extraordinary feat with the equipment at his disposal.

He did have one renowned figure to look on as a role model. In the early decades of the century there had been no one to touch Harry Vardon, and he, too, had evolved a singular method of his own through endless hours of lonely trial and error. As a child growing up in Jersey, far from the centre of golf, he began by nailing a square of scrap metal on to the face of a sawn-off stick until he could knock marbles around the edge of the new course – Royal Jersey – that appeared outside his bedroom window in 1878. In the process he came up with a new grip, with overlapping fingers, that is still used by more than 90 per cent of the world's golfers more than a hundred years later. This famous 'Vardon Grip' gave him more accuracy and control than his rivals, and led to his scooping 62 tournament victories, including six Open Championships.

Perry's originality was clear. In training himself to take the ball early, on the rise – a skill he took from table tennis – he placed himself in the highest group of all-time greats: the rare few who have genuinely altered the central essence of their games.

Does something similar hold true for other giants? Maybe. In 1919 Lord Harris wrote that W. G. Grace had developed the ability to work straight balls into the leg side with a vertical bat – a new and risky skill in the era of bumpy, unprepared wickets. It was 'entirely unique', and meant that 'his cricket did not resemble that of any other player'. At a stroke, Grace became impossible to bowl at, since naturally he would deal roughly with anything wide of the off stump. Bowlers were bemused: unprepared for so unconventional an approach, they had no clear way to prevent him scoring.

Don Bradman, perhaps the greatest of them all, also ignored the usual rules in favour of a personal, custom-made method based on quick hands, twinkling footwork and more horizontal-bat strokes than were recommended by the coaching manuals of the time. His grip was strong (devised as a way to keep the ball down) and his stance was low – with the bat between his feet, not behind his back boot. His pick-up was new: he lifted the bat away with an early cock of the wrists and a downward press of his left hand, with his elbows quiet and still – he did not *swing* at the ball with his arms. And he clubbed the ball with a good deal more right hand than anyone at the time thought wise. Combined with his odd, low posture, it made him a maddening opponent – how on earth was one supposed to bowl at a fellow who insisted on wielding a bat like *that*?

All of these small manoeuvres were enough to give these very gifted sportsmen a firm advantage over their contemporaries. Dorothy Round's case was different. In the two-part film *How I Play Tennis* that she made for Pathé Pictures, she was at pains to stress the importance of the acknowledged basics. In a voice that sounded like the Queen, but with a Midlands twang, she added that there was 'plenty of room for team spirit' when you played doubles, and that the main thing to remember was that it is 'only a game'. But even she had the unusual luck of having learned the game playing with her three older brothers on her very own tennis court. From the word go she was comfortable with a harder-hitting game than most of her women opponents were used to.

Fortune does not always favour the brave – lots of risk-takers fall by the wayside. But it may be that some degree of fresh thinking is a prerequisite for sporting greatness. It is not certain that Verity, Cotton and Perry knew exactly what they were doing, but the variations they came up with turned out, in Darwinian ways they could not predict, to be splendid adaptations. Natural selection, in the glare of competition, did the rest.

CHAPTER FOURTEEN

Here We Go Again

Less than a year after the high noon of 1934, on 11 March 1935, Hermann Goering, a pilot who had flown on the wingtips of the Red Baron in the First World War before going on to found, in 1933, the *Geheime Staatspolizei* (Gestapo), proclaimed the creation of a new air force: the *Luftwaffe*. It had been reported for months that the Dornier factory on Lake Constance was blazing night and day turning out 'freight aeroplanes' – and everyone knew that the 'freight' in question was high-explosive bombs. Two weeks later the Führer himself ordered up a dozen submarines. After such blatant contraventions of the Versailles agreement there could no longer be any hiding from the fact that blasted old Churchill was right: Germany really *was* becoming a military power all over again. In August it would formally adopt the Nazi badge, the swastika, as an aggressive symbol of the new Germany. A nation was on the march.

Sport would soon be implicated in this fearful pageant. It had long been agreed that Berlin would host the 1936 Olympic Games and, though Hitler was mild on the idea, thinking it a frivolous distraction, he could see that it might make a good display case for wholesome Aryan virtues. Leni Riefenstahl was asked to forge the imagery, and she did a splendid job. Her film *Olympia* licked its lips over the Aryan physique, creating a triumphant succession of tall, blond, muscular athletes, some of whom (the rowers) actually gave a synchronised Nazi salute as they passed the winning post.

Riefenstahl was given 80 cameramen to make this great work, and one of her ideas was a novel gimmick: the Olympic torch relay. In one fiery sequence she depicted a glowing marathon, run from the Parthenon to Berlin, with wondrous Greek sculptures and nude athletes throwing javelins or hurdling mountains. When modern sportspeople grow emotional about such rituals, they do not always realise that they are honouring not a classical ceremony but a modern *son-et-lumière* conceived, in Wagnerian terms, as a way of giving ancient-world polish to Adolf Hitler's dream of racial supremacy.

But sport being sport, the black athlete Jesse Owens derailed this nationalist project by sprinting away to four wins. 'The Americans should be ashamed of themselves,' the Führer was quoted as saying as he refused to demean himself by placing the gold medal around Owens's black neck: 'letting Negroes win their medals for them.'[1]

Naturally we right-thinking moderns see Hitler's gambit – using games to boost a political fantasy – as ugly. But few complained when Nelson Mandela did virtually the same thing in enlisting the Springboks to the cause of the new South Africa. Donning the green and gold uniform of the apartheid state was a profound gesture of reconciliation, and how we all cheered. Scrum-halves wept openly; prop forwards covered their eyes. But even Mandela was seeking to exploit sport's tenacious grip on the public imagination. His purpose might have been wholly different, and more obviously magnanimous – but we ought at least to register the fact that he did pursue it through similar tactics.

We should notice, too, that Britain's own modest performance in those 1936 games was greeted with chagrin at home. Not

[1] Owens's four gold medals were rightly hailed as symbols of America's freedom-loving spirit, and compared to Nazi Germany this was beyond doubt. But back at Ohio State University he was not, thanks to his skin colour, allowed to live on campus. And inter-racial sprinting was banned in many Southern states, including his own, Alabama.

everyone believed that playing up and playing the game was more important than winning. On the contrary, many felt that the taking part was a *lot* less important than the doing badly. The *Daily Express* called the team's effort 'an insult to all Britons', while the *Observer* argued that if no steps were taken to change things we were in severe danger of achieving 'national second-rateness'.

When war did come in 1939, top-level sport was again suspended. The West Indies tour of England was abandoned when news of the Molotov–Ribbentrop Pact broke in August; and The Oval, venue for the third Test (Constantine 'surpassing Bradman in his stroke play', according to *Wisden*), was requisitioned and turned into a prisoner-of-war camp. England's upcoming tour of India was cancelled, too. The skipper, Sussex's Jack Holmes (nickname: 'Sherlock'), joined the Royal Flying Corps in 1918 and was about to come back as a Wing Commander in the Battle of Britain – he would win an Air Force Cross before retiring to tend his mink farm in Sussex.

His last match in that fateful 1939 season came when he led Sussex against Yorkshire at Hove. The game was nearly cancelled, but because it was a benefit both sides agreed to go on – though Sutcliffe, for one, had already received his call-up papers. Yorkshire were fresh from winning a seventh championship in ten years by beating Hampshire at Bournemouth, so it wasn't a major journey. As so often, Verity excelled, taking seven for nine (in six overs) as the home side fell for 33 in their second innings; indeed, one of his scalps was Holmes himself. 'I wonder if I shall ever play cricket again,' said Verity as he walked off. Afterwards the Sussex scorer handed a slip of paper to Brian Sellers, Yorkshire's captain, but he thrust it into a pocket and forgot all about it.

The date was 1 September 1939, a day that would go down in the annals of infamy: the assault on Poland was under way. W. H. Auden's poem caught the *Zeitgeist* when he sat in one of the dives on 52nd Street (New York) inhaling the 'unmentionable odour of death' as he watched the 'clever hopes' of a 'low, dishonest decade' go up in smoke.

Hedley Verity did not have the luxury of brooding in a New York dive. As Sir Home Gordon put it in *The Cricketer*: 'England now began the grim Test against Germany', and the change was instantaneous. When the coach to Yorkshire crossed the A4 out of London the players could see that the road was crowded with people fleeing the big city.

Verity had been preparing for this day since 1938, when he bumped into a friend in the Headingley pavilion; this was Arnold Shaw, a Lieutenant Colonel in the Yorkshire Regiment (the Green Howards). He had known Shaw since a reception following the Madras Test of 1934 (in which Verity took 11 wickets) but there were more serious things to talk about now. Shaw sent him some military manuals, which Verity read carefully. Then he joined the Officer Cadet Training Unit. On completing the course in late 1941, he became a captain and company commander. He wasn't the only Yorkshire player in the Green Howards: Bowes, Hutton and Sutcliffe were brothers in arms. And in that same year his old England team-mate, the fast bowler Ken Farnes, was killed shortly after qualifying as an RAF flying officer, on a night-flying exercise over Oxfordshire.

For his part, Shaw was impressed by Verity's approach to soldiering. 'I have seen him talking to royalty, generals and private soldiers,' he said. 'And his bearing never varied. He had the respect and admiration of them all.' He added that Verity was 'clean-living and clean-speaking, charitable and a quick help to others'.

While Verity was training, his old captain Douglas Jardine was also tasting war as part of the ragged Expeditionary Force that fled France at Dunkirk and Boulogne. As he pushed his way on to the destroyer waiting to take him home to safety, he heard a voice at his side. 'We'll be all right now, Sir.' He looked to where his batman was pointing, to the letters on the cold grey hull of the ship. It was called HMS *Verity*.

In a letter to his young sons Verity wrote: 'Always remember to do what's right, and to fight for it if necessary.' With that he sailed off to Persia, Syria and Egypt.[2] Soon afterwards, in July 1943, the Green Howards took part in the invasion of Sicily – an attack on the Third Reich's 'soft underbelly'. The attack was led by General Patton's Seventh Army, and once the landings had been made the Green Howards drove north up to the Strait of Messina, the slim band of bright blue water that led to the toe of Italy's mainland. Verity was ordered to lead an attack on an isolated farmhouse that was blocking the path to the sea. His old team-mate Norman Yardley ran into him an hour or so before the assault, and judged him to be 'very fit and in good spirits'.

It was a dark night, but the enemy was ready and waiting; the Green Howards found themselves crawling through an exposed cornfield with machine-gun fire sizzling over their heads. Verity rose to urge his men forward, and (by this time it was about three o'clock in the morning) was smashed in the chest by shrapnel. 'Keep going,' he was heard to shout – but he himself could not move. When the attack failed he lay wounded close to the enemy line, attended by his batman, a private from Durham who had never even seen a game of cricket. The Germans carried Verity away to a nearby field hospital, performed a rough-and-ready operation, and put him on a railway truck for evacuation to Naples. He made it as far as Caserta, where a fellow trooper recognised him and spread the word. But his wound was infected, and after three days of grievous pain one of England's greatest sporting heroes died. He was 38 years old.

When Bill Bowes heard the news he was not far away, in another Italian prison camp. He was dumbstruck. 'Hedley dead!' he cried, recalling the shock in his memoir. 'It was unbelievable. For a long time I walked up and down the road, time stilled …'

[2] Verity actually played a game of cricket on the eastern bank of the Suez Canal at this time, bowling, according to one bystander, 'as near perfectly as made no difference'.

It was an even sadder story at the Verity household in Yorkshire. His sister Grace said that she would 'never forget the sight of father's face' when the news came. 'We had been assured that Hedley had been picked up and was a prisoner of war,' she remembered, 'and then came the letter from the Red Cross ...'

The nature of his death made it inevitable that Verity's life would be cast in terms of noble sacrifice, but even by these standards the obituaries were lavish. 'So passed a great Yorkshireman and a great cricketer,' ran the *Green Howards Gazette*, 'in godly company, as a real knight should.' His old headmaster, William Rigby, testified that Verity had been a boy 'unspoiled by the highest successes'. F. S. Jackson, the President of Yorkshire, recalled a 'fine and generous personality ... a delightful and charming man', while Herbert Sutcliffe said simply: 'I don't think I have ever played with so fine a sport.' Hutton added that he radiated goodwill: 'If you dropped a catch off him he just smiled.' And *Wisden* echoed him by saying that Verity 'combined nature with art to a degree not equalled by any other English bowler ... He was tireless, but never wild ... as sensitive in observation as a good host, or as an instrumentalist who spots a rival on the beat; the scholar who does not only dream, the inventor who can make it work.'

Brian Sellers, Yorkshire's captain, also dwelt on Verity's singular character. Though he seemed 'a very quiet type of man', it was clear he could be steely when firmness was called for: 'It was not his nature to be ordered about.' Above all, he was level-headed: 'His character and disposition never changed amidst his many triumphs.'

These were rare tributes even for so popular a cricketer, and it is noticeable that they focused on the man's moral as much as his cricketing qualities. And they gushed in from all quarters. 'If a side that included Verity got 60 runs,' ran one heartfelt tribute, 'it reckoned the match was won.' Another one, catching the Cardus style, was adamant that 'bowling, to Hedley, was like poetry to Burns, or sculpture to Michelangelo.' And George Hirst wrote: 'Anyone who came into contact with Hedley had but one thought.

He may be a fine bowler but he is certainly a fine man. I am so glad I knew him ...'

The *Bradford Telegraph and Argus* had the last word: 'Wherever cricket is appreciated, wherever sportsmanship is an indication of character, wherever men are honoured not because they are wealthy or gifted but because they are, in the true sense of the word, men – there will the name of Hedley Verity be ever respected.'

The effusiveness of these remarks speaks volumes for the affection in which Verity was held by those who knew him. But his death moved strangers, too. In a hospital for soldiers in the north of God's own county, a wounded cricket lover scratched out his feelings in a poem which the *Yorkshire Post* was happy to publish. It ended:

> *Never a doubt that somewhere you still play*
> *The game you loved upon a summer's day.*

And a 22-year-old officer named Drummond Allison, fresh out of Sandhurst, added another verse in recalling Verity's imperishable triumph at St John's Wood in 1934:

> *On this great ground, more marvellous than Lord's*
> *– Time takes more spin than nineteen thirty four.*
> *You face at last that vast, that Bradman-shaming*
> *Batsman whose cuts obey no natural law.*

Drummond wrote these lines in Ireland, where he was training; he himself would soon fall victim to the war, dying in Italy, a few months later, in December 1943.

The 1944 *Wisden* found space, in a terrifying list of casualties, for something like a service of remembrance. Among the contributors was Don Bradman, who stated that Verity was 'one of the greatest if not THE greatest left-hand bowlers of all time'. That amazing spell in the Lord's Test, he said, was 'a performance to which even the statistics could not do justice'. And he wanted to stress that Verity was no one-game wonder; for years he had been 'the foundation stone of England's bowling'.

He was right. But the statistics did say *something* about Verity's powers as a player: in ten seasons of cricket for Yorkshire and England he took 1,956 wickets at an average of 14.90 (by way of comparison, Graeme Swann, England's best spinner of modern times, took 739 at an average of 32.12). Verity topped the national bowling averages five times, capturing 200 wickets in each of the three seasons following his great feat. He took all ten wickets twice, nine seven times, eight 13 times and seven 34 times – no need to write home about *them*. And this was in a career cut short by war.

He had a particular hold over Bradman – to a greater extent than any other bowler. In all he dismissed him eight times, for 401 runs, in 16 Tests – giving The Don an average of only 50, half his usual tally. Robertson-Glasgow might not have been wrong when he wrote, in *Wisden*, that had it not been for Verity The Don might have averaged 150.

Some years later, the Australian paid another tribute to his old adversary when he contributed a generous introduction to Sam Davis's 1952 memoir, *Prince with a Piece of Leather*. Verity was not only a 'very great England-Yorkshire cricketer' but 'a gallant soldier and chivalrous gentleman'. Years later he did the same for Alan Hill's *Hedley Verity: Portrait of a Cricketer*. Verity had an 'ideal physique', he remembered, with 'a lovely, curving, sinuous flight'; but his finest quality was his 'sportsmanship and manly bearing ... I never once heard him complain or offer a criticism.' In short, the Yorkshireman 'exemplified all that was best about cricket, and I deem it an honour and privilege to have been on stage with him in those golden days'.

There was one last chance for Verity to make his presence felt on the cricket pitch. When the game resumed after the war Yorkshire's captain, Brian Sellers, dug his gear out of the wardrobe and was relieved to find that it still fitted, since he was down to play for the Army. But what was this in his blazer pocket? He pulled out a scrap of paper, looked at the scribbled numbers – 6-1-9-7 – and, after the briefest of frowns, suddenly knew what they signified. His mind drifted back to that sombre September day at Hove before the war, when the Sussex scorer had handed him this same slip of paper as a souvenir. It was Hedley Verity's last bowling analysis for Yorkshire.

Verity was buried in a military cemetery at Caserta, beneath a simple stone with a white rose, and in 1954 Len Hutton's England team paused en route to Australia to pay their respects. Someone draped a Yorkshire tie – blue with white roses – over the grave. But there were other ways of remembering Hedley. Ten years earlier, in 1944, a match had been held at Headingley to mark the first anniversary of his death. All the greats turned out – Hammond captained one side, Sutcliffe the other and Rhodes umpired, all wearing black armbands. A plaque bearing Verity's name was later placed at the Hutton Gates, and in 2009 another was put on his birthplace in Burley. In front of various county legends, his son Douglas spoke of 'a humble house on a humble street … a street where he would first learn to take a ball in his left hand'. A year later a pub called the Hedley Verity opened in the city centre, with scoreboards over the bar and a large photographic portrait of the great man, demonstrating how to grip a cricket ball.

His name lives on in more discreet ways. When Adrian Allington needed a name for an England bowler in his satirical caper, *The Amazing Test Match Crime* (1939), he paid tribute to Verity by calling one of his characters 'Truth'. And Jack Sheffield's *Please, Sir* (2011) includes a man born on 25 June 1934, the last day of Verity's Test at Lord's, and is named Hedley Verity Bickerstaff into the bargain. Finally, Verity lives on as the middle name of the England batsman (and commentator) Nick Knight, in honour of the fact that he is a distant relative of the great left-armer.

One of the most pleasing echoes of Verity's triumphant day, however, arose in an unexpected *quartier*. At the end of a 1989 TV episode of Agatha Christie's *Poirot*, the great detective is dining in a restaurant to celebrate the solution of another baffling murder case when news comes through of Verity's bowling analysis. The English men at the table assume that here at last was one thing the Belgian brainbox might not know – but as usual he astounds them. But of course, he murmurs. 'Are you surprised, *mes amis*?' Doesn't everyone know that Monsieur *Verité* is the 'greatest exponent alive' of spin-bowling on a sticky wicket? What on earth did zey *sink* would 'appen?

High-level golf ground to a halt in the war, too, but golf courses still had a role to play – and not only as peaceful spaces for rest and recreation. Many became caught up in the conflict. Balmoral became an impromptu POW camp while Turnberry, on the Ayrshire coast, hosted an RAF airstrip; those famous rumpled fairways became a base from which Liberators flew anti-submarine patrols over the North Atlantic sea lanes.

In the south, a former Cambridge golfer, now a fighter ace, 'Laddie' Lucas, landed his wounded Spitfire on the links at Prince's, where Sarazen had won the 1932 Open, and which abutted Royal St George's. Prince's had been turned into an anti-aircraft battery, and was bombed as a result; and other nearby clubs performed similar duties: there were pillboxes at Rye and Deal, and Folkestone was a centre for naval mine control. A maze of tunnels was dug under Wentworth to build a shelter for Whitehall, and the fairways were allowed to run wild so they would not attract any passing Luftwaffe pilots. At the end of the war the overgrown course was cleared by German prisoners, and when someone remarked that this was their 'Burma Road' – a reference to the Burma–Thailand railway line laid by British POWs in Asia – the name stuck for good.

There were other connections. Dwight D. Eisenhower, a devoted golfer, planned the Normandy landings of 1944 from a cottage beside the 14th fairway of Coombe Hill in Kingston; and after the invasion itself (in which Bobby Jones waded ashore at Omaha Beach) he set up a new HQ in the clubhouse at Guex, near Reims, in France's Champagne region.

These warlike intrusions on this most pastoral of sports gave rise to a noted instance of British sang-froid under fire when Richmond Golf Club responded to the Blitz in 1940 by publishing 'temporary rules', including the following amendments:

> *Players are requested to collect bomb and shrapnel splinters to save these causing damage to the mowing machines ... While bombs are falling, players may take cover without penalty ... A player whose stroke is affected by the simultaneous explosion of a bomb may play another ball from the same place. Penalty, one stroke.*

These were widely taken as examples of, how you say, the famous British stiff upper lip. But it is at least *faintly* possible that they owed as much to another national reflex: dry humour. Keep calm, the merry old codgers seemed to be saying over their pink gins, and here's to Drake. Let's not let a piffling thing like a bomb spoil the game.

Henry Cotton didn't experience the war like Verity; indeed, it put him in marital rather than martial danger. Though Argentina was not an enemy, the conflict threatened to turn 'Toots' into an alien in Britain, a status fraught with discomfort. Until now it had been hard to get past the Roman Catholic injunction against divorce, but in this crisis, under pressure, they managed to have her first marriage annulled by a district court in Latvia. Cotton had himself received into the Catholic Church, and they were married in London, at Farm Street. His timing was excellent: the wedding was in December 1939, just before the fighting began. One of the witnesses was that lucky fighter pilot, P. B. ('Laddie') Lucas.

Cotton had done officer training at Alleyn's, so was a natural for the RAF. But though technically a flying officer, he was at first assigned to catering, and spent most of his time in the officers' mess at various aerodromes. No one objected when he began to devote himself to raising money at golf days – in the autumn of 1939 and the spring of 1940 he travelled far and wide, playing his old adversaries in front of good-sized galleries and generating tidy sums for the Red Cross. It was a small irony that in becoming one of the few RAF officers to avoid the Battle of Britain, he was awarded an MBE for charitable deeds. But only a small one. In truth, he contributed more to the war effort by playing golf – those matches raised some £70,000, enough for several Spitfires – than he could have done making bread and butter pudding on air bases. And he had his own cross to bear: had it not been for the war he would have been captaining Britain's Ryder Cup team in the away fixture at Ponte Vedra Beach, Florida.[3]

This war work was playing hell with his stomach, too. Cotton rather fancifully put his painful innards down to the rationed diet and the absence of 'proper food', though the RAF doctors diagnosed a plain duodenal ulcer. He was operated on, invalided out of the service and given instructions not to touch golf clubs for a year. One way or another, the war was costing him his prime years as a professional golfer.

Not surprisingly, neither he nor 'Toots' had much enthusiasm for the austere ways of ration-era Britain when the war finally ended (despite living in a suite at the Dorchester Hotel) so he was more than happy to accept a job in Monte Carlo, to revive its now-overgrown golf course – also with the help of German prisoners of war. He built a new driving range in front of the Casino from which golfers (including the young Crown Prince Rainier) could thump balls out to sea, using nets to trawl them up. And he loved the life – the climate, the food, the social scene. He wasn't exactly match fit, though, so it was a surprise when he went north in 1946 and won the French Open by a mile, playing as well as ever. It reminded everyone, including himself, that he was too young to give up high-level golf, so he returned to London, accepted a

---

[3] Cotton was given his chance to captain the team in the first post-war Ryder Cup, in 1947. But it turned out to be the worst showing by a British team in the history of the contest: Britain lost the 12-game series 11-1; Cotton himself lost his doubles match by an astounding margin (10 and 9) and was beaten in the singles by Sam Snead.

professional's position at Royal Mid-Surrey (J. H. Taylor's old home), found a luxury flat in Eaton Square, and started to think about winning again. He continued to winter in the South of France for many years, in Mougins, but in 1948 he crossed the Atlantic to play the Masters at Augusta, and a few months later, at Muirfield, put on a grand display (in front of George VI, who was walking in the Open gallery – the only British monarch ever to do so) and won his third claret jug by five strokes – the same margin as in 1934. He was 41, and second only to Vardon on the top plinth of English golf.

To the end, however, he remained a man whose face didn't quite fit. When a *Daily Telegraph* tournament in 1949 asked him at short notice to add some star quality to the field, many of his fellow professionals threatened to strike in protest at the favourable treatment he was receiving (he had skipped past the usual qualifying process). 'There is a feeling,' wrote the *Sunday Express*, 'that he gets too much publicity.' This was true – and not all of it was down to his golf. He and his wife were well known for being, shall we say, highly strung. When Temple Golf Club refused to pay for the fixtures and fittings 'Toots' had added to the apartment they had been given, she smashed the damn place up. And when Henry seemed to be dancing a little *too* enthusiastically with someone else's wife, she strode out and punched him on the jaw.

Nor was Cotton himself above courting controversy. 'I am a legend,' he would say when fusspot stewards interfered with his dining arrangements at golf tournaments, 'and we can eat wherever we like'. At a PGA dinner he spoke too vehemently against the hidebound ways of British golf and had to apologise. When he angrily withdrew from a tournament at Sunningdale after the organisers refused to change his tee time, he was fined. And things came to a head when he was made honorary secretary of a breakaway group within the game that sought to give top players a stronger voice. He blotted his copy-book further at the US Open in 1956 when his playing partner, Jimmy Demaret, refused to sign his card following a dispute over the score – a very rare and damaging snub in a game that made such an ostentatious fetish of honesty.

As his ability and desire to play the game dwindled (and his waistline spread[4]) he turned his attention to course design, helping to create or enhance a dozen layouts in Britain (like Abridge, Farnham Park, Sene Valley, Gourock and St Mellons) as well as Bologna and Torino in Italy, Megève in France and Vale do Lobo in Portugal. His most significant project, however, fell into his lap in 1963 when he was invited to inspect a stretch of swampy coastland on the Algarve. It didn't look promising, but Cotton, heartened by memories of golf on the French Riviera, took the assignment and went on to build Penina, the first great winter-sun golf resort in southern Portugal. He even used a patient camel to lug sand up from the beach for the new bunkers.

Always a loner, he became a keen painter in his later life, knocking out golfing views in bright oils – and of course, as in golf, he was self-taught. He had plenty of other eccentricities, too: he believed that swimming was 'bad for golf' – a pity, since there was an enormous pool at Penina, which Tony Jacklin loved – and preferred to dangle from a trapeze bar in his sitting room to strengthen his arms. But he was always a dedicated teacher both at Royal Mid-Surrey and in Portugal; and an evangelist for the method he had discovered on his own – he would get students to whack away at rubber tyres till their arms ached, to strengthen their hands. Even when he moved to Penina full-time he came back to London for Test matches, and it was partly thanks to his love of cricket that the headquarters of the PGA were based at the Kennington Oval.

He had no great interest in the commentary booth, so he never became one of golf's presiding voices; but he did help create the

---

[4] The entry on Henry Cotton in *Peter Alliss's Golf Heroes* speaks of his 'secret vice of stuffing his face full of cream cakes smothered in strawberry jam'. But Alliss didn't hesitate to think of him fondly as a 'great man' as well as a legendary golfer.

Golf Foundation for young players, and put his name to the Henry Cotton Rookie of the Year award for newcomers. Over the years the list of winners – Tony Jacklin, Sam Torrance, Sandy Lyle, Nick Faldo, José María Olazábal, Colin Montgomerie, Sergio García and others – amounted to a Who's Who of European golf. When he presented Tony Jacklin, the first winner, with his cheque for £100, he urged him to spend it on clothes, so he would 'look the part'.

He was awarded a knighthood in 1987, shortly before his death (making him Britain's first golfing knight) and though the honour was not public, it came just in time for him to be delighted. He was buried in Portugal, beside 'Toots', and at the memorial service in London Bill Deedes (of the *Telegraph*) said he had always felt unappreciated – had believed, from Waterloo onwards, that 'a prophet is not without honour – save in his own country.' His life, said Deedes, had been 'a lonely voyage to the stars'.

The obituaries felt much the same way, though few of them omitted to mention his awkward side. 'A conversation with Cotton was invariably one way,' said one golf magazine. 'He spoke, and you listened.' And the *Observer*'s Pat Ward-Thomas spoke of a fragile perfectionist driven by 'anguish' to succeed. 'The conquest of himself was Cotton's greatest victory.' But there was no disputing the man's greatness. Cotton had won two further Opens, in 1937 and 1948, three British Matchplay titles, and had captained the Ryder Cup team twice. Neither was there any arguing with the resolve it had taken to achieve so much. If Cotton rarely appeared to have been looking out for anyone except Number One, the drive to liberate himself from the suffocating constraints of old-time golf did make him a notable freedom fighter for the game as a whole, one of golf's pioneering and emancipating figures. His friend (and biographer) Peter Dobereiner wrote in a *Guardian* obituary that, yes, Cotton was a man whose ambition reached 'demonic proportions', and, yes, he made himself a maestro through 'a frenzy of self-improvement'. But while admitting that his driven manner inclined some people to think him 'an insufferable snob', Dobereiner declared that through it Cotton had seemed to him 'an absolutely bloody wonderful person'.

The Henry Cotton course at Penina still bears his name (as does a restaurant and an annual trophy) and the hand-forged Benny putter that helped him win the 1934 Open stands in a cabinet of golf memorabilia in the corridor at Royal St George's. A painting of his escape from the bunker at the eighth hangs on the wall of the professional's shop.

A few months before his death he attended the Open at Muirfield and startled one young player, Brandel Chamblee, by bumping into him at breakfast, congratulating him on his good play so far and giving him, impromptu, a detailed tutorial on ball-striking – the placement of the fingers, the 'dime-sized' spot on the clubface that needed to be found time and time again ... That was Cotton: obsessive to the last.

Fred Perry cannot be said to have had a glorious war either – he stayed in America, playing exhibition tennis and living the high life. When German bombs started to fall on London there was, not surprisingly, some comment to the effect that he had skipped town at a less than brave moment – indeed it was probably this rather than anything in his social background that led the officer class of Wimbledon to shake its head at the mention of his name (and the Palace to resist the temptation to bestow a knighthood on one of England's greatest ever sportsmen). But no one liked a 'bomb dodger',[5] and there was no getting away from the fact that, while Britain was cowering under German raids, and raging firestorms lit up the night sky over London, Perry was swearing

---

[5] He wasn't the only one. The back trouble that kept Don Bradman out of harm's way raised eyebrows even among his own team-mates. The all-rounder Keith Miller, who flew sorties for the RAAF, couldn't help noticing that the back seemed fine during the famous 'Invincibles' tour of England in 1948, and never quite forgave him.

an oath to a foreign flag. 'I absolutely and entirely renounce and abjure all allegiance and fidelity to any foreign prince, potentate, state or sovereignty,' he said – and meant it.

He made this declaration on 15 November 1940. Only weeks earlier, Cotton had raised £300 for war charities in Perry's own childhood neighbourhood, Wallasey, and on the very day of Perry's oath incendiary shells rained down on Coventry in a 500-plane bombardment that lasted ten hours, destroyed 4,000 homes, wrecked three-quarters of the city's factories and killed 1,000 people. A glorious medieval cathedral was smashed to dust. It was a shift of strategy by the Luftwaffe, which had spent the previous 57 nights unloading explosives on London. One bomb, in October, crashed through the roof of the old Centre Court and wrote off a thousand seats – the lawn itself was now a farm for hens and pigs. Those stuffy old Wimbledon types could perhaps be forgiven, at a time like this, for not looking *too* fondly on their absent champion, who was playing Don Budge at Madison Square Garden for big money, and scandalising New York by handing in an eye-watering expenses claim. Even when it came to the Blitz his luck held: Coventry was the home of Dunlop, and he was a Slazenger man.

In Perry's defence, he was embroiled in a bad-tempered divorce from Helen Vimson at this time, which wasn't resolved until 1941. But he was also busy with the romance that would lead to a second brief marriage, concluded before the divorce was finalised. He was conscripted a year after Pearl Harbor (he didn't volunteer) and stayed in California as a fitness adviser of low rank. When he went up before a board for officer selection, his prickly attitude to authority did not greatly impress the interview panel.

But in the post-war years a mellower Fred Perry made peace with his past. He returned to Wimbledon in 1947 to report on the event for the *Evening Standard*, and went on to become a regular voice for the BBC – part of the furniture. He was there to see the world change in 1968 when Wimbledon became the first grand slam event to hand out prize money – Rod Laver picking up £2,000 for beating Tony Roche. By now Perry was a major player in the rag trade, thanks to a tennis shirt inspired by the successful designs of the French musketeer Réné Lacoste. It says quite a lot about Perry's feelings for Wimbledon that after first plumping for a crossed pipe design, he then borrowed the laurel wreath logo of the haughty old club as his insignia.[6] He sold the clothing line in 1964, but stayed on as its ambassador – or, as he liked to put it, 'chairman of their friendship department'. Always restless, never a homebody, he wintered in Jamaica, entertaining cricketers from England and Australia, and West Indians, while following the global tennis tour energetically as a popular pundit and raconteur.

When the Duke of Kent unveiled a statue – a three-quarter-size representation of that famous forehand drive – in 1984, he attended in person and said, with feeling, that it 'meant more to me than all the prize money in the world'. It sits in the heart of the All England Club today, garish as a work of art, but resonant as a monument to a truly great player. In 2013, when Andy Murray became the first Briton to bring home the title since Perry completed his hat-trick in 1936, it made a fitting backdrop for the morning-after picture. Thanks to an enviable Adidas deal, Murray was no longer wearing Fred Perry clothes (in 2009 he wore Perry gear but failed to reach the final) but who said life was perfect? By then the Fred Perry shirt was a global bestseller and fashion statement – what we might call rebel-casual: the laddish uniform of bad-boy pop culture.

Stockport honoured him with a Fred Perry House (a government building) and a Fred Perry Way; and two houses bear plaques in his name: one in Wallasey, one in Ealing. Dorothy Round has been less forthrightly remembered, though in 2013 a newly commissioned bronze statue of her, with a giant tennis ball as a

---

[6] Just as the Dunlop 65 ball inspired by Cotton featured in a Bond story, *Goldfinger*, so, too, did this shirt: Sean Connery wore a blue one with white laurels in *Thunderball*.

pedestal, was unveiled outside the public tennis courts at Priory Park, in her home town of Dudley.

With respect to the Second World War, a telling space opens between the three men in this story. Though all sprang from similar backgrounds in the north of England, Verity had the humblest origins, with his roots in the Yorkshire coal trade. While Cotton, with his private-school polish, and Perry, with his metropolitan swagger and political father, had bigger ambitions, Verity never lost the quiet habits of his Yorkshire past. Yet it was he who possessed the commanding and considerate personality required to lead soldiers in battle. Cotton and Perry may on paper have been closer to being gentlemen, but neither seems to have quite been officer material.

Confusing? Not really. Most people today would laugh at the idea that cricket has any moral qualities – what a comical Victorian boast! But there is no disputing the fact that golf and tennis are individual sports which do put personal ambition above the team ethic. That is why, when Cotton was bickering with his headmaster at the age of 13, the headmaster was so bemused and bewildered. In a letter to Cotton's father he advised earnestly that the boy should resist the temptation to take such a momentous step, lest some people 'jump to the conclusion that your son preferred playing golf for himself to playing cricket for the school. Of course this could not be true …'

We can smile at the stuffiness of such views now (and they are certainly contradicted by the saintly example of Dorothy Round) but what if, in the case of the three male sportsmen who reached their superb peak within a few days of each other in that hot midsummer daze of 1934, the *esprit de corps* fostered by boring old cricket really did inspire a keener sense of duty than the go-go mentality required by more individual pursuits? Maybe they are not so dumb after all, those hoary old clichés of yesteryear.

Shooting Minus the War

What is it about sporting miracles, and the men and women who deliver them, that so waylays us? Is it simple admiration for people who perform feats beyond anything we can dream of? Is it just the fun of the thing? Or is it that we feel them to be emblems of something, ideal versions of what we as a club, a city, a country or a people stand for?

It is a commonplace of anthropology to say that when a society venerates something, it is really venerating itself. So if sport is a form of theatre, a dramatic spectacle whose ending only discloses itself at the last minute (we do not know whether it will be a comedy, a tragedy, a farce or a fairytale) then sports stars are 'characters' with whom we can identify in the same way we empathise with the people we meet in novels and plays. They 'represent' us, which is why sport is often a focus for national validation, but so whole-hearted is this identification that they do more – they almost *become* us. When we cheer or groan at their mistakes, we are cheering or berating ourselves. And there is a dose of fantasy involved. Most of us are happy to delude ourselves that we would be just as good as the idiots out there given more time, more practice, a bigger slug of money behind us, a larger dollop of luck or simply better contacts.

The excitement provided by Verity, Cotton and Perry in the summer of 1934 did much to brighten the national mood. As relayed through the news-stands, wireless sets and cinema reels, it suggested that Britain was still a world-beater, that grand deeds *were* possible. In the phrase mocked by *1066 and All That* (1930) we were, at a time of freezing self-doubt, still 'top nation'. In cricket's case this made sense: the game had long seen itself as expressing all the best aspects of the national character, just as ice-hockey seemed to grow out of the white Canadian winter. But the idea that individual sports could also stir such strong emotions – this was a new and unfamiliar pleasure.

It is easy to say, with Churchillian loftiness, that sentiments like these are childish dreams. We only have to glance at the intensity of the flag-waving at the World Cup and the Olympic Games to know that there is more to it than a babyish thirst for fabricated escapism. Something deep grinds away beneath the playful surface, and in 1934 it was connected with war – the war in the past and the war in the future. Sport was a way to celebrate the fact we were at peace – indeed it was one of the things we had fought for. But it was also a way of warding off fears that worse was yet to come.

It may be overstating the case – it is a cliché to speak of sportsmen being 'lifted' by the crowd – to imagine that the players themselves could be swayed by forces of this sort. One can hardly see the success of Verity, Cotton and Perry as the inevitable by-product of some deep national craving. It doesn't work like that. If anything, when Perry walked on to Centre Court, the knowledge that Cotton had won *his* Open the week before, or that Verity had just bamboozled the Australians, might have held him back. It was not national fervour that drove the sportsmen, but the opposite; their achievements inspired the fervour. They roused passions that had long lain dormant.

In the end, moments of triumph such as these reverberate loudest when they marry individual deeds – cheering human interest stories – into a bigger picture. On such occasions there truly does seem to be, as the saying goes, something in the air. In this case, a deep, long-suppressed wish could finally be given voice, and the fact that it was mixed with dread only made it more resonant. All times seem in retrospect to dangle between two poles, the old and the new. But at this midway point in the struggle with Germany, in this heavy lull, it really did seem like the calm between two storms.

These were the emotions that pulsed through the summer of '34, in those three heady weeks that shook the sporting world. Britain was at peace, but a peace that would not last long. The Great War had been an unthinkable nightmare, and if the war to come was no more than a fearful suggestion of cloud in the blue summer sky, there were plenty of hints that it would soon be winter again. Might as well try to enjoy it while it lasted.

In November 1945, just two months after the end of the Second World War, a team of Soviet footballers, Dynamo Moscow, came to Britain as part of the post-war fun and games. A number of fixtures against leading clubs – Chelsea, Arsenal, Cardiff and Rangers – were arranged with a view to demonstrating how sport could bring people together.

That was the idea. In the event, the trip was acrimonious. The Soviets looked to their footballers to show their ideological superiority, and England's journalists were slow to extend anything much in the way of consideration. The visitors, advised the *Sunday Express*, were 'earnest amateurs ... so slow that you can almost hear them think'.

The tour did catch the public attention, however. Some 85,000 fans, starved of big-game viewing, squeezed into Stamford Bridge to see the first match, some of them perched high on the roof. And there was a strident nationalist agenda in the air. When the Muscovites presented *flowers* to the home players during the playing of the anthems, the Chelsea lads looked shocked. Flowers? Was this football, or what?

Dynamo astonished everyone that day by coming back from 0-2 down to draw 2-2. Then they beat Cardiff 10-1, and the papers had to change their tune: the *Daily Sketch* hailed the Russians as 'without a doubt the greatest club side ever to visit this island'. In truth it was clear now that they were rather more than a club side – this was a major national XI. So by the time they prepared to face Arsenal, British pride was prickling too. Arsenal even invited two guest players, Stanley Matthews and Stan Mortensen (the two finest footballers in the land), to help put the brakes on this damned Soviet juggernaut. It was a compliment – and a sign that they didn't intend to lose.

The match was played in thick fog. There were more than 54,000 fans at Highbury, and most couldn't see a thing. An odd groan after 30 seconds was the only sign that – incredible, but true! – Moscow had scored. Arsenal recovered to lead 3-2 at half-time, but then things went downhill. The English FA had obligingly agreed that the game could be refereed by a Russian, but regretted it when he allowed the visitors a goal which *anyone* could see – even in the fog – was a mile offside. Soon afterwards he let another one stand while ruling out a perfectly fair Arsenal strike. And hang on a minute? It was hard to see, but didn't the Russians have an extra man on the pitch?

The atmosphere seethed with rancour, and Arsenal's captain, Cliff Bastin, accused the referee of cheating. Dynamo Moscow pretended to be affronted, but didn't really care. They had beaten England's best – they were Heroes of the Revolution! For the final act of their tour they went to Glasgow, drew with Rangers in front of 90,000 fans (the tour was a ripping success commercially, if not culturally) and went home to be garlanded as grand superstars of the Soviet experiment. Goodwill? Yeah, sure.

It was with respect to these hot-tempered events that Orwell delivered, in *Tribune*, his famous disparagement of sport. He hated the way it was used as a beacon of national prestige, and despised the cant that gathered round the idea that it was ennobling. 'Now that the brief visit of the Dynamo team has come to an end,' he argued, 'it is possible to say publicly what many thinking people were saying privately before the Dynamos ever arrived. That is, that sport is an unfailing cause of ill-will, and that if such a visit as this had any effect at all on Anglo-Soviet relations, it could only be to make them worse.' The entire spectacle of this insidious football tour had led him to only one, pungent, conclusion: sport was nothing less than 'war minus the shooting'.

We can respect the context in which Orwell wrote. His essay 'The Sporting Spirit' was a specific swipe at the way totalitarian leaders such as Hitler and Stalin sought to mobilise sport in the service of national propaganda. But though he was entitled to reject the old-school idea that cricket and football were character-building, like cold showers, he may have been giving his own feelings (he disliked sport) too free a rein. Even if he was right to see it as no more than a playful imitation of angrier rivalries, what is wrong with that? Sending David out for a trial of strength against Goliath is less lethal (and a better story) than letting two armies hack each other to pieces.

Orwell didn't say many foolish things. But in seeking to taint sport with the shrill and rivalrous manners of war, and sarcastically emphasising the similarities between the two, he overlooked the far more telling difference – 'shooting' is a very big thing to subtract; one might as well say that war is merely games with bullets. If anything, the way that playful combat can ignite hot emotions while causing only fleeting distress might be taken as a token of its civilised ability to draw stings without drawing blood, not the opposite. And our own tastes are of little importance. No one would suggest that war doesn't matter simply because we don't *like* it. Sport presents combat as theatre, yes – but the visitors from Moscow left a few footballers with nothing worse than bruised shins and injured pride. It was pantomime violence. Much worse things had until very recently been happening at sea – and on land, and in the air.

It is easy to overdo the resemblance between sport and war. The self-help shelves in airport bookstalls are full of eager volumes recycling the wise sayings of Sun Tsu and Clausewitz as sporting maxims, and mashing the leftovers into a recipe for succeeding in business. But sport and war have a number of mannerisms in common, and certainly share a sizeable vocabulary. Many of the metaphors we use for sport derive from the long history of armed conflict: shooting, striking, punching, attacking and defending. Both involve advances, retreats, battles, digging in, sieges, wings, thrusts, parries, feints, duels, assaults, risks, rearguard actions, *esprit de corps*, triumph, disaster, and much else. Few sports have quite so exact a military resonance as modern pentathlon – the routine of riding, running, swimming, throwing and shooting was fully designed to mimic the skills of a soldier on the run. But nearly all of them touch in some way on the quieter essentials of martial life: teamwork, fitness, loyalty, bravery, sacrifice.

Metaphors are treacherous: they have a foot in both camps. There is something awry in the way sport borrows the language of war to give it life-or-death importance, just as there are dismaying aspects to the way military leaders use sporting language to soften the brutal edge of *their* proposals. But this should not obscure the breadth of what they share: conflict, dispute, argument, difficulty, codes of conduct, the overcoming of obstacles ... these are facts of both their lives. If sport does no more than mimic, in a playful way, the bloody extremes of war, it answers some sort of cultural need.

But which came first? Is it sport and war, or war and sport? Which is the original, which the proxy? Is war a game that got out of hand, or is sport a mock-battle? The only thing we can be sure of, perhaps, is that the two are strangely intertwined.

What we are left with is a sequence of tumbling images, a flickering spool that spins in the mind's eye like those tattered prayer wheels outside Himalayan monasteries: the bold warrior dreams (spear-throwing, sword-fighting) of the ancient Olympics ... the more bloodthirsty 'games' of the gladiators in Roman arenas ... the annual battle re-enactments on British Bank Holidays ... the yeoman archers of Crécy and Agincourt ...

Drake kneeling over his bowls as Spanish sails appeared on the southern horizon ... old-fashioned children's frolics (King of the Castle, Capture the Flag) ... Newbolt's hearty lads urging each other to play up, play up and play the game ... Sassoon's traumatised boys crouching in their 'foul dug outs' and 'dreaming of things they did with bats and balls' ... British and German troops punting leather footballs into the smoke of no man's land ... the officer who booted *his* ball high over the Somme like a flare, to kick off the advance ... the cricketer Lionel Tennyson, wounded three times on the Western Front before batting one-handed in the 1921 Ashes ... the subalterns of *Journey's End* hero-worshipping their old rugby captain ... Walter Tull of Spurs and Northampton breaking the embargo on 'Mulattos' and 'Negros' to become an officer on the Western Front ... Hitler glaring at the wrong-coloured whirlwind that was Jesse Owens ... E. W. Swanton's 1939 *Wisden* being passed around a Japanese POW camp ... the Nazi swastika flying over White Hart Lane in 1935... Jardine grimacing as he boarded HMS *Verity* in France ... Verity himself shouting 'Keep going' as he led his men across that field in Sicily ... the annual 'cavalry charge' that launches the Grand National ... the obituaries in the wartime *Wisden*s ('Wood, Sergeant-Navigator, E, a useful all-round cricketer, killed flying over Essen') ... Douglas Bader scooting round golf courses on two tin legs ... Cotton in his RAF uniform, missing his prime years ... the suburban hackers playing golf out of bomb craters, unperturbed ... the barrage balloons over Lord's ... the anti-aircraft gun emplacement at Prince's ... those cold warriors Spassky and Fischer duelling over a chess board in Reykjavik ... the Kiawah Island Ryder Cup styling itself 'the war on the shore' ... the Olympic motto ('The essential thing is not to have conquered, but to have fought well') ... the chant ('Two World Wars and one World Cup') that rocked English football grounds in 1966 ... the war memorial at Turnberry, where Tiger Woods lost his ball ... the 'Soccer War' in Honduras and El Salvador, when a girl stabbed herself because her team conceded a goal... the ferocious-eyed Maori *haka* before All Blacks matches ... the USA and Soviet Union letting off superpower steam in Olympic basketball ... Mandela launching the Rainbow Nation by dancing in the green and gold ... the ceremonial tug-of-war on sports days... the lists of dead comrades in gloomy school chapels ...

On it flaps, this never-ending spool, and round go the ghostly figures, glowing and fading like shadows in a magic lantern. Sometimes, in the background, we can hear the crackle of the crowd, echoing like the cries of children on an empty carousel.

Of all these enduring images of sport and war, few are so resonant as the glittering montage of the 1936 Berlin Olympics created by Leni Riefenstahl just two years after Verity, Cotton and Perry had reached their summits. And there was a nice coda to those Games. Though golf was not part of the syllabus, Hitler himself launched the Great Golf Prize of Nations, a World Cup of golf, donating a showy silver and brass salver as a trophy. Some 36 countries were invited to send a two-man team, and though only seven accepted (the event became known as the 'Hitler Invitational') the thing went ahead at Baden-Baden in August. The Master of Ceremonies was an up-and-comer named Von Ribbentrop, and when, after three rounds, Germany looked certain to win – with a clear five-stroke lead – he cabled Berlin. Hitler promptly set off in a motorcade to present the heroic Aryan winners with the salver, only for the English pair to come with a late surge and pass their German hosts. Ribbentrop raced off to meet his furious leader, who ordered the Mercedes to be turned around – he had no interest in giving anything to a pair of smart ball-strikers from Lancashire.

The winners – Arnold Bentley (whose brother Harry had conceded that four-foot putt to halve a match with Cotton in 1934) and Tommy Thirsk – found their own plucky-Brit way to return Hitler's compliment. Along with the Führer's glittering silver plate they were given a small fir tree, which they took home and planted at Hesketh Golf Club (where none other than Henry Cotton had set a new course record with a 62, posted in 1932). The fir became known as the 'Hitler Tree' and a few years later, when war did come, the members made a point of relieving themselves on it as they passed.[1]

Cotton himself had his own golfing brush with the Führer as war descended. In August 1939 he went to play the German Open in Bad Ems, even though the political situation was 'pretty black'. After winning the tournament for the third time, he had to leave his prize money (£120) with the German Golf Federation, since it was absolutely forbidden to take money out of Germany at that time. He contemplated buying a few cameras and binoculars with his winnings, but decided against it and turned his car for home. But crossing the border was by no means easy. It was 25 August, the very day that Britain and Poland were signing the treaty that bound them to one another, and though Cotton was armed with a letter from the German Golf Federation, written on their 'most imposing stationery', crossing the border to France was still a hair-raising trial. And the queue of cars at Calais, waiting for the ferry, was enormous. Luckily, the knowledge of the area gained at Waterloo stood Cotton in good stead. He slipped up the coast to a little place called Dunkirk, and boarded the boat home from there.

One week later Germany invaded Poland, and that was the end of all such adventures for a while. But war, like form, is temporary, and in 1948 Cotton heard from the secretary of the German Golf Union that she had not forgotten him, that his winnings had been kept safe, and that he was welcome to come and collect them one

---

[1] It is possible that the detail about Hitler's dash to the course and the turning of the car is fanciful. There is no official record of his having made such a trip. But the tale was much enjoyed at the time, and there is a school of thought that – so keen was the humiliation – the records may have been expunged. Either way, the 'Hitler Tree' still stands close to the clubhouse at Hesketh. All that extra watering did it no harm at all.

day. It meant that just as the sporting glories of 1934 had been a happy distraction, a half-time entertainment in the midst of the tumultuous ongoing struggle with Germany, so the war would turn out to be nothing more than a stormy hiatus in the long, continuing and irrepressible story of games. For life indeed is short, as Horace almost said ... but sport is long.

Acknowledgements

Since no one below the age of 90 can have anything resembling a first-hand memory of the sporting whirl of 1934, this account of that year and its remarkable midsummer was drawn from libraries. Particular thanks are owed to the London Library, the British Library, the Kenneth Ritchie Library at the All England Club, Neil Robinson of the MCC Library, Kensington & Chelsea Library and the Cheshire Record Office.

For the lives of the principal characters I relied on the autobiographical writings (not always the wisest move) of the players, and on the many newspaper reports about their various triumphs. I depended also on the biographies of Verity, Cotton and Perry – by Alan Hill, Peter Dobereiner and Jon Henderson respectively. Nothing was added or invented, but for dramatic effect I have at times rendered words and phrases that our heroes were reported as saying (or claimed to have said) as ordinary speech. The banter between Henry Cotton and Reg Whitcombe at the Open, for instance, the words Fred Perry and Jack Crawford exchanged in the Wimbledon dressing-room, or snatches of conversation in Verity's house ... all these were recorded and published elsewhere.

Similarly, when I say that Verity tucked into extra strawberries at lunch, that Cotton helped himself to spaghetti and ice cream, or that Perry was heckled by Marlene Dietrich, these are not fanciful inventions but reported details. In the case of Cotton's spaghetti and ice cream, they may not be gospel – the man himself denied tucking in to such a feast. But this is normal: history vibrates with conflicting versions of itself.

Particular thanks are due to Charlotte Atyeo, David Godwin, Hermione Davies, Richard Collins and Graeme Wright for their shrewd and observant advice. To Graeme I owe the salutary reminder that Don Bradman, contrary to the myth, never did score that famous century before lunch at Lord's, though it sounds like the kind of thing he really *should* have done. Thanks also to Tim Checketts, of Royal St George's, for allowing us to walk in Henry Cotton's footsteps. Of course it is impossible to travel back in time, but on a cold December day, on a deserted golf links beside a slate-grey sea, with gulls on the wind and frost in the hollows, the decades do fall away, as if by magic.

Bibliography

The following books were especially useful.

History

Black, Jeremy, *The Great War*, Continuum, London, 2011

Blythe, Ronald, *The Age of Illusion*, Hamish Hamilton, London, 1963

Churchill, Winston, *The World Crisis 1911–1918*, London, 1931

Corrigan, Gordon, *Mud, Blood and Poppycock*, Orion, London, 2003

Engel, Matthew, *Tickle the Public*, Gollancz, London, 1996

Gardner, Juliet, *The Thirties: An Intimate History*, HarperCollins, London, 2010

Harris, Clive, and Whippy, Julian, *The Greater Game: Sporting Icons Who Fell in the Great War*, Pen and Sword, Barnsley, 2008

Hochschild, Adam, *To End All Wars*, Pan, London, 2011

Jenkins, Alan, *The Twenties*, Heinemann, London, 1974

—, *The Thirties*, Heinemann, London, 1976

Johnson, Paul, *Modern Times*, Weidenfeld & Nicolson, London, 1984

Keynes, J. M., *The Economic Consequences of the Peace*, Macmillan, London, 1919

Kitchen, Martin, *Europe Between the Wars*, Pearson, 1988

C. F. Masterman, *England After War*, Taylor and Francis, 1922

Marwick, Arthur, *The Deluge*, Macmillan, London, 1965

—, *Britain in the Century of Total War*, Bodley Head, London, 1968

McKibbin, Ross, *Classes and Cultures: England 1918–1951*, OUP, Oxford, 2000

Morris, James, *Farewell the Trumpets: An Imperial Retreat*, Faber & Faber, London, 1978

Mowat, C. L., *Britain Between the Wars*, Methuen, London, 1955

Oakes, John, *Kitchener's Lost Boys*, The History Press, Stroud, 2009

Overy, Richard, *The Morbid Age: Britain Between the Wars*, Allen Lane, London, 2009

Pennell, Catriona, *A Kingdom United*, OUP, Oxford, 2012

Pugh, Martin, *We Danced All Night: A Social History of Britain Between the Wars*, Bodley Head, London, 2008

Simkins, Peter, *Kitchener's Army*, Pen and Sword, Barnsley, 2007

Simmonds, Alan, *Britain and World War One*, Routledge, London, 2012

Priestley, J. B. *English Journey*, Gollancz, London, 1933

Seaman, L. C. B., *Life in Britain Between the Wars*, Batsford, London, 1970

Stevenson, John, *British Society 1914–1945*, Pelican Books, London, 1984

Taylor, A. J. P., *The Origins of the Second World War*, Hamish Hamilton, London, 1961

—, *English History 1914-1945*, OUP, London, 1965

Van Emden, Richard, *Boy Soldiers of the Great War*, Headline, London, 2005

Winter, J. M., *The Great War and the British People*, Macmillan, London, 1988

General Sport

Barthes, Roland, *What Is Sport*, Yale University Press, New Haven, 2007

Birley, Derek, *Playing the Game: Sport in British Society 1910–1945*, Manchester University Press, Manchester, 1995

Barnes, Simon, *The Meaning of Sport*, Short Books, London, 2006

Bose, Mihir, *The Spirit of the Game*, Constable, London, 2012

Natan, Alex, *Sport and Society*, Bowes, London, Ontario, 1958

Huggins, Mike, and Williams, Jack, *Sport and the English 1918–1939*, Routledge, London, 2006

Smith, Ed, *What Sport Tells us About Life*, Penguin Books, London, 2009

Cricket

Ames, Les, *Close of Play*, Stanley Paul, London, 1953

Rajan, Amol, *Twirlymen: The Unlikely History of Cricket's Greatest Spin Bowlers*, Yellow Jersey, 2011

Birley, Derek, *A Social History of English Cricket*, Aurum Press, London, 1999

Bradman, Don, *My Cricketing Life*, Stanley Paul, London, 1938

Bowes, Bill, *Express Deliveries*, Sportsman, Stanley Paul, 1949

Cardus, Neville, *Good Days*, Rupert Hart-Davis, London, 1948

Davis, Sam, *Hedley Verity: Prince with a Piece of Leather*, Epworth Press, London, 1952

Fender, Percy, *Kissing the Rod*, Chapman & Hall, London, 1934

Fingleton, Jack, *Cricket Crisis*, Cassell, London, 1946

Hammond, Walter, *Cricket My Destiny*, Stanley Paul, 1940

Hendren, Patsy, *Big Cricket*, Hodder & Stoughton, London, 1934

Hill, Alan, *Hedley Verity: Portrait of a Cricketer*, Mainstream, London, 1986

Hobbs, Jack, *The Fight for the Ashes 1933 and 1934*, Harrup, London, 1934

Hodgson, Derek, *The Official History of Yorkshire Cricket*, Crowood Press, Ramsbury, 1989

James, C. L. R., *Beyond a Boundary*, Stanley Paul, London, 1963

Jardine, D. R., *Critical Accounts of the 1934 Test Matches*, Hutchinson, London, 1934

Lynch, Steven, *The Lord's Test*, Spellmount, 1990

Moult, Thomas (ed.), *Bat and Ball: A Book of Cricket*, Magna Books, 1935

Rice, Jonathan, *One Hundred Lord's Tests*, Methuen, London, 2001

Sutcliffe, Herbert, *For England and Yorkshire*, Edward Arnold, London, 1935

Verity, Hedley, *Bowling 'Em Out*, Hutchinson, London, 1936

Warner, Pelham, *Cricket between the Wars*, Chatto, London, 1942

Waters, Chris, *10 for 10: Hedley Verity and the Story of Cricket's Greatest Bowling Feat*, John Wisden, London, 2014

Wisden, London, 1934, 1935

Wyatt, R. E. S., *Three Straight Sticks*, Stanley Paul, London, 1951

Yardley, Norman, *Cricket Campaigns*, Stanley Paul, London, 1950

Golf

Allis, Peter, *Peter Alliss's Golfing Heroes*, Virgin Books, London, 2007

Braid, James, *Advanced Golf*, 1908

Cotton, Henry, *Golf!*, 1930

—, *This Game of Golf*, Country Life, 1949

—, *My Swing*, Country Life, 1952

—, *A History of Golf*, Lippincott, 1975

—, *Thanks for the Game*, Sidgwick & Jackson, London, 1980

Cousins, Geoffrey, and Scott, Tom, *A Century of Opens*, Frederick Muller, London, 1971

Darwin, Bernard, *Golf Between Two Wars*, Chatto, London, 1944

—, *Historic Courses of the British Isles*, Duckworth, London, 1987

Dobereiner, Peter, *Maestro: The Life of Henry Cotton*, Hodder & Stoughton, London, 1992

Hargreaves, Ernest, *Caddie in the Golden Age*, Partridge Press, 1993

Mortimer, Charles, and Pignon, Fred, *The Story of Golf's Open Championship*, Warrolds, 1952

Sampson, Curt, *Royal and Ancient: Blood, Sweat and Fear at the British Open*, Villard, New York, 2000

Taylor, J. H., *Golf: My Life's Work*, Jonathan Cape, London, 1943
Vardon, Harry, *How to Play Golf*, Methuen, London, 1912

Tennis

Henderson, Jon, *The Last Champion: The Life of Fred Perry*, Yellow Jersey, London, 2009
Perry, Fred, *My Story*, Hutchinson, London, 1934
—, *Fred Perry on Tennis*, Hutchinson, London, 1936
—, *Fred Perry: An Autobiography*, Hutchinson, London, 1984

Index

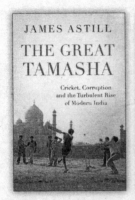